"Almost inadvertently, the workforce has become the big owner of the world's most significant companies. If we can work out how we use our new powers responsibly, we have a enormous opportunity to create sustainable development. This book is a roadmap. No-one who seeks to influence company behavior should be without it."
    —John Monks, General Secretary, European Trade Union Confederation

"This book offers an escape path around the quicksand of corporate misconduct. At last, we have a guide that gets past the hand-wringing angst, passive abdication, or even the mechanical irrelevant "good governance" recipes. The authors reveal how owners can reassert the voice they've inadvertently yielded to their expensive hired hands."
    —Jeffrey Sonnenfeld, Senior Associate Dean, Lester Crown Professor
        of Management Practice, Yale School of Management; and founder
        and President of The Chief Executive Leadership Institute

"Everyone interested in corporate governance should buy this well-written, anecdote-packed treasure. It is an exciting story of what is possible—a virtuous corporate regime."
    —Robert A. G. Monks, founder, Lens Governance Advisors, LLP

"This book effectively spells out who the true beneficiaries of today's capitalist world should be—us. It's a call-to-action must-read for anyone and everyone with a stake in today's investor-owned society."
    —Ira M. Millstein, Senior Partner, Weil, Gotshal & Manges LLP; Senior
        Associate Dean for Corporate Governance, Yale School of Management

"An ambitious and optimistic manifesto, written by three authors whose insights have been enriched by their active participation in the growth of shareholder activism, *The New Capitalists* is a valuable addition to the debate on corporate governance and accountability."
    —Lucian Bebchuk, Friedman Professor of Law, Economics, and Finance
        and Director, Program on Corporate Governance, Harvard Law School

"This work is an engaging and complete account of the origins and goals of modern shareholder activism. It is also, more importantly, a primer for action as boards and shareholders confront the reality of a market dominated by the new capitalists."
    —Charles Elson, John L. Weinberg Center for Corporate Governance,
        Lerner College of Business and Economics, University of Delaware

The New Capitalists

The New Capitalists

How Citizen Investors Are Reshaping the Corporate Agenda

STEPHEN DAVIS

JON LUKOMNIK

DAVID PITT-WATSON

Harvard Business School Press

Boston, Massachusetts

Library of Congress Cataloging-in-Publication Data

Davis, Stephen M., 1955–
   The new capitalists: how citizen investors are reshaping the corporate agenda / Stephen Davis, Jon Lukomnik, David Pitt-Watson.
       p. cm.
     ISBN 1-4221-0101-0   978-1-4221-0101-8 (ISBN 13)
     1. Investments. 2. Capitalism—Social aspects. I. Lukomnik, Jon. II. Pitt-Watson, David. III. Title.
     HG4521.D184 2006
     338.6'041—dc22

                                                                                      2006011146

We thank Clo, Lynn, and Ursula,

and dedicate this book to our children,

Gabriel, James, Jacob, Julia, Aidan,

Eleanor, Jimmy, and Isabel.

We hope they have the chance to thrive and

contribute in a civil-economy world.

Contents

Acknowledgments

Scores of people around the world are contributing to the civil economy. There are, however, a few whose wisdom and counsel have particularly helped our own understanding of the possibilities and pitfalls it presents. We take the liberty of dubbing them, in this context, civil economists. They include Jamie Allen, Philip Armstrong, André Baladi, Marco Becht, Igor Belikov, Pierre Bollon, Gordon Brown MP, Matt Brown, Steve Brown, Tim Bush, Peter Butler, Sir Adrian Cadbury, Jonathan Charkham, Peter Clapman, Bill Crist, Frank Curtiss, J. Sanford Davis, Peter Dey, Sandy Easterbrook, Jesus Estanislau, Harrison J. Goldin, Jeff Goldstein, Peter Gourevitch, Sandra Guerra, Jim Hawley, Alan J. Hevesi, Patricia Hewitt MP, Marianne Huvé-Allard, Mats Isaksson, Hasung Jang, Jeff Kindler, Paul Lee, Pierre-Henri Leroy, Michael Lubrano, Bob Massie, Alan McDougall, Colin Melvin, Ira Millstein, Nell Minow, Bob Monks, Carol O'Cleireacain, Taiji Okusu, Bill Patterson, David Phillips, Iain Richards, Alastair Ross Goobey, Howard Sherman, James Shinn, Anne Simpson, Tim Smith, Christian Strenger, John Sullivan, Raj Thamotheram, Dario Trevisan, Shann Turnbull, Paulo Conte Vasconcellos, David Webb, Ted White, Ralph Whitworth, John Wilcox, Andrew Williams, and Ann Yerger. We are also indebted to Mikael Lurie for his research and Josie Reason for her support to our efforts.

We would also like to thank Gail Ross, Howard Yoon, and Jacque Murphy for their assistance in helping *The New Capitalists* mature from a series of articles to a fully envisioned and documented book. Whatever errors remain, whether of omission or commission, are the responsibility of the authors.

Preface

Look at your savings account. You may not know it, but your share of more than $3 trillion is missing. A colossal pool of wealth should be there to feed prosperity, but it isn't. Then flip through the newspaper to the employment ads, where another mystery lurks. Many more jobs should be available around the world, but they aren't.

This book has two main goals. First, it seeks to expose the mechanisms that have historically driven corporations and citizens apart, trying to solve the riddle of missing savings and jobs. Second, it identifies a powerful countervailing phenomenon that is pushing corporate executives, investors, politicians, activists, and citizens to hone new skills for a reengineered capitalism. What we call the *civil economy* is materializing for a simple reason: a population of *new capitalists* is seizing influence over the corporate agenda.

Who are these new capitalists we're talking about? Corporate power used to be wielded either by wealthy tycoons or by the state. In some places, that is still the case. But in North America, Europe, Japan, and increasingly throughout the world, the owners of multinational corporations are the tens of millions of working people who have their pensions and other life savings invested through funds in shares of the world's largest companies. Their nest eggs constitute majority ownership of our corporate world. Each pensioner owns a tiny sliver of vast numbers of companies. From IT pacesetters in Silicon Valley to the oil wells of Nigeria, from breweries in Mexico to the chemical giants of Germany, citizens collectively are now the ultimate owners.

Of course, these citizens have neither known that nor acted the part. Indeed, until recently, this historic transfer of ownership has been effectively immaterial—a peculiar factoid rather than a development of genuine significance to companies or countries. Real power remained in the hands of a small cadre of distant and unaccountable players on Wall Street, in Tokyo, and in the City of London, or in the cabinet rooms of governments, merely because the citizen owners have been unaware that ownership has become democratized. Until now. In this book we track the present awakening of a consciousness of civil ownership—of new capitalists—that promises to make those traditional power brokers accountable, or kick them out of the way.

Rubble and Revenue

Consider two stories that we think sketch the *past* and the *future* of enterprise.

Deep into a chilly April night in 2004, New York City police officers muscled former Enron chief executive Jeffrey Skilling into custody. Several night owls had phoned the 911 police hotline to report that Skilling was drunk and aggressive, accosting strangers, pulling up a woman's blouse in search of a wiretap, and accusing passersby of being FBI agents. En route to the precinct lockup, the police cruiser drove Skilling past the skyscrapers he had once frequented as a power broker during Enron's heyday, before hubris and apparent deceit brought an onslaught of criminal fraud charges and turned his company into rubble.

Just hours later, around the water coolers in those tower offices, Skilling's behavior was the topic of executives' chatter. Some groused about a prosecutorial inquisition. Others expressed relief that they had dodged the bullets that had brought their ex-colleague so low. Enron, they agreed, was an exception. Either the energy trader had suffered singular bad luck in getting caught, or it was a thoroughly bad apple in an otherwise well-functioning marketplace.

But those are the wrong lessons. The forces that had brought Skilling low had less to do with poor luck or extraordinary transgression than with the rise of a new populist class of citizen investors who counted on stock in Enron and other firms to finance their retirements. In a break from the past, Enron's nosedive proved not some bloodless casualty among magnates. Gigantic losses, this time, ravaged the accounts and future dreams of millions of middle- and working-class savers. The scandal naturally fueled an angry nationwide—ultimately worldwide—backlash against corporate misconduct. Skilling's arrest, then, was not an eccentric moment. Instead, it was a gritty symbol of how the new citizen owners of corporations are calling an end to old ways of business.

What new ways of business do they want? For one answer, consider a second story that draws an unlikely line between General Electric, one of the world's mightiest corporations, and an obscure coalition of Catholic nuns. In 2002 the pension funds of various religious orders, holding an infinitesimal stake in the company, petitioned what appeared to be a quixotic resolution onto the agenda of GE's annual shareowner meeting. The nuns asked directors to report on greenhouse gas emissions and steps the board could take to promote energy efficiency and combat climate change. The nuns argued that environmental responsibility would be good for GE's bottom line.

CEO Jeffrey Immelt at first dismissed the resolution and authorized a routine rebuttal. But the meeting proved a stunner. A lofty 23 percent of GE's investors rebuffed management for the nuns' business case. Chastened executives decided to take a second look at what their new capitalist owners were telling them. They ordered detailed internal studies of what it would take to reduce emissions. The results of these studies were astonishing. If GE changed course to make energy efficiency a core business mission, it could both bolster its market reputation and add at least $10 billion in fresh revenue in just five years. In 2005 it unveiled a milestone, companywide project dubbed "ecomagination" to do just that.[1]

Circle of Accountability

GE is no anomaly. New capitalists are beginning to compel radical change across the globe as they build a civil economy. We find the evidence, first, in a circle of accountability:

Individual shareowners—the new capitalists—are awakening to citizen investor power around the world, **spurring**

Institutional investors to adopt responsible portfolio and activist strategies, **which prompt**

Boards of directors to embrace sweeping reform making them accountable to shareowners, **creating an agenda for**

Corporations and corporate executives, who are turning to a new "capitalist-manifesto" path to corporate success, **which, in turn, hands**

The new capitalists unprecedented clout.

This book is not designed as the definitive text on board operations, audit functions or investor governance. We suggest resources that do just that in the bibliography. Instead, we offer a fresh insight: that all these pieces of the marketplace now fit together. Our aim is to decipher the unwritten code that links them into a civil economy. We then suggest practical tools that corporate managers, investors, citizens, and policy makers can use to navigate the revolution and shape it.

Entering the Civil Economy

What exactly do we mean by the term *civil economy*? In political life, we use the term *civil society* to define the vast array of institutions needed to maintain democratic governments accountable to public needs. Think of a free press, a fair judiciary, civic groups, political parties, unions, religious institutions, and involved citizenry.

The civil economy is a phenomenon that involves a similar range of parallel institutions—but trained on business, not politics. Today, they are combining in ways that propel the rise of a new species of corporation. The successful enterprise is increasingly skilled at cultivating commercial dynamism, but in a context of accountability to shareowners.

That context remains alien to some corporations. Businesspeople are often demonized as apostles of greed and short-term thinking. A few are. But a larger number of forward-thinking corporate leaders understand that popular resentment of globalization, divisions between the shop floor and executive suites, and recurring clashes between corporations and social interests cannot help but drain energy from competitiveness, costing jobs and undercutting public confidence in institutions critical to growth.

This transformation from conventional to civil economy is not merely what some *hope* will happen. It *is* happening, today. Whether it persists, and in what direction it evolves, is of course open to question. But neither corporate managers nor investors nor involved citizens can ignore it.

Financial Amphetamines

Stop for a moment, though, and ponder three points you *won't* find us making in this book. For one, we are under no illusion that changes forced by the ownership revolution are readily embraced by those with stakes in the status quo. In fact, we outline in each chapter the barricades thrown up against new capitalists. Defense of convention cannot be underestimated. But in this book we consciously set out to stress the many *solutions* new capitalists are forging well out of the public spotlight. Not all such innovations succeed; progress is sometimes overshadowed or overcome; sometimes it comes two paces forward at the cost of one pace back. But progress is made because the hard-nosed new realities of capital ownership are inexorable, as we try to demonstrate in this book.

Second, we do not argue that corporations that embrace social responsibility automatically outpace competitors. They might, but we leave that judgment to scholars, who are divided on the question. Instead, we make a different case: that new capitalists are rewriting the rules that have long defined how we have judged winners and losers in the commercial world.

Think of sprints in the Olympic Games as an analogy. If all we onlookers truly cared about was watching our favorite athletes win a single race, we would insist that they inject as many performance-enhancing drugs they could lay hands on; we would even applaud them for trip- ping and kneecapping opponents. But we don't, because we care about athletes competing fairly, about the health and safety of runners in this and all future sprints, and about the social lesson of what an individual can achieve through sheer unaided willpower, talent, and discipline. So we celebrate winning athletes as heroes—but *only* if they compete within limited bounds.

In the business world, the financial equivalents of amphetamines and kneecapping include loose stock options, aggressive accounting, short-term management, short-changed pensions, pollution, and influ- ence buying. When owners care little about how the stock price game is played, unscrupulous corporate executives can use these deceptive tech- niques at will to speed ahead—even if their enterprises flame out after short-term bursts or cause damage to their firm or others.

New capitalists demand fair competition because their interests, like those of Olympic spectators, are broad and long-term. So the civil economy they are building isn't about individual companies making a choice to leave the main path in search of a benevolent route to success for this reporting period. It is about redirecting the path itself so that incentives and penalties *compel* marketwide change over the long haul. That means new ways executives manage, directors oversee, shareowners own, intermediaries behave, accountants measure, and citizens lobby.

Finally, we do not contend that the emerging civil economy heralds a kind of "end to history" in which social conflict over control of eco- nomics might magically vanish. Why should it? The ownership revolu- tion rebalances power to force different means of resolving problems; it cannot abolish the problems themselves.

Fueling Change

Look again at that savings account. We try to show that capital is the fuel driving reform. As big investment funds act more as new capital- ists, reflecting the interests of their grassroots savers, they increasingly compel boards and CEOs to operate in a pragmatic new framework. Yes, citizen investors fiercely press corporations to seek profit. After all, no profit, no pension. But new capitalists are just as fiercely bent on scrutiny that ensures that corporate profits are real, not a result of accounting tricks. Focus is shifting to sustainable, *long-term* corporate performance and away from firms configured to generate only short-term highs. And more funds insist that corporations gain profit without shifting expenses—such as pollution—to society at large because, as taxpayers, citizen investors will have to pick up that tab, too.

The civil economy, to be sure, is still in gestation. Formidable obstacles slow its spread. But the clock has started. Jeffrey Skilling's nocturnal arrest sealed the end of his run as a master of the business world. GE is among those exploring fresh paths ahead. Leaders that fail to reorient themselves and their institutions will be left behind. Those who adapt have a greater shot at success. That will benefit everyone, for a civil economy, managed right, offers new capitalists a positive prospect: higher chances of a prosperity that is sustainable, more widespread and equitable, and rooted in public trust.

To find out how, let's return to the mystery with which we began. How could $3 trillion have slipped through the hands of capital-hungry companies and unwitting citizen investors? Break that secret, and we decipher the roadmap to the new corporate agenda.

The New Capitalists

1

The Civil Economy

The Democratization of Ownership

Few of us feel like tycoons, able to sway the destinies of huge multinational companies. But we should, at least according to the numbers.

Take GE, the largest company in the world. The international energy giant was worth a staggering $350 billion—more than a third of a trillion dollars—in 2006.[1] If the entire population of Indonesia, 200 million people, were to toil for a year and consume absolutely nothing, they would still not have saved enough rupiahs to buy this giant corporation.

Who owns GE? Not the tycoons. Dig out the investors' register and you will find not a single tycoon among top ranks. Instead, the largest holders of GE shares are Barclays Bank, State Street, and Fidelity, mammoth financial houses. Funds like these represent the owners of GE. But their capital is not their own. They act on behalf of, and in trust for, tens of millions of people who pool their investment savings and routinely hire such firms to provide professional investment management services.

That means that, most likely, *you* own GE. Most readers of this book will have some sort of retirement savings: a traditional pension, a defined contribution plan such as a 401(k) in the United States or an ISA in the United Kingdom, an investment in a mutual fund, or a life insurance annuity. If so, each of us, through our banks, brokers, fund managers, and insurers, is a part owner of a small slice of GE.

This kind of ownership is a global phenomenon. Two of the largest owners of company shares in Britain are not Sir Richard Branson or the Queen (or even J. K. Rowling), but the British Telecom workers' pension plan and the mineworkers' pension plan; combined, they represent eight hundred thousand individuals. In the United States, the top one thousand pension funds own nearly $5 trillion in assets, with the top five funds representing civil servants of the states of California (two funds), New York, and Florida, as well as the federal worker retirement system.[2] In Denmark it's the ATP, the workers' pension fund; in the Netherlands it's ABP, the public service fund. Each of these holds stakes in literally thousands of companies.

Taken collectively, working people through their savings today hold the majority of stock in the most powerful enterprises in the world. It wasn't always this way.

As recently as 1970, a handful of wealthy individuals controlled corporations. At the typical U.S. company, financial institutions speaking for small investors owned just 19 percent of stock, far less than the percentage owned by individuals, most of whom were among the richest 1 percent of the population.[3] Today, by contrast, funds own more than half of all U.S. stock. In fact, the largest one hundred money managers alone control 52 percent of all U.S. equity.[4] Moreover, that trend shows no sign of reversing. According to the Conference Board, institutional investors owned 69.4 percent of the largest one thousand U.S. public companies in 2004, up sharply from 61.4 percent in 2000.[5] A similar tectonic shift of economic power took place in Britain. Private individuals, most of them wealthy, owned 54 percent of U.K. stock in 1963. They now control less than 15 percent, while institutions hold more than 70 percent, up from around 25 percent in 1963.[6] In Australia, France, Germany, Japan, the Netherlands, Sweden—in fact, in many major markets around the world—the capital of institutional investors is beginning to dwarf that of the individual rich.

The power to sway whole nations' economic fortunes—once exclusively the province of the state or of merchants and princes such as the Rothschilds or the Medicis—is now held by those institutional investors representing policemen, autoworkers, and computer programmers saving for retirement.[7] The premise of this book is that this change has been revolutionary. It is profoundly affecting our world, from the amount each of us counts in our retirement nest eggs to the vigor of national economies. Management guru Peter Drucker predicted such a money transfer as long ago as 1976 in *The Unseen Revolution*.[8] Now the day of the "new capitalists" is visible.

Grassroots Tycoons?

Let's not get carried away, though. By no means does everyone have the kind of savings that qualifies him or her as a citizen investor. Swaths of societies remain in poverty. A living wage, let alone a retirement nest egg, is over the horizon for millions. Moreover, everyday headlines track how companies are cutting back on retirement benefits. Part-time or low-wage workers often get no retirement benefits at all. Even those with long-standing full-time jobs are growing insecure about resources they once counted on to pay their living expenses upon retirement.

But if universal saving remains admittedly distant, an unprecedented transformation of ownership has nonetheless come about. The statistics noted earlier indicate that institutional investors have replaced the rich in stock ownership. But let's dig deeper to see whether those big funds are just the wealthy by another name, or whether they really reflect a new and broader public engagement in capital.

Here, then, are the bedrock questions: Whose money do these institutions manage? To whom are these institutions accountable? Let's look first at the United Kingdom and the United States, where data is easier to unearth.

How many British families are contributing to pensions and insurance policies that are invested in equities? Approximately 55 percent of the U.K. working population is putting money into private pensions, and an additional 10 percent have partners who are contributing, according to a recent government survey. In addition, other workers may not be contributing today but did so in the past. Therefore, even allowing for the fact that some public-sector pensions may not be backed by investments in securities, around two-thirds of the nation's population has an interest in equity investment through their pensions.[9] Other surveys show similar figures for life insurance. Some 47 percent of British families have life insurance; another 15 percent have a pension provided by an insurance company.

Statistics tell a similar story in the United States, where in 1989 less than a third of families owned stock. Today, somewhere between 50 percent and 60 percent have savings in the stock market directly or through mutual funds or retirement accounts. This shift even carries over into self-identification. In the early 1990s only about 20 percent of U.S. voters identified themselves as investors; now more than half do.[10] That trend is bound to continue if only because corporations are fast replacing traditional pension plans with defined-contribution plans. They transfer investment decisions and risks to individual employees.

To be sure, millions—between 35 percent and 45 percent of the population in the United States and Britain—have no provision for future savings backed by equity investment. But a huge proportion of the population—55 percent to 65 percent, more than turn out to vote in many political elections—is in the capital market in some fashion. Pundits and politicians proclaim that an "investor class" is arising in North America, Europe, Australia, and now in parts of Asia. We call the people in it the *new capitalists*.

Neutralizing the Wealth Gap

Granted, citizen investors have unequal pension entitlements. Highly paid executives have far more invested on their behalf than do shop-floor employees.[11] But both are likely to be invested through a collective investment scheme, such as a company pension fund. And the fund owes duties to all its savers, not just to the richer ones. Under most trust laws, a pension fund cannot pursue investment policies that benefit wealthy pensioners while doing damage to poorer ones, or vice versa.

In other words, the influence of small owners is magnified through collective savings and investing vehicles. The board of California's CalPERS pension system, or a portfolio manager at Fidelity, or the president of insurance company AXA has the same fiduciary obligation to all participants in pension funds, mutual funds, or annuities. The board or manager may not distinguish between a lower-paid, newly hired worker who might have a balance of only $500 in the pension plan from an about-to-be-retired senior manager whose balance exceeds $1 million. When such funds speak to corporations and countries, they do so on behalf of teachers and bus drivers as well as executives. And with so much capital aggregated, they get heard.

All very well for the United States and Britain, some may say. Companies are generally widely held there, giving funds greater sway. What about continental Europe, Japan, Brazil, Korea, and other parts of the world? In many markets, large families and banks often have a dominant voice, though not necessarily because they own controlling stakes in corporations. Instead, they frequently rely on strategies that resemble political gerrymandering to artificially inflate their influence. Think nonvoting shares, restrictions on voting, blocks held by allied ventures, phantom stock, multiple votes, and pyramid ownership schemes. But gerrymandering techniques are in retreat in Europe and elsewhere, a retreat both caused by, and exposing more companies to, the global spread of new capitalist funds.

Let's neither overstate nor understate the case outside the United Kingdom and the United States. Data on real ownership is "simply not available" as yet for places such as continental Europe, according to scholars Marco Becht and Colin Mayer.[12] But we do know some facts about the level of equity ownership—if not the breadth of ownership—that suggest that the same dynamic is at play in much of the developed world. In the Netherlands, for example, institutional investors increased their allocation to stocks by 27 percent between 1992 and 1999. In France, the change was 23 percent during that same time period. In Germany, the number was 18 percent.[13] Those changes have made stock markets important to ordinary investors. In France, for example, equity ownership as a percentage of household disposable income was 144 percent as of 2001, higher even than in the United States and nearly double the figure in the United Kingdom. Among other G7 nations, both Italians and Canadians owned more stock, as a percentage of household income, than did Britons.[14]

Moreover, the influence of nonresident institutional investors, usually those of the United States and United Kingdom (and, increasingly, the Netherlands), is climbing, and it compounds the effect of the rise of a domestic equity culture in many markets (see box, "Case in Point: Citizen Investors Move a Nation"). In France, Belgium, Sweden, Germany, Netherlands, and other European Union countries, nonresident institutional investors now own between 30 and 75 percent of the largest public companies.[15] In Japan the figure hit a record 24 percent in 2004.[16] No wonder multinationals such as Shell and Unilever—once thought impregnable to shareowner activism—recently scrapped age-old governance traditions to satisfy investors.

In other words, the starting point may be different in countries outside the English-speaking world. The rate of change may be different. The regulations, laws, and collective savings vehicles may be different. But the direction of travel toward a civil economy is the same.

The Money Tide

Now let's ask *why* stock ownership has spread from elites to broad populations. Reasons for the transformation boil down to a mix of demographics and economics.

The demographics are straightforward: An ever-expanding world population, and an ever-expanding working- and middle-class, create an insatiable appetite for more retirement resources. Meanwhile, advances in health care and standards of living increase the number of years people spend in retirement. The economics of transformation are similarly manifest. The tidal wave of workers approaching pension age, swelled in North America and Europe by the post–World War II baby boom, has forced politicians and citizens to face a brutal macroeconomic reality: government retirement programs are inadequate. They need to be supplemented by prefunded retirement systems. Those prefunded systems need to invest years in advance of an individual's retirement so they can build wealth over time. Governments around the world have therefore spurred a mind-numbing variety of programs to

CASE IN POINT: CITIZEN INVESTORS MOVE A NATION

In February 2002, the Philippine Manila Composite Index tumbled 3.3 percent in a day. The reason: the California Public Employees' Retirement System (CalPERS), the largest pension plan in the United States, announced it would not invest in the Philippine public equity markets. The fund had determined that the country's market infrastructure, laws, and procedures were below acceptable risk standards.

For two years, the Philippine government waged a campaign to reverse the ruling. During that period, it reformed laws, changed procedures, and sent its ambassador on a special pilgrimage to CalPERS's Sacramento, California, headquarters to plead for relief. Was it worth it? Well, on the day CalPERS reversed its boycott decision, the Manila exchange closed at a three-month high. "It's important that the portfolio investment of CalPERS remain," said Albert del Rosario, Philippine ambassador to the United States, explaining that the pension fund's decision represented a seal of approval to investors around the world.[a]

While del Rosario might want individuals to invest in Philippine companies, the real investment clout is held by institutions that aggregate the investments of individuals. CalPERS, like most pension funds, represents the retirement savings of people who are far from rich. Ambassador del Rosario would not have visited any of the CalPERS members—bus drivers, sewer workers, firemen—individually. But that is exactly the point: more and more people who are *not* rich own stock through various collective savings/investing vehicles. The amount of money CalPERS was talking about removing from the Philippines represented only 0.05 percent of the fund's assets, the equivalent of a nickel out of a hundred dollars. You probably have that amount tucked under the cushions on your sofa. However, multiply it by the $172 billion then controlled by CalPERS, and those nickels add up to $85 million.[b]

a. Andy Mukherjee, "CalPERS Flips and Flops in Philippines—Again," Bloomberg News Service, April 22, 2004; CalPERS press release, April 19, 2004.

b. Embassy of the Philippines, "Philippines Is Retained by Calpers in Its Permissible List," press release, January 31, 2005.

prefund citizens' retirements at least partially. Further, policy makers are heeding studies that consistently point to equity ownership as a way to generate higher total returns over the long term than bond ownership would generate.

The result: expansion of stock ownership and an equity culture.

Moreover, institutional capital has become global. Institutions in the United States and the United Kingdom are leading the charge. North American and U.K. capital alone account for approximately 61 percent of assets in the world's three hundred biggest pension funds.[17] Funds in the United States, Canada, and the United Kingdom together speak for 70 percent of the $32.1 trillion pool that constitutes institutional capital assets in the ten largest international stock markets.[18] Put simply, when the typical French multinational traded on Paris's Euronext stock market now needs a cash infusion, it must try to sell its equity as much to agents representing retirees in Texas, Yorkshire, or Ontario as to investors at home.

So even though you alone may not feel like an international tycoon, citizen investors together own the commanding heights of the world economy.

"Capitalism Without Owners..."

A key reason citizen investors may be numb to a sense of power is that they have shifted ownership functions to others. In each chapter of this book, we illustrate how, by imperfectly delegating responsibility, all of us as investors have failed to make companies accountable. We then spotlight the many new ways in which that accountability is being reestablished, giving rise to a civil economy. But there is no doubt that dysfunction, when it occurs, produces devastating consequences.

When savers don't feel and act like owners, corporations are free to behave as if they are unaccountable. Absent accountability, the inevitable result is abuse of power. At the extreme, scandals emerge: Maxwell and Polly Peck in the United Kingdom; Enron, Tyco, WorldCom, and Adelphia in the United States; Parmalat, Ahold, and Skandia in continental Europe; HIH and One.Tel in Australia; Livedoor in Japan.

To be sure, few corporate misdeeds reach the level of criminality. But lack of accountability manifests itself in less newsworthy but possibly more corrosive everyday actions that affect shareowner capital, employees, and the environment. Count the ways. Corporate managers can hold onto unneeded cash, or invest in dubious acquisitions, so as to enlarge dominion rather than returning cash to owners through share buybacks, dividends, or other means. CEOs can defer strategic action; they can protect executive expense accounts and perks; they can siphon shareowner capital to controlling investors; they can stifle entrepreneurship for fear of jeopardizing the steady and predictable, even if rivals gain ground. Companies can meander unnecessarily to obsolescence, shedding employment and value and goodwill along the way. They can act, in short, as if no one is minding the store.

In capitalism, that's lethal. The success of any enterprise in the market economy depends on owners alert enough to drive change when times turn ill, or to reward tactics that perform. Thought leader Bob Monks famously put it this way: "Capitalism without owners will fail." When accountability breaks down on a market wide scale, the cost is staggering.

How do we calculate the amount that is lost when owners don't own? We have to do it by inference. Harvard's Michael Jensen estimated that between 1977 and 1988, some $500 billion in value was lost by poor management in just a handful of companies. It took a takeover bid to change the management, and the removal of the company from the stock market to release that value. This is a huge sum attributed to the better management or financing of only a few companies. Jensen reckoned that value had been trapped because of "the central weakness of the public corporation—the conflict between owners and managers over the control and use of corporate resources."[19]

If ever there were a call to action to improve the performance of company boards, this was surely it. Jensen's findings showed that remaking boards so that the companies were indeed run in shareowners' best interests could produce enormous paybacks.

Study after study confirms it. Management consultants McKinsey & Company for example, found that fund managers holding shares in U.S. companies said they would be willing to pay 14 percent more for well-governed companies than for poorly governed ones. U.S. corporations, in aggregate, are worth around $15 trillion, so if we were able to add 14 percent to the bottom half of this group, that would add over $1 trillion of value.[20] The numbers are striking no matter where you look around the globe. In the United Kingdom, investors would pay 12 percent more. In Italy, 16 percent. In Japan, 21 percent. In Brazil, 24 percent.

The $3 Trillion Gap

Of course, it is unlikely that investors will automatically make more money simply by investing in "well-governed" companies, any more than they will by investing in "profitable" companies. The stock market is not stupid. Shares of well-governed companies will be priced higher than those in poorly governed ones. But the weight of academic and industry studies—four of the most prominent by the University of Michigan, Stanford University, McKinsey & Company, and Deutsche Bank—show that funds enhance the value of their investments if they are activist players in the marketplace.[21] The groundbreaking shareowner stewardship fund managed by Hermes in the United Kingdom can claim not only to have created a surplus for its own investors, but also to have helped add billions to the value of the companies in which it has invested.[22] And those benefits flow directly to corporations themselves. Companies that respond to watchful shareowners by improving governance can lower their cost of capital.

Research further demonstrates that activism—and accompanying improvements in corporate governance—significantly boosts a country's economy. The reverse is likewise true. Countries with poor corporate governance lose out on wealth and jobs. ANZ Bank calculated that in 1998 alone poor corporate governance cost New Zealand the equivalent of 7 percent of its GDP in shareowner value.[23]

Let's then run some speculative numbers. A one-time revaluation as the market changes its opinion of previously poorly governed companies could add 10 percent to the value of company shares. That, in turn, would be worth $3 trillion on a global basis. In other words, if we saw a wholesale change of boardroom behavior so that companies truly operated to meet shareowner interests, the world economy would get a $3 trillion boost: on average, the equivalent of every one of the 6.4 billion men, women, and children on the planet gaining some $500, not to mention a range of other nonfinancial benefits.[24]

But that multitrillion-dollar ownership gap is only one prize of the civil economy. Early studies show that corporations aligned with shareowners create more jobs over time than those managed for the special interests of managers or controlling shareowners. McKinsey & Company estimated that a country could expect to cut its unemployment rate by some 2 percent if corporations were structured to pursue shareowner value.[25] Or look at the opposite perspective. In 2005 the Economic Policy Institute reported an "employment deficit" of 3.2 million jobs in the United States alone—in other words, jobs that should be created in a comparable phase of the economic cycle, but which simply had not materialized.[26] A major culprit, a new study argues, is financial manipulation—the kind that toppled Enron and forced about one of every ten U.S. corporations to issue restatements of earnings. Add the nearly 600,000 jobs lost in 2001–2002 as wayward corporations retrenched to indirect job losses, and you can see the employment penalty when owners do not or cannot act like they own.[27]

Steadily, more observers are waking to the implications of widespread citizen ownership. James Hawley and Andrew Williams argue that very large pension funds act as "universal owners," of necessity concerned about the overall economy as much as their specific investments.[28] They get it. We now live in an economic system in which everyone involved wears many hats: workers, owners, consumers, interest groups, regulators, competitors, suppliers. Where the relationships were once one-dimensional and linear, today they are profoundly interrelated. We have a new circle of accountability that both starts and finishes with the investor-pensioner-employee-consumer-citizen.

The New Capitalist Circle of Accountability

Part 1 of this book focuses on exactly that. Management gurus have written whole libraries demonstrating that internal accountability—

wherein every employee reports to someone for his or her perform-ance—makes companies efficient. But they gloss over a key question: to whom does the stock-traded company *board* report? In the era when both directors and shareowners acted liked ornaments, the issue was virtually irrelevant. But in an era of awakening new capitalists, real lines of accountability are coming into view that affect the corporation as a whole.

Figure 1-1 shows what these lines of accountability look like. Cor-porate executives report to the board, which reports to shareowners, who are represented by fund managers, who are often hired by pension trustees or other fund administrators. These decision makers, in turn, are responsible for the finances of the employees whose retirement and other savings they seek to invest.

In aggregate, therefore, the workforce of public companies reports up the chain to owners, who are in turn the workforce, the retirees, and the dependents of the workforce, as well as the suppliers, competitors, and customers. Companies face incentives to seek to efficiently maxi-mize the complex, long-term interests of all of us.

FIGURE 1-1

Circle of accountability

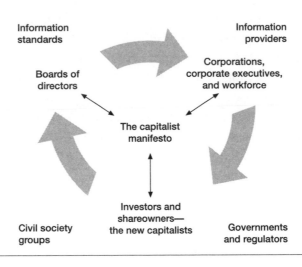

Information standards

Information providers

Boards of directors

Corporations, corporate executives, and workforce

The capitalist manifesto

Civil society groups

Investors and shareowners— the new capitalists

Governments and regulators

Many senior business executives are aware that the rise of citizen investors is mandating a new focus on accountability. But as figure 1-1 implies, this is not just about the accountability of corporations. It is also about the accountability of investment institutions and how well they perform the role of overseeing the companies in which they have invested our capital. When all stations on this accountability circuit operate unhindered, the result is a phenomenon that we call the *civil economy*. Let's unpack what we mean by a civil economy.

Step by step, the spread and awakening of new capitalists has produced dozens of little-noticed innovations—changes to rules, assumptions, and behaviors—that in effect "constitutionalize" the marketplace. That is, they have built a new doctrine of standards of accountability in the corporate world. Frameworks—some voluntary, some mandatory; some explicit, some unstated—redefine the role of the board, expand transparency, enfranchise shareowners, and overhaul director appointments. They also divert law and regulation from trying to impose specific results and toward reinforcing weak links in the circle of accountability, so that market forces can carve responsible paths.

We have now arrived at a point where we can identify a budding civil economy that mirrors civil society. In the political sphere, civil society is served by democratic institutions, separation of powers, and protection of individual liberties. If handled correctly, these can be the foundation stones of a society most likely to benefit most of its members, thereby establishing grounds for progress and social cohesion over time. The constitutionalization of the marketplace means that an equivalent structure is emerging in the economic sphere—a framework that could promote growth in employment and equitable prosperity.

The civil economy is not a singular invention so much as a frame of reference allowing us to connect the myriad dots of individual developments bubbling up in international enterprise. Interpreting these changes as part of a widespread phenomenon gives us insights into what is happening, how we can benefit from it, and how we can help it along if we choose.

Constitutional and accountable political institutions supported by political parties, an independent judiciary, a free press, impartial law, civic bodies, and an involved citizenry are the core sustainers of democracy in a civil society. Parallel institutions of a civil economy can be under-stood to be constitutional and accountable corporations, supported by engaged shareowners and their accountable representatives, indepen-dent monitors, credible standards, and community organizations partic-ipating in the marketplace. (See figure 1-2.) Change occurs when these agents are mobilized, thus altering the infrastructure and rules, the un-written constitution, of commerce.

In a nutshell, the global market ideal implicit in a civil economy is this: institutional owners accountable to their savers push corporations toward sustainable prosperity through responsible management.

We see the market potentially transforming into a civil economy by means of the circle of accountability, which is all about how citizen in-vestors are steadily clearing conduits to influence. In part 1 we spotlight the main way stations along that circuit. But we also contend that ac-countability is maturing thanks to what we call a *new capitalist eco-system* that is keeping the circle working effectively. That's the focus of part 2. For now, let's take a summary tour of where the book is heading.

Corporations and executives: from an uncivil economy to the capitalist mani-festo. In chapter 2, we examine the civil economy at the most obvious station on the circle of accountability: the corporation. What does the owner revolution mean for the way the corporation operates? In a con-ventional economy, corporate executives often only paid lip service to owners or else assumed investors wanted mainly to maximize short-term profit. Today CEOs confront different impulses. New capitalist owners are speaking up; more are flexing newfound clout to press for company performance. How then does a "civil economy corporation" adapt? What should corporate managers do?

To answer those questions, we retrace some history to spell out where we've come from before projecting where we're going. The role and activities of corporations were fundamental to how we thought about global politics and economics in the twentieth century. But the change in ownership brings a profound change in thinking. In chapter 3 we outline the demands of the new owners in a *capitalist manifesto,* com-plete with strategies that executives can tap for advantage. It opens by affirming that any company must strive to be profitable, but just as important, it defines what profitability means in an accountable civil

FIGURE 1-2

Comparison between institutions of a civil society and a civil economy

Civil society

Civil economy

Accountable government	**Accountable corporations**
• Constitution	• Constitution of board (i.e., board charter)
• Elections	• Election of boards
• Limitation of powers	• Powers of executive limited

Informed electors	**Engaged shareowners**
• Voters understand and able to choose between coherent political programs at elections	• Owners' fiduciaries (e.g., fund managers) informed, skilled, and appropriately engaged with the companies they invest in

Independent monitors	**Independent monitors**
• Free press, independent judiciary	• Fully independent annual audit giving information owners need
• Independent statistics, freedom of information	• Voting advisory services, remuneration consultancies transparent and unconflicted

Credible standards	**Credible standards**
• Relevant and independent statistics and other ways to measure performance	• Relevant and independent statistics and other ways to measure performance

Civil society organizations	**Civil economy organizations**
• Freedom within the law and the constitution to campaign to change government policy	• Freedom within the law to campaign to change company policy
• Acceptance of the right of others to scrutinize background and motivation of any such action	• Acceptance of the right of others to scrutinize background and motivation of any such action

economy: investing in projects that return more than the return available from deploying capital elsewhere. If such projects are unavailable, a company should return surplus money to its owners. Creating a surplus on its invested capital is the primary purpose of the corporation. If we ever forget that, we undermine the whole system of equity savings and investment.

But it no longer makes strategic sense for a company to profit at the expense of society at large. This declaration is the logic not of some do-gooder ethos, but of changed assumptions born of the ownership revolution. Classical economists use the term *externality* to signify the cost of a transaction that affects a third party. For example, a coal-burning utility scrimping on pollution-control devices may boost its next quarter's profits by decreasing capital spending. Traditionally, regulators tried to legislate against harmful externalities; they levied fines for pollution. Predictably, companies would oppose such regulation since they could save cash by shunting costs to outsiders.

But new capitalist collective investment vehicles hold stakes in many companies; they can have no interest in abetting behavior by any one company that yields a short-term boost while threatening harm to the economic system as a whole.

In short, corporate management styles acceptable to the conventional economy can today do damage to the interests of citizen savers who entrust their capital to big funds. By contrast, management in a civil economy involves corporations pursuing sustainable profitability since such practices match the interests of their new capitalist owners, thus raising stock value over time and reducing a company's cost of capital.

Institutional investors: mobilizing ownership. In civil society, we talk of voters. In a civil economy, we address owners. Institutional investors form the backbone of activist networks. Think CalPERS in the United States, Ontario Teachers in Canada, Hermes in Europe, Sparx in Japan, ARIA in Australia, Dynamo in Brazil, Templeton in various emerging markets. These investors have made activism on behalf of members the hallmark of their investment styles. In this respect, they represent a sharp break from conventional investment, in which the shareowner was encouraged to think of his or her stake in each company as a "tradable security," not as a fractional ownership share with rights and responsibilities. Even the nomenclature—*shareholder* as opposed to *shareowner*—conveyed ambiguity. If the company performed badly, the shareowner would simply sell. (In this book, we use the term *shareowner* because it more closely reflects appropriate behavior for modern fund managers.)

Of course, many financial institutions remain hobbled by conventional practices. Funds may operate, for instance, without sufficient regard for their roles as fiduciaries for millions of savers. They may be opaque and fail to reveal how they deal with corporate managements or how they vote their ownership interests. Pension plans, mutual funds, or unit trusts may be conflicted and do little to challenge wayward companies in which they own stock. A mutual fund, for instance, may be less likely to vote shares against a company's management if it wants business from the CEO. Moreover, mutual funds, hedge funds, and the like are often (though not always) judged and marketed by their short-term performance, leading to many of the same short-term pressures as affect their corporate brethren. We review these dysfunctions in chapter 4.

Following that, we illuminate how—through market innovation, grassroots pressure, voluntary codes, and law or regulation—institutional investors are becoming more accountable and, as a consequence, playing a more active role as owners.

Boards of directors: a new accountability. Chapter 5, last stop on the circle of accountability, returns to the corporation through the boardroom door. Until the last decade or two, little effort had gone into thinking through the roles and responsibilities of a board member. We profile some of the consequences: ways corporate boards, asleep or co-opted, have failed citizen investors. New capitalists, though, tag the board as the principal gateway to ensuring that companies strive for long-term performance. This dynamic is invigorating the relationship between investors and the agents who are supposed to act on their behalf, adding another pipeline to the civil economy.

The New Capitalist Ecosystem

In part 3 of this book, we spotlight barriers embedded in the conventional economy and show how they are giving way, making it possible for citizen investors to compel corporate change.

Circuits don't run without external catalysts. In home wiring, it is electricity zapped in from the local utility. In the circle of accountability, it is an array of information services and pressures that constitute what we call a civil economy ecosystem. In the conventional economy, monitors and accounting standards were supposed to cater to investors—but did so only rarely. Civic organizations mostly ignored capital, focusing instead on government to achieve their social ends. Today this ecosystem has undergone a quiet evolution, with all parties starting to focus on the new capitalist dynamics of the market.

Monitoring the market: the information moguls. In civil society, we expect the surveillance of a free press and the brawn of an independent judiciary to guard against tyranny. Citizen investors depend on a wide range of monitors to help make corporate behavior transparent. After all, information is essential to the efficient working of the marketplace, as more than one economist has observed. But, as we note in chapter 6, historic conflicts of interest limited the value of traditional "information moguls" such as investment analysts, auditors, consultants, credit-rating agencies, and the press, who were supposed to monitor the market fairly.

That, too, is changing as the civil economy takes hold. The information moguls are now swiveling: from catering to corporate managers to serving new capitalists. Traditional capital market intermediaries have responded by devoting fresh, critical scrutiny to corporate boards and managers. Thus corporate credit-rating agencies now have corporate governance staffs to evaluate corporate governance risks. Executive recruiting firms boast corporate governance practices. Law firms from Los Angeles to Johannesburg have created corporate governance services.

Then there is the new breed of specialized services that analyze corporate governance for a fee. They are the eyes and ears that shareowners needed, but never had, until now. And these services literally span the globe.[29] Still more firms probe companies on their social or environmental performance.

These new civil economy monitoring institutions hand portfolio managers, for the first time, the ability to define "investment-grade governance"—in other words, to measure a company's capacity to align with new capitalist interests—when making buy and sell decisions. And companies are able to benchmark their own accountability practices against peers at home or anywhere in the world.

Accounting Standards: Escaping Brother Luca's Boxes. Civil society depends on information attuned to the concerns of the electorate. It helps voters benchmark progress so citizens can hold those in power to account. Public data on crime, productivity, jobs, and housing let citizens debate the merits of policy using validated measures.

In the ecosystem of owners, accounting and other standards serve alongside law as a rough equivalent. Such rules—first framed five hundred years ago by Franciscan friar Luca Bartolomeo Pacioli—pilot executives and accountants toward how and what to manage and measure. But do these reflect the views and needs of today's new capitalists and their agents? In chapter 7 we review how conventional measurements ill suit an era where citizen investors require different markers to assess corporate performance. We profile the fresh standards being propelled into the market—and how they are altering the behavior of investors and CEOs alike.

Civil economy–style reporting standards offer a chance to measure shareowner value creation properly. When companies begin releasing accounts based on such standards, stock prices begin to reflect a company's ability to manage all its assets—both tangible and intangible—and all its liabilities—whether long-term or short-term, absolute or contingent, measurable to the second decimal point or only able to be guessed. Ultimately, the goal of these new civil economy standards is not just to help the stock market assign a price to a company's stock, but to allow corporate executives to better manage their assets, and to allow citizen investors to take timely, remedial action where companies fail to do so.

NGOs and capital: civil society meets the civil economy. The success of a civil society rests in part on the proliferation and clout of nongovernmental organizations—political parties, organized religion, trade unions, big business, advocacy groups, or academia—working within the law for change.

So too the civil economy is arising in part from the involvement of community organizations, which we profile in chapter 8. Some groups are new; others are veteran civil society entities adapting their strategies to suit channels afforded by capital. Of course, some traditional organizations still shun the market, hewing to the conventional habit of seeking solutions only at the political level. Others—Japan's *sokaiya* gangsters, say—champion violent protest or use muscle for corrupt purposes, placing themselves decisively beyond the bounds of a civil economy. But many more NGOs understand the latent power of citizen-owner capital peacefully marshaled. They are paving fresh paths.

Conclusion: The New Capitalist Agenda

In a Darwinian sense, the worst of the traditional economy's capital market structure—submissive owners, marginal or conflicted monitors, absent civic groups, and blinkered accounting standards—could not help but give rise to companies that celebrate shortsighted stock price jumps instead of sustainable growth. Creatures of a flawed economic terrain, many firms by their actions understandably provoke public resentment of globalization.

By contrast, a new species of corporation naturally evolves when citizen-owners are energized, monitors are girded with safeguards against conflict, performance yardsticks help managers and investors gauge real drivers of value, and civil society organizations become a constructive market force. This kind of civil economy terrain spawns corporations skilled at cultivating commercial dynamism in a context of accountability and responsibility. For early indications of how this works, just look at the extent to which intense consumer and investor pressure on some of the world's big multinationals—BP, Nike, and GE—has convinced them to become vocal, if still perhaps imperfect, apostles of socially responsible management.

Evidence coming in from diverse markets already shows that the circle of accountability is a virtuous one. Companies with active long-term shareowners introduce more responsive governance and are more likely to produce higher returns, drawing in turn more long-term—and loyal—investors. Such corporations gain access to capital at a lower cost, giving them advantages over rivals. Accountability in all parties, in short, is surfacing as one of the most effective keys to unlocking sustainable value. This accountability is the core of what we mean by a civil economy.

Still, only a fraction of the world's listed companies have what we might identify as hallmarks of the civil economy enterprise: a professional, independent board; a culture of disclosure; and executives skilled at recognizing and drawing value from management of corporate responsibility.

For that reason, we offer in chapter 9 a set of action memos to directors, executives, shareowners, information brokers, and civic lobbies. After all, the revolution wrought by new capitalists is merely an opportunity to be seized or lost by market players. Our recommendations are crafted to give each the best shot at optimizing stakes in the civil economy as it grows.

We also spell out an agenda for policy makers in government. Lawmakers and regulators are necessary partners in creating conditions for accountable commerce. Their aim should be to clear obstacles to the circle of accountability, not to predetermine outcomes. They can empower funds to play an active role as owners on behalf of their citizen investors, while at the same time arming grassroots new capitalists with adequate and credible information to hold their funds accountable.

With new capitalists inheriting influence, both public- and private-sector policy makers are coming to understand that the emerging civil economy represents a prudent path to a worldwide "constitution of the marketplace." In it, institutional investors can promote a fusion of accountability and commerce, pressing our large public companies to seek a broader and more sustainable prosperity.

Business Past

The Uncivil Economy

S truggles for control of economic power have driven the world to the brink of nuclear conflict. Cold War clashes between communists and free marketers have today given way to risks of a new divide, this time between citizens and multinational corporations. But new capitalists are setting the stage for thinking about corporations in a different way.

Communications were cut with naval command in Moscow, and the B-59 submarine captain was feeling light-headed in the heat and thin air. Thuds from depth charges were getting closer, rocking his silent vessel. U.S. warships cruising above seemed determined to force him to surface. This was clearly no drill. But the Soviet captain had no way to get orders, or even to find out what was going on. It was October 1962, off the coast of Cuba. The two superpowers were at loggerheads over whether Moscow would keep nuclear missiles on the island, pointed at cities in the southern United States. "Maybe the war has already started," the captain declared to his officers. The U.S. Navy could not know that the Russians' secret undersea arsenal included nuclear missiles. The captain now ordered one armed for launch. "We're going to blast them," he pledged. "We will die, but we will sink all of them."[1]

In the end, of course, the commander did not launch, and the Cuban missile crisis came to an end. But if he had, he would have triggered a worldwide atomic conflagration, killing tens of millions of people either from direct blasts, tidal shock waves, or lethal radiation. Things can get nasty in the struggle for economic power.

Two superpowers were poised on the brink that day in the confusing seas off Cuba largely because they held opposing notions about how we own and control capital. On the one hand, the Soviet Union advocated the abolition of private property. Communist doctrine held that the only way to achieve human equality and development was through common or state ownership of the ways and means of production. As Karl Marx wrote in *The Communist Manifesto*, "The theory of the Communists may be summed up in a single sentence: Abolition of private property."[2] On the other hand, the United States believed that the ability of individuals to own and control capital was a fundamental civil liberty. If this were breached, other freedoms would quickly disappear. In his inaugural address just twenty-one months before the Soviet submariner sweated over the launch button, President John F. Kennedy had set the stakes. America would "pay any price, bear any burden, meet any hardship, support any friend, oppose any foe, in order to assure the survival and success of liberty."[3] During the Cuban missile crisis, that price was nearly paid—by all of us.

Throughout history, conflicts over economic power have shown a ferocious potential to destabilize. Today some have suggested that such conflicts are over. Yet confidence in globalized free enterprise is low. Now, in the early twenty-first century, we are witnessing a new clash. On the one hand are populations of citizens, the new capitalists, who have come to own our great companies only to find them difficult to make accountable. On the other hand is a potent establishment that benefits from this lack of accountability.

We contend that there is a third path: the revolution in ownership is quietly laying foundations of an accountable capitalism capable of winning public trust. Corporate executives, political leaders, and working people alike have everything at stake in this outcome. If the collision between citizens and corporations escalates, there is a potential for unsustainable economic development and social unrest, with the price paid in lost jobs and ebbing income, rising poverty, environmental destruction, and spreading curbs on business life.

Pins and Poverty

The Cold War is long over. But Cold War attitudes still permeate the way many economists think and the way many companies operate. That is no surprise. A culture of management divorced from broad shareowner interests has deep roots—and, until recently, businesses have avoided change. But unbeknownst to many, such old-style corporate stewardship is as obsolete as the Cold War itself. Executives who cannot soon extract their companies from the "uncivil economy" will find their enterprises ever more at risk from companies led by executives who can.

Where did we get our model of how business works? For that we need to wind the clock back to the beginnings of factory life, around 1770.

The Industrial Revolution reordered society. Its effects were so profound that historians would argue that they had "completely eclipsed" all other social shifts over the previous thousand years.[4] Contemporary thinkers sought to make sense of change, predict its outcomes, and recommend policies to improve them. Their brainstorms helped shape the way we think about today's business world.

One of those eighteenth-century thinkers, Adam Smith, was a professor at Glasgow University in Scotland. Although he was one of history's most outstanding economists, he did not teach economics but rather moral philosophy. In part, this focus reflected Smith's wide-ranging interests (he was, for example, an enthusiastic advocate of American independence). It also reflected the fact that, for centuries prior to Smith, matters involving money had been largely considered questions of ethics. In the Middle Ages, for instance, the proper price anyone could charge for goods and services was a question of what would be considered "just."[5]

Smith illustrated how factories were making jaw-dropping advances in productivity, thanks to the division of labor. In The Wealth of Nations, he famously described a pin factory with ten employees. With each worker doing a specialized task, the factory could produce forty-eight thousand pins a day. Had they toiled independently, as in the old days, "they certainly could not each of them have made twenty, perhaps not one pin in a day."[6] He concluded that the world had entered a wholly new era. The larger the market demand for any good, the more scope a manufacturer had to specialize. And the more specialization, the greater the increase in productivity and wealth.

Adam Smith also had a second breakthrough insight: there is no one "correct" price for goods; the price will be determined by the law of supply and demand. Open competition in the marketplace will automatically bring supply and demand into balance and ensure that prices reflect the cost of manufacture. It was this effect of competition that Smith dubbed his "invisible hand." For Smith, and more particularly for his followers, economics would become less a matter of philosophy and more a pragmatic matter of supply and demand.

Fifty years after Smith's death, his predictions about productivity had come true—with a vengeance. In his hometown of Glasgow, merchants had built fortunes trading textiles, tobacco, and other goods. But most citizens—even those working daily jobs—remained poor, crammed into the increasingly crowded and unsanitary slums that grew up around the great factories that exploited the benefits of the division of labor. And many Glasgow merchants were callously indifferent to the consequences of their actions. One even tried (and failed) to corner the market in slaves. We can only imagine the human suffering that arose from such an action.[7]

To some, the poor conditions of working people, even the slums themselves, were the result of supply and demand; in this case, the supply of people. The laboring poor lived in such conditions, critics argued, simply because there were too many of them. Unless the government worked to curb the birth rate or encourage people to emigrate to the colonies in North America, the masses would remain in degradation. In the meantime, the authorities needed urgently to keep control for fear of rebellion.

Workers' Rule

Here is where the schism leading to today's battles over the corporation's mission began. Not everyone accepted this analysis. Some concluded that laborers were poor because industrial moguls had kept the surplus of workers' productive labor for themselves. In the Middle

Ages, communists would explain, when land was the source of wealth, barons controlled the estates and wielded their power to make serfs of the working people. Now capital was the prime source of wealth. "Capitalists" were controlling the levers of economic and political power and exploiting the labor force.

The only solution, so the communists and socialists thought, was for workers to seize control of productive capital. For socialists, control over capital would be achieved through evolution. For the communists, it would be achieved by revolution. But for both, ownership of property was the key to creating a fair and decent society where all would have equal dignity and equal freedom and would live in community.

Keir Hardie, founder of the British Labour Party, stated the case in ringing terms in 1907:

> The boundaries of freedom have been widening with the progress of the ages. The slave of 1,000 years ago, with no more right than the swine he tended, has fought his way upward from serfdom to citizenship. The modern workman is theoretically the equal in the eye of the law of every other class. His vote carries equal weight in the ballot box with that of the millionaire who employs him; he is as free to worship when and how he pleases as the noblest baron . . . But his task is not yet finished; the long-drawn-out struggle is not yet over. There is one more battle to be fought . . . He has yet to overcome property and win economic freedom. When he has made property his servant, not his master, he will literally have put all his enemies under his feet.[8]

"Crass Inequality"

Socialists and communists had a harder time gaining traction in the United States. Perhaps that was because the country had such a long tradition of smallholdings and small business, a heritage of suspicion of state power, and a constitution that protected property rights. The preferred path for progressive politicians was not to nationalize the huge new enterprises, but to break up the trusts and monopolies deemed to be abusing market power, and to extend the authority of trade unions to protect workers' rights.

Even in the United States, however, political debate over corporate power raged. When President Franklin D. Roosevelt spoke to the unemployed millions in the 1930s about "unscrupulous money changers [who] stand indicted in the court of public opinion," he had in mind a small elite who had amassed vast fortunes.[9] President Theodore Roosevelt, in an earlier decade, had described vividly an era of "crass inequality":

> The great coal mining and coal carrying companies could easily dispense with the service of any particular miner. The miner, on the other hand, could not dispense with the company. He needed a job; his wife and children would starve if he did not get one. What the miner had to sell—his labor—was a perishable commodity. The labor of today—if not sold—was lost forever. Moreover, his labor was not like most commodities, a mere thing; it was part of a living, breathing human being. The workmen saw that the labor problem was not only an economic but also a moral, a human problem.[10]

In the event, the transforming political episode destined to crystallize debate about the control of capital took place neither in Europe or America but in Russia, with the Bolsheviks' 1917 seizure of power. Within a few years the Bolsheviks had established the Soviet Union, a state based on the abolition of all private property. Here, they claimed, was the end of the uncivil economy.

State Rule

In destroying private enterprise, and in trying to overturn the laws of free-market economics, the Communists showed ruthless indifference to human life and liberty. The Soviets made it illegal for individuals to own any productive capital and, hence, to undertake any commercial activity. The state controlled all decisions regarding production. Businesses could not "sell" to one another; instead, they delivered and received goods according to quotas. Business did not earn a profit that could be spent. Central planners—rather than Adam Smith's laws of supply and demand—dictated what goods went onto shop shelves.

For workers, changing jobs was difficult, not least because residency rights required a permit, the *propiska*. On the other hand, you were unlikely to lose your job, since enterprises had little incentive to reduce labor costs. Thus the Soviets controlled the mobility of labor, but at a great cost both to productivity and to personal freedom.

People could save. But money did not give access to goods as it did in a market economy. Planners paid little heed to frivolities. They permitted few restaurants and simply outlawed anything like sidewalk food stands. You could not buy a house; if you wanted to rent a larger home, or acquire a car, you had to enter a bureaucratic process of allocation based on need—or else pull strings. A culture of corruption developed, further decreasing productivity, as pervasive graft served as a "tax" on economic growth. Business was effectively a branch of government, providing housing, education, and transport—even arranging holiday accommodation for employees.

In short, in reaction to an uncivil economy of freewheeling but profoundly unequal capitalism, the Soviets built an uncivil economy of authoritarian oppression. And this uncivil economy worked—for a time. The Soviet Communist Party proved to be efficient at delivering simple goods, at least initially. Many around the world saw Russia's model, despite its many drawbacks, as a valid challenge to Western-style free-market capitalism. But it was about to implode.

Moral Vacuum

By the time of the Cuban missile crisis, the gulf between the superpowers over the control of capital had come to dominate global politics. Ironically, throughout the Cold War, both communists and capitalists shared one fundamental belief: Neither saw business as incorporating much to do with morality.

Communists and Socialists subscribed to theories that tended to view private capital as immoral, oppressive, and exploitative. Across the divide, free-market economists viewed capitalism as "amoral." Economics faculties in every major university were now long divorced from the moral philosophy departments of Adam Smith's day. Experts branded economics, including the study of how business works, the "queen of social science" and even the "dismal science," at least partially because its theoretical models had little need for ethics or the discussion of social responsibility.[11]

Pity the corporate executive grappling with modern conflicting demands. Cold War management theory simply assumed that the purpose of production was the maximization of profit. The key questions—what constitutes profit, and how can it best be made?—were too often left unanswered.

In fact, by the 1990s, with the end of the Cold War and the defeat of Communism, many thought leaders embraced what became known as the "Washington Consensus": the great economic issues of ownership, capital, and finance that had set the world on the brink of nuclear war in the twentieth century had now been resolved. Free-market economics had triumphed. Prosperity now was a function of market forces unleashed through deregulation, privatization, and letting business just get on with it.

Not everyone agreed, of course, but few offered a viable alternative. During antiglobalization demonstrations in 1999, one protester waved a placard urging onlookers to "Destroy Global Capitalism and Replace It with Something Nicer."

"Something nicer" was hardly a blueprint for reform. On the other hand, the message accurately caught an important strand of popular conviction. The collapse of Communism's uncivil economy had not just signaled the triumph of market capitalism. The chief inheritors of financial power were multinational corporations—and they were failing to earn universal confidence. Small wonder. The end of the Cold War had prompted no sweeping reconsideration of business culture. The corporation, tapping roots stretching back four centuries, had become, all too often, unaccountable.

"The Pathological Pursuit of Profit"

Slide your finger down a map of the Western Hemisphere to the tip of South America, where Argentina's Tierra del Fuego juts toward Antarctica. There, in violent seas at the very edge of the world, is an unlikely memorial to one of the earliest attempts to control the activities of the corporation.

The Strait of Le Maire marks the wild ambitions of a Flemish merchant and investor. Swashbuckling isn't a word normally applied to corner-office fund managers of the twenty-first century. But four hundred years ago, Isaac Le Maire fit that bill. His nemesis was the Dutch East India Company—*Vereenigde Oost-Indische Compagnie*, or VOC—the first enterprise ever to be listed on a stock exchange. It raised 6.45 million guilders from over one thousand people. But its managers were ruthless, paving a path that ultimately led straight to Enron, WorldCom, Parmalat, and other debacles. Complacent insiders enjoyed opulent perks while systematically demolishing shareowner value. Directors acquired substantial fortunes overnight "in the manner of mushrooms," as contemporaries noted.[12] Directors kept financial accounts secret. Investors had no say in selecting managers or voting on policies. The board refused to pay dividends—or it would disburse them in the form of bags of surplus nutmeg rather than cash.[13]

Enter Isaac Le Maire, father of twenty-four and the VOC's largest minority investor. Fed up with anemic returns, he submitted history's first recorded dissident shareowner petition on January 24, 1609. The Amsterdam trader slammed VOC management as "absurd and impertinent" and claimed that its chronic squandering of investor capital was "a kind of tyranny." In the rhetoric of umbrage alone Le Maire kicked off a rich tradition. "Pigs at the trough" is how author Arianna Huffington would brand similar boardroom behavior four hundred years later.[14] *Nieten in nadelstreifen* ("nitwits in pinstripes") is how journalist Günter Ogger would put it in a German bestseller.[15] For others it is not just management greed or incompetence that is in the dock. It is the corporation itself. According to Canadian professor Joel Bakan, corporations are organizations aiming for "the pathological pursuit of profit and power."[16]

VOC executives were unmoved by Le Maire's complaints, however. So the determined financier recruited a coalition of investors and speculators to drive VOC shares down through massive selling, hoping to force management capitulation.

In the event, the Dutch government hastened to save the skins of the VOC's directors with special concessions to the company and curbs on investor power. The assault did force the board to make token concessions to shareowners. In an uneasy compromise, the VOC committed to paying regular dividends, and by keeping its shares tradable, it allowed shareowners to realize their capital by selling their shares to someone else, thus creating the world's first permanent publicly traded company. But, equally, it convinced managers to erect formidable statutory walls against future investor attack.

The VOC bided its time before striking back at Le Maire. Defeated but even more obsessed with thrashing the company, Le Maire challenged its stranglehold on shipping to lucrative spice markets in Indonesia. In 1615 he financed—and charged his son Jacob to command—a bold expedition, "Goldseekers," which discovered an uncharted channel to the Pacific two hundred miles south of the VOC's monopoly-controlled Straits of Magellan. Le Maire's caravel pushed triumphantly through to Jakarta, its captain heady with visions of a new commercial empire. The VOC, however, would have none of it. Three days after Le Maire's ship sailed into port, officials threw the crew into prison and confiscated the vessel. The company flatly denied Le Maire's claim that he had found a new route to Asia, and packed his son Jacob off to the Netherlands. He died during the long voyage home. The VOC had its revenge.

For the next two years, a furious Isaac Le Maire waged legal war on the company. Against the odds, he won. He recovered his vessel and earned the right to match the family name with the strait Jacob had discovered at the bottom of the world. The VOC shrugged off the challenge and continued to grow.

Brilliant and Dangerous

The corporation had emerged as a new player that was to change the nature of commerce profoundly. But it did not have auspicious beginnings. The model was brilliant because it allowed a company to raise capital from a multitude of sources, permitting it to become permanent while its investors changed. Dangers, though, stemmed precisely from this separation of ownership from the management of capital.

First, managers faced a grave temptation to act in their own best interest rather than in the interests of the firm's shareowners. Economists call this the principal-agent problem. Second, if the company's securities were subject to speculation, its managers could take advantage. And they did.

In 1720, scandals from exactly this sort of abuse sent the London and Paris stock markets into cataclysmic tailspins that stifled company growth for more than a century. The Enrons and Parmalats of the day were the Mississippi Company in France and the South Sea Company in Britain. Each proved uninterested in trade. Instead, they bought government debt and artificially ramped up their share prices. Some insiders and investors made fortunes, but for most the schemes brought only tears. The public grew to see companies as little more than seedy speculative devices. Even Adam Smith was wary. Companies were useful where large amounts of capital were required and the mission was the common good—for example, building a canal. But "to establish a joint stock company, for any undertaking, merely because such a company might be capable of managing it successfully . . . would certainly not be reasonable," Smith concluded. His logic was clear: "The directors [of joint-stock companies] being the managers rather of other people's money than of their own, it cannot be well expected that they would watch over it with the same anxious vigilance with which [owners] watch over their own. Negligence and profusion, therefore, must always prevail, more or less, in the management of the affairs of such a company." [17]

Despite Smith's concerns, the corporation prospered. Indeed, such corporations are central to the free-market culture and have expanded globally, as if beyond the power of national governments.

We have seen how corporations have wrought benefits and ignited controversy over the course of four hundred years. Today, as they have risen to unprecedented worldwide power, corporations are at the center of the debate. But before we praise or condemn their activities, we need to ask a more basic question. What is, or should be, the purpose of a corporation? And how does the revolution in ownership affect the answer?

- Near-nuclear conflict in the Cold War demonstrated how dangerous the struggle for economic power can be. Today, instead of superpowers at loggerheads, we have a worrying gulf between citizens
  and globalized corporations. To map the future of the corporation
  in an era of new capitalists, we need to understand its evolution.

- Adam Smith framed the most influential economic case for the Industrial Revolution. In the nineteenth century, debate over free markets polarized. Communists and Socialists considered private
  enterprise socially divisive, while free-market advocates defended
  its capacity to generate wealth.

- Soviet Communism countered an uncivil economy of freewheeling
  but profoundly unequal capitalism with an uncivil economy of authoritarian oppression.

- The end of the Cold War prompted no sweeping reconsideration of
  business culture. Private-sector corporations inherited economic
  power but failed to earn universal confidence. Executives faced
  public pressure to make the corporation into a good citizen. But few
  critics spelled out what that meant.

- The emergence of new capitalists creates a new basis for answering
  the question at the heart of today's economy: what is, or what
  should be, the purpose of a corporation?

PART TWO

The New Capitalist Circle of Accountability

The Future Corporation
A Capitalist Manifesto

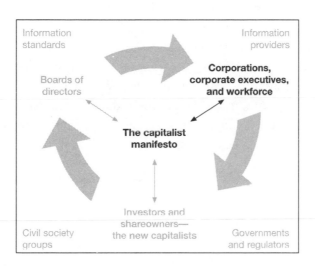

Regulation, markets, and culture constrain the corporation, keeping it from trampling on social interests. And new capitalists are becoming a powerful force driving long-term value so that corporations work *for* social benefit. In this chapter we outline a ten-point *capitalist manifesto*, which allows successful executives to align their companies' interests with those of their citizen owners.

"**G**reed is good," purrs Wall Street trader Gordon Gekko to fawning investment bankers in the 1987 Hollywood hit *Wall Street*. In real life, Nobel Prize winner Milton Friedman put it almost as bluntly: "The social responsibility of business is to maximize its profits."[1]

With that dictum, Friedman won the hearts of those pledged to fight government interference in the economy and social fetters on companies. Equally, it earned the economist special disdain from many others. Friedman seemed to advocate that a company's primary mission should be to satisfy its own economic appetite regardless of the harmful consequences it might cause others. Why would a civilized society, they argue, ever foster such self-interested institutions?

It is the old debate of left and right, each fiercely convinced that corporations are amoral, and equally fiercely convinced that the other side's vision of "morality" is dangerous and inefficient. Now it is time to escape that dead end and discover a fresh way of framing the mission of the corporation in a twenty-first-century era of new capitalists.

Lord of the Ring

Corporations are remarkably simple yet powerful legal creations. They allow individuals, who may not even know one another, to contribute capital to an enterprise but take on no liability for any action of that enterprise, beyond the cash they originally put in. That collective action of pooling capital allows for economies of scale and efficiencies of expertise, enabling corporations to drive the world's economy.

But as we have seen, the corporation is also potentially dangerous. Consider the ethical question a student by the name of Glaucon posed to Socrates some twenty-five hundred years ago. Imagine you have a ring with magical powers; Glaucon called it the ring of Gyges. With this ring, you can become invisible and do whatever you want to further your own self-interest without any fear of discovery or punishment. How would you behave? "Surely," Glaucon thought, the common view would be that "any man who possessed this power . . . [and] nevertheless refused to do anything unjust or rob his fellows, all who knew of his conduct would think him the most miserable and foolish of men."[2] Socrates countered that it is better for the person—invisible or not—to behave morally, because such behavior would reflect his true nature and hence lead to happiness.

What if the ring-bearer is not a human, but a company? Whatever you think of Socrates' argument, it is difficult to apply it to the legal construction known as the limited liability company. It has no nature or conscience or beliefs that would encourage it to behave morally. It will do what it will, with the only sanction being a loss of its capital. After all, you may jail executives, but you cannot put a corporation in prison; you cannot even make it feel guilty! In extreme cases, corporations may be put out of business (take, for example, the accounting firm Arthur Andersen). But for the most part, companies can allow the investors who own them to behave as if they were all wearing rings of Gyges.

Fear that Glaucon's perspective will prevail in business has haunted society for centuries. When governments first awarded companies charters, the terms of those charters strictly limited business activities to specific opportunities, for example, to conduct trade with a particular part of the world or to form a bank or to build and operate a canal. Corporate charters were also limited in duration; if a corporation wanted to keep shareowner capital past the expiration of its charter, it needed special permission. Indeed, throughout the early part of Britain's industrial revolution (1720–1825), a special act of Parliament was required even to establish a company.[3] Lawmakers worried that such powerful creatures, if left uncontrolled, could be a licence for fraud and waste.

License to Harm?

Why would an economist such as Milton Friedman apparently want to hand corporations even greater license? The answer is that license is the opposite of what Friedman intends. His aim is to ensure that corporations do *not* use their power in ways that are arbitrary and potentially harmful.

Imagine if the boards of directors of powerful companies were to decide to wield financial clout arbitrarily and for their own self-interest rather than to deliver profit for their owners. They might begin, say, with inoffensive infringements of their profit mandate: for example, giving money to some noble institution, with the CEO receiving personal recognition for his company's generosity with shareowner cash. They might stray further by, say, inflating pay and perks for top executives. They might expand their empires into high-profile trophy businesses that come with political influence or social status—newspapers and television, or sports franchises, for example. They might give money to political candidates who would ensure that their personal interests were protected and promoted. In the extreme, they might use their companies' bank accounts to "buy" the government of the land.

This behavior is of course all too common in the business world. That is why so many observers echo the thoughts of U.S. Supreme Court Justice Louis Brandeis, who once described the corporation as a Frankenstein's monster that has escaped the lawmakers who originally created it and is now taking control of them.[4] Milton Friedman, believe it or not, would be on the side of those who wished to reharness the monster. The goal of the corporation, he would argue, needs to be clearly and narrowly defined: to serve its shareowners by simply maximizing profit.

The paradox is that Friedman suggests that solely maximizing profit is a legitimate social objective. Yet it does not sound like one. Perhaps what Friedman means is that *if* corporations were to maximize profit, this in turn would naturally lead to other positive social consequences, such as the production of desired goods and services, and to economic growth and employment. And, certainly, a cursory review of the economies of the Western world would suggest that corporations have been extraordinarily successful in producing all these outcomes.

So Friedman may have formulated the equation the wrong way around. The issue is not whether the social goal of corporations is to maximize profit; profit maximization is a private goal. What he might have said instead is this:

> Corporations, run in the interests of their shareowners, can be vehicles
> for generating the sustainable prosperity that society demands.

Leashing Frankenstein's Monster

Despite the natural fear that corporations might behave like Franken-stein's monster, corporate misconduct remains the exception, not the rule. This is because at least three important constraints channel corpo-rations to a social purpose: the market, the state, and the societies within which they operate. It is worth reflecting first on how each helps tame the corporation. Then we will look at how the rise of new capital-ist owners compels a root-and-branch overhaul of the very purpose and goal of corporate behavior.

First Constraint: The Market and the Invisible Hand

What is to stop a profit-maximizing enterprise from cheating its customers? Well, in a pure free market, cheated customers will simply take their business elsewhere. If a corporation charges too much for its goods, another will try to take the business from them until the price settles down to a level that reflects the costs of the goods to be sold plus a reasonable profit. This is the breakthrough insight Adam Smith called the "invisible hand." Competition among suppliers will ensure that prices equal the cost of production plus reasonable profit. If any producer of-fers shoddy goods, customers will soon learn of it and reduce the prices they are willing to pay.

The same is true, in theory, for employment. If an employer offers poor working conditions, the best workers will go elsewhere and the poorer employer will be driven out of business.

Indeed, apostles of free markets believe the invisible hand will en-sure that every transaction meets these social goals. They contend that if all economic actors are forced to compete, price will approach cost. Therefore, they argue, government must ensure that all markets are as competitive as they can be. Thus no corporation should be allowed to enjoy a monopoly position. That is why, particularly in the United States and the European Union, governments have put enormous effort into trying to eliminate "trusts" or monopolies.

As a result, government has become involved in all sorts of ways in ensuring that, where corporations exist, they do so under conditions that reflect free markets, with open competition, full information, and contract laws.

But that is not enough to discipline corporate behavior. Why? Because, in large part, it is extremely rare to find the conditions where Adam Smith's invisible hand can operate as theory predicts. Natural monopolies can frustrate a free market. Sometimes significant economies of scale, special location advantages, or technology confer advantages to one producer rather than another. Or information is restricted, so the supplier knows more about the product or service than the customer. Or labor mobility is limited by language, law, demographics, or culture. When these situations arise, enter the regulator.

Second Constraint: Regulation

Go into any shop, buy any good or service, and you will probably find that the good or service has been produced, distributed, and sold only if it meets reams of regulations. Across the world, robust debate is under way about how much regulation is appropriate. But whatever the level of regulation, rules are as essential for defining the market as they are for playing football. The size of the field, shape of the ball, number of players—none of these issues is negotiated before the start of each game. Similarly, essential rules of the marketplace are decided well in advance of each business transaction.

How much do regulations affect corporate behavior? Objects in our homes need to pass stringent tests to ensure that they are safe against fire hazards. The building itself must be constructed according to certified standards. The same applies to our cars, to the restaurants and hotels we patronize, the insurance and savings products we buy. In short, regulatory standards constrain each and every product or service in the marketplace.

Roll back the clock 150 years, and we see why this regulation is so necessary to sustain a market economy. In those days, unscrupulous businesspeople would routinely adulterate food, put chalk in flour, or add sulfuric acid to beer. It was commonplace for products to have addictive ingredients; one of the most famous was Coca-Cola, which contained trace amounts of cocaine.

Regulation was not the only answer to the problem of consumer protection, of course. The cooperative movement was an alternative. By the early twentieth century, it dominated the retail trade in Britain because people uniquely trusted coops to offer reliable produce at reasonable prices.[5] Perhaps if government had chosen to remain dormant, coops would have become the prevailing form of enterprise. But lawmakers intervened with a web of standards, so that today most profit-seeking corporations are also reliably trusted to sell goods of quality.

Goods, though, are not the only subject of rules. Regulations address the way things are made. Minimum wages are controlled in many countries, as are maximum hours, health and safety protection, the right to trade union representation, and the rights to equal opportunity, holidays, overtime pay, and protection from arbitrary dismissal.

Every factory, every office, every restaurant and hotel, every form of transport is subject to inspection. Limits are set on pollution. Zoning and planning determine where production can be located. Regulations even determine whether a corporation can establish a nightclub or a casino. And to raise capital in the world's capital markets, corporations are subject to an abundance of rules and regulations, with breaches subject to sometimes draconian penalties, to ensure fair and equal treatment of investors.

The point of all this regulation? To ensure that businesses, in maximizing their profit, are doing so in a way that creates social as well as private benefit. In addition, regulation enables all market participants to know they are playing by the same set of rules. The one brewery that delivers the promised beer should be confident that it won't be driven bankrupt by a competitor who adulterates its product.

Regulation is not the only tool that governments use. They also create systems of taxes, subsidies, or incentives for business to undertake more or less of a particular activity. For example, a carbon tax may try to curb greenhouse gas emissions, or a subsidy may spur biotechnology employment or training. But beyond the effects of markets, regulation and incentives, there are other, equally powerful forces that influence the way corporations behave.

Third Constraint: Corporate Culture

Most senior businesspeople know that what holds large corporations together for success is a common understanding of the business culture, of what are and are not the right ways to behave. Large businesses, like large organizations, simply cannot exist without their own sense of culture, one key foundation of which is ethics.

Cultures help explain why organizations and the individuals within them behave the way they do, how they treat each other, and how they treat those outside the organization. Like anthropologists, analysts describe business organizations in terms of the symbols, stories, and legends that employees tell about their company; the lines of authority, both formal and informal, that allow decisions to be made and action to result; and the types of behavior that are considered positive or negative.[6]

Ask business leaders. They will tell you that culture is often the most intractable obstacle to engineering change. Executives at former state-owned enterprises—though privatized for nearly a generation—can still be heard complaining of an entrenched "civil service" culture that values care and caution and, as a result, impedes rapid innovation. Mergers often fail because corporate cultures clash. It is one thing to revamp the legal structure of a business and quite another to alter the fundamental ways it influences individual behavior.

The challenge is even harder for companies operating across borders. Corporate cultures do not exist in a vacuum. Workers who make up the corporation are themselves part of one or more national cultures. For example, when Wal-Mart introduced a policy forbidding employees from dating each other, which was central to its U.S. controls against sexual harassment, a Düsseldorf court struck it down, finding the policy in conflict with German custom.

Company cultures cannot ignore the culture of the society in which they operate. One of the reasons that most companies do not lie, cheat, and deceive as a matter of policy is because most of their employees are not liars, cheats, or thieves. Indeed, cultures inherited from outside can impose practices to which many would object. Consider that business organizations have an overwhelming incentive to promote staff on grounds of merit alone. Yet many turn out to be poor at promoting women and ethnic minorities. Their failure arises from the beliefs and expectations of the societies within which they operate, not from direct economic pressures; business doctrine would encourage them to hire and promote from the widest talent pool available.

Critics outside the business community often believe that the profit motive will lead ineluctably to unethical behavior. Most within the community know, however, that in order to conduct business, a clear sense of ethics and the highest degree of trust are essential. The ability to do business on a handshake is critical to the operation of any market. A reputation for openness and honesty is central to long-term business success. Conversely, a reputation for duplicity can at best retard growth or, at worst, doom an enterprise.

In fact, evidence generally suggests that profitable companies are also ones that treat their workforce well, and that focus on delivering value to their customers. That is why, by the late 1970s, the best-selling management textbook would declare that "excellent" companies "treat [their employees] as partners; treat them with dignity, treat them with respect. Treat them—not capital spending and automation—as the primary source of productivity gain."[7]

Weak Chains

We don't mean to suggest that corporations are or will be perfect. We have come a long way, however, in creating a nuanced view of Friedman's dictum that "the social responsibility of business is to maximize its profit." What we have discovered is that corporations are highly constrained by competitive markets and by regulation. In addition, successful company cultures tend to promote positive social behavior. Bear in mind that all three of these forces interact. A regulation to provide knowledge to consumers, for instance, forms the basis of a campaign for or against a product, which in turn affects its success in the marketplace. These interwoven pressures have channeled the energies of Frankenstein's monster to a more positive social purpose than critics of unfettered corporate capitalism fear.

Is that still good enough in today's world, as national frontiers fray under the weight of globalization? Although the monster may be constrained, it is still a monster, and it may at any time break the chains that any one country drapes around it. Some people who take this view advocate greater regulation of business. Others argue for a new corporate constitution in which stakeholders affected by the company collaborate to decide corporate strategy. Some countries, notably Germany, have cemented a portion of "stakeholder capitalism" into law: workers' representatives sit on supervisory boards.

The stakeholder idea has appeal, in theory. But in practice, as many commentators have warned, it risks making management the servant of many masters, with the unintended consequence of handing executives excessive power to mediate among them. Other problems are equally daunting. How do you adjudicate which stakeholders get board seats? German multinationals, for example, allot board representation only to *German* workers, not to those they employ in the rest of the world. And when stakeholders are on the board, can they really serve the best interest of their constituency if those interests conflict with those of the company over the short term? Finally, how could you implement such a solution without riding roughshod over company owners' existing rights? All these issues present real challenges for advocates of a stakeholder solution.

But the old argument for stakeholder power hinges on the conviction that companies, however constrained they are, will tend to ignore the wider social interest if they focus on satisfying their shareowners. In a world where there is now broad ownership of major companies, and funds represent the pooled capital of citizens, that doctrine may no longer carry as much weight. Let us see how new capitalists upend the equation by setting new goals for business.

The Path to the Civil Company

Let's switch analogies. Let's think of the corporation not as a monster, but as a common lawnmower. All the constraints of markets, regulation, and culture affect the safety, pollution, performance, appearance, and fuel economy of the motor, as well as how and where it is manufactured. But the engine will sit uselessly in tall grass without someone to push and steer it, to give it direction. That is where the shareowners, the new capitalists, come in.

From the perspectives of economists and lawyers, a corporation is the property of its stockowners and should serve their interests. As we have seen in earlier chapters, beneficial shareowners today are, by and large, not the wealthy few. They are millions of pension holders and other savers. We, the people, own the world's giant corporations. We, the people, are the new capitalists and will be more than happy to agree with Milton Friedman when he asserts, "A corporation is the property of its stockholders. Its interests are the interests of the stockholder."[8] But that begs the bedrock question that we must ask ourselves: What are our interests? And having defined them, what behavior should we demand of the corporations we own?

The rise of citizen investors means we need to find answers in light of two standpoints that divide this age from those past. First, new capitalists are likely to be highly "diversified" in their investments. Second, the biggest powers in the global capital market are funds representing millions of savers. These millions have different ideas about speed, direction, and mission when they push that lawnmower. How does a company change its objective to incorporate these basic facts of the civil economy?

The Power of Diversification

Most well-managed pension plans, mutual funds, and other collective saving programs are invested in many companies. Rather than holding a large share of one company, they hold a tiny share in hundreds, perhaps even thousands, of companies around the world. The success of the plan is not determined by the success of one company, but by the success of its investee companies in aggregate. Indeed, one of the principal reasons for diversifying the investment is precisely to avoid exposure to the success or failure of any one particular organization.

How does diversification change an investor's interest? Well, imagine that all your savings were invested in one company. The success of that company alone would be your only interest. You would want it to survive, prosper, and grow, even if that did damage to the economic system as a whole. But your perspective would change if you had investments in lots of companies.

Let's look at an example. Say company X is trying to win a large contract in a country abroad. The purchaser has made it plain that it will award company X the contract if it makes a cash payment to a numbered bank account. Although the payment appears to be a bribe, lawyers have found a loophole by which the payment can be legitimized. What should company X do? If it takes the perspective of an investor who is interested only in the company's success, it may make sense to pay the bribe. But if company X does so, it will open a Pandora's box; in the future, all companies operating in the country will be asked to make such payments—which would damage the diversified shareowner's interests.

The best solution from the diversified investor's point of view is to close any loopholes that harm open and fair market trading. Although, in this instance, company X will find it galling to refuse the bribe and hence risk the loss of the contract, it would be in the interests of its diversified shareowners to do so, provided that no other company then exploits the loophole to win the contract. In other words, new capitalists have an interest in creating rules that lead to the success of the economic system as a whole even if, in particular circumstances, those rules may tie the hands of an individual company.

Naturally, the chief executive and managers of a business may see things differently. Their charge is, quite properly, to maximize the profits of *their* organization—and they will be rewarded on that basis. From a practical perspective, it would be foolish to change the focus of individual business managers. We would want to have them concentrate single-mindedly on the success of their own organizations. To do anything else would make it nearly impossible to manage these organizations. However, they will not be serving their shareowners' interests if they undertake activities that may be good for them individually but damaging to the larger economic system.

Moreover, as most businesspeople understand, a successful business community needs rules if it is to be commercially successful. Earlier we discussed how the government imposes rules to try to protect society from inappropriate corporate behavior. In fact, businesses need rules to ensure that the economic system allows them, in aggregate, to be economically successful, and to protect them from rogue behavior. Let's return to the earlier example. The initial "bribe" might be economically profitable, but the inevitable result of participating in such a scheme is to encourage increased corruption. The invitation will soon be offered to competitors, driving up the amount the company needs to send to the numbered account so as to stay the preferred vendor, which then encourages still higher demands. Thus the spiral of corruption begins to add costs, not advantages, for the individual company as well as the economy as a whole.

Many would argue that much suspect behavior is, at its heart, anti-competitive, designed to win short-term advantage at the expense of well-understood rules of competition, akin to an athlete's using illegal performance-enhancing drugs. The athlete may gain a temporary advantage but could suffer a shortened career, serious long-term health deterioration, or even death. And, of course, once the athlete is exposed, his or her records and reputation become tainted. (Not surprisingly, athletes generally support widespread drug-testing regimens.)

The corporate equivalent would be to support marketwide practices that outlaw bribes or other unethical competitive tricks for every company. Let's move from the theoretical to the real world. Recently, a number of companies involved in oil exploration and mining in emerging markets signed an agreement known as the Transparency Initiative. This accord commits them to make public all payments to country governments and officials. It was announced to the press as a contribution to helping eliminate corruption and hence promoting development. But a diversified new capitalist shareowner would have wanted to support this agreement whether or not it helped with development, because business success is more likely to be promoted by clear and ethical rules than by corrupt practices.

Diversified investors thus have different economic requirements from focused investors. But new capitalists are not only diversified across multiple companies, they are millions of citizen investors. And they have different requirements, in aggregate, from the kind of lone shareowner that bestrode capital markets in earlier times.

The Universal Owner

Citizens own equity because they want to save for their long-term future, whether for retirement, or for higher education, or for a home purchase. In technical terms, they want to "hedge" a long-term real liability (the money we need to spend in retirement, on tuition, on a house) by investing in a long-term real asset (shares of a number of companies). Therefore, although traders on the stock market tend to focus on short-term performance, the ultimate objective of companies should be to manage themselves in such a way that they maximize long-term value for their ultimate owner. This objective might often be the same whether a company has one owner or millions of owners.

What is different for a company with many owners is the way the owners will decide what constitutes value and time frame. If there is just one owner, that person, family, company, or state will alone define what it wants from the enterprise and when. If such an owner is particularly sensitive to social duties, it may well make the company behave in a highly responsible fashion. Alternatively, the owner may happily retire to Palm Springs and encourage his or her manager to generate the greatest possible private profit without any concern about the consequences for society at large.

For new capitalists, the situation is quite different. To a significant degree, they *are* society at large. It makes no sense for citizen investors to encourage a corporation to make a great profit for their shareowners, but then to ignore the damage they are doing, for example, by polluting the environment. If they do, they are simply stealing from one pocket to put it in another. The same is true for any corporate activity that freeloads costs onto society at large. Of course, not all damage is disqualifying. But by understanding the needs of diversified owners, we create a different range of action for civil economy corporations than if they were owned by an individual. Effects once thought to be no business of the corporation turn out to be very much the business of its citizen investors.

In the 1930s, management gurus Adolf Berle and Gardiner Means depicted a world where corporate economic power was enormous and unaccountable. To maintain public goodwill, they encouraged chief executives to behave voluntarily as if the goal of their companies was to benefit society at large.[9] In the twenty-first century, we argue that listed companies' shareowners reflect the demands of society at large. What we are arguing is consistent both with the view of Milton Friedman—that the interests of a company are those of its shareowners—and with the view of those who argue that companies should be more socially responsible. Society and shareowners are becoming one and the same.

But what exactly will such universal owners expect of companies? Can we define the goals of new capitalists clearly enough to create a tough, measurable benchmark that CEOs can use to navigate a course?

The New Capitalist Manifesto

Here are our ten rules for corporate boards, what we call the *capitalist manifesto*.

1. Be profitable—create value.

2. Grow only where you can create value.

3. Pay people fairly to do the right things.

4. Don't waste capital.

5. Focus where your skills are strongest.

6. Renew the organization.

7. Treat customers, suppliers, workers, and communities fairly.

8. Seek regulations that ensure your operations do not cause collateral damage and your competitors do not gain unfair advantage.

9. Stay clear of partisan politics.

10. Communicate what you are doing and be accountable for it.

This list is not a random set of "golden rules." Each of these requirements flows necessarily from the needs of the new capitalist.[10] And although the principles may at first seem simple, motherhood-and-apple-pie statements, each can raise considerable complexities for business managers, both in theory and still more in their practical execution. Take a closer look.

Rule Number One: Be Profitable and Create Value

Or, put formally, corporations should seek to *maximize* the value they generate for their shareowners.

Why is this a central goal for a diversified universal owner? Because a citizen investor fund has purchased shares to create a store of value to pay incomes in the future.[11] So the first goal of a company acting on behalf of the new capitalist is to maximize that value. It needs to make a profit. After all, as we said earlier, no profit, no pension. Companies are not social services. They did not raise share capital so that they could arbitrarily spend their investors' wealth on good causes. If they did, they would be undermining the reason that pension funds invested in them in the first place. Milton Friedman was right: there is a responsibility for business to maximize its value.

But a practical problem arises: it is often tough to discern whether a company is maximizing its value. Success in business is uncertain, and usually occurs slowly, over a very long period.

An example helps illustrate the difficulty. Imagine Marco Polo before he set out on his epic journey from Venice to China and back. Before casting off, he raises thousands of ducats from his backers, using proceeds to purchase goods that he will sell to the Chinese, as well as food and money for lodgings. After thirty years he has used up much of his investors' capital. He is in China, loaded with goods that are not worth much in Beijing, but he reckons they will earn a fortune in Venice. Of course, between China and Venice lie hills and valleys, floods and storms, brigands and thieves, tolls and taxes. Has Marco Polo maximized value for his investors? Or has he just taken a twenty-nine-year holiday in the court of Kublai Khan at his backers' expense?

Today's accountants would try to answer that question with a complex system of calculations to arrive at a "true and fair" view of Marco Polo's profits in each year. But as we can imagine, it is pretty difficult to decide whether he has made any money until he gets back to Venice and sells his goods. That said, if Marco Polo knows how the accountants perform their arcane arithmetic, he might do things that benefit him, provided they make his accounting returns look good—even if it does not deliver value to his shareowners.

Now for Marco Polo, substitute a company manager. All too often companies chase accounting goals such as "growing earnings per share," or "maximizing returns on capital." They can even use accounting measures to hide the fact that value is not being created. They may fail to identify where and why value is being created—sometimes because it is complex to do so, but often just because it's embarrassing to review why plans did not turn out as anticipated.

A civil economy company should seek to maximize value. That means, all other things being equal, it should seek to generate the greatest cash surplus (adjusted for the cost of capital) sustainable for the longest possible time.[12] After all, what new capitalists need to offset their long-term liabilities is, in the aggregate, real investments that return above the rate of inflation.

Rule Number Two: Grow Only Where You Can Create Value

In other words, corporations should seek growth, but *only* where that growth will create a surplus above the cost of capital.

Diversified universal owners can invest their money in thousands of companies, not to mention other assets such as property and bonds. They will seek to invest where their capital can be most productive, where they can get the highest return. If investors behave according to these rules, then money will be readily available for companies when investment opportunities arise.

But there is a corollary. If companies do *not* have good investment opportunities, they should return the surplus cash, so that shareowners can invest it elsewhere. Too often, a CEO will repeat, as a mantra, that the aim is to deliver shareowner value (and mean it), only to wind up doing the exact opposite. He or she will base an acquisition, for instance, on optimistic earnings projections, or on how much cash the company has in its reserve pool, rather than the true merits of the case. Study after study has shown that the majority of acquisitions fail to make a proper return for the acquiring company, losing their investors billions of dollars.

So why do boards continue to pursue such wasteful strategies? Often it is just optimism or overconfidence but, on occasions, other motivations play a key role. Some CEOs doubtless succumb to the temptation to use shareowners' money injudiciously rather than undertaking the hard work necessary to create real growth. Investment banks push deals for the huge payoffs awaiting them. Further, executive pay is often more closely linked to the size of the business than to the returns it has delivered. In addition, boards routinely deliver outsized bonuses to executives when they consummate a deal, whether it is configured to produce value or not. Together, these amount to a potent brew of incentives to merge, buy, or sell out.

Take Bass plc, owner of Bass Brewers. In the early 1990s it was not only Britain's biggest brewer but also the owner of literally thousands of English pubs. It was extremely profitable. But the demand for its beer and pubs was dwindling as consumers spent more time at home and switched their drinking habits from beer to wine.

What was Bass to do? One possibility was to return profit to its shareowners until management came up with more creative plans for growth. Instead, using its huge cash hoard and the most prestigious advisers in the City of London, Bass bought chains of international hotels—Holiday Inn, Intercontinental, Crowne Plaza, and others—for which it paid top dollar.

Of course, running a pub in Birmingham, England, is different from running an upscale hotel in New York. Not surprisingly, the great acquisition spree failed to deliver a proper return. Yet the company still seemed intent on further deals, optimistic that they would be less value-destructive.

By the time shareowners intervened, Bass, now renamed Six Continents, had spent almost as much on acquisitions as the entire value of the company's shares. It took three years of investor engagement to persuade the board to unwind its strategy. Finally, the company sold its breweries, split the pubs and hotels divisions in two, and returned over a billion pounds to shareowners.

Bass spotlights a chronic error corporations may make in finding paths to value. They spend profits on diversifying their business, on becoming a conglomerate, because executives believe that doing so will reduce risk. The universal owners' investments are already diversified, however; they do not gain any value from the company diversifying on their behalf. This perspective may be wholly different from that of management, which may wish to own several businesses so that, if one fails, the other will sustain the company's head office. Indeed, this is a typical practice of managers, particularly in low-growth businesses. They may seek what they perceive as the excitement of running a new business rather than sticking to their knitting, and exploring more creative routes for expansion of their existing one.

Rule Number Three: Pay People Fairly To Do the Right Things

Payment and incentives should be designed cost-effectively to maximize long-term value.

Almost no business controversy has received more headlines than the outsize salaries some public companies pay their chief executives and other senior managers. Some wage packages are now measured in tens of millions of dollars per annum, orders of magnitude larger than the salary of the president of the United States.

One reason compensation is out of control is that company directors decide who their CEO should be before they ask what salary he or she will request. And there is little incentive for them to negotiate strongly. Non-executive directors—many of them CEOs themselves—have rarely found their lives made easier by opposing a CEO's salary increase. Similarly, remuneration consultants paid by the company get no business boost from urging curbs on top executives' salaries.

It is not just the sheer size of these salaries that fails the interest of new capitalists. It is that wage scales are often unrelated to the individual executive's performance, or to his or her success in creating long-term value for the company's owners. Further, salaries may be massively higher than average workforce pay. That is a potential staff morale killer in good times. It can be poisonous to a company when CEO wages, bonuses, and perks rise even as shop-floor jobs and benefits are cut.

Pay is not the only significant contributor to value creation or destruction, but it's a barometer above all else of the degree to which companies have become the plaything of their managers rather than a service to their owners. What is true for all company employees should also be true for the CEO. The aim should be to compensate CEOs fairly, and in a way that will encourage them to behave in their citizen investors' interests.

Rule Number Four: Don't Waste Capital

Corporations should have an efficient capital structure that minimizes cost.

Diversified new capitalists want their savings to generate the greatest possible surplus. Yet many corporations raise more money than they need and keep a large store of cash for their company's own use. This practice tends to make life easier for the managers, who have a cushion against poor performance. But by featherbedding themselves this way, managers are denying their owners the opportunity to invest in other profitable ventures.

By contrast, some companies borrow too much. If things go well, having the extra cash might generate higher returns, and perhaps high value for the CEO's stock options. But if things go badly, the shareowner (and, in cases of insolvency, the lender) picks up all the losses. Indeed, in some jurisdictions (particularly the United States), it is even common for bankruptcy courts to grant special pay packages to executives of companies that fail. Judges believe that retention bonuses will encourage managers to revive the fallen company, even when they are the very same individuals who led the enterprise to bankruptcy. That is the epitome of a managerial "heads I win, tails I win" paradigm, with all the risk placed on the owners and lenders.

Rule Number Five: Focus Where Skills Are Strongest

Companies should develop coherent strategies based on their ability to generate customer value better or at lower cost than competitors. Companies should be the "best parent" of all the operations within their portfolio.

In a competitive market, the greatest profit will go to the producer who can meet the customers' needs better or at lower cost. Those who meet needs better will gain sales or be able to charge premium prices. Those who have lower costs will make higher profits or be able to gain sales by reducing prices. In a competitive market, therefore, a company will create the greatest capital value for its owners by concentrating on activities where it has the most advantages over its competitors. By doing so, the company not only uses its cash effectively, it also implements Adam Smith's great insight that specialization and competitive markets will tend to use resources efficiently. So focusing on those areas where a company has greatest advantage benefits customers and new capitalist owners alike.

There is another corollary, however. If a company has business activities for which it is not the best operator, it should seek to sell them (at an appropriate price) to someone who is better able to run them. In that way, a company is the "best parent" for its operations.

Rule Number Six: Renew the Organization

Always plan to develop management, staff, product, processes, and technologies to meet the challenges of the future.

Running a business is among the least static activities in the world. Markets, technologies, infrastructure, and society are constantly changing. Indeed, if they were not, our free market economy would rapidly freeze into Soviet-style sclerosis.

Companies need to respond, and rapidly. They need to be on a constant search for renewal, for new ways to meet customer needs better or at lower costs. If they fail to do so, competitors will overtake them, and their owners' capital will disappear.

Such renewal is not just about spending more on research and development. It's a mind-set that should pervade the whole organization. Starting at the top, the company board of directors should be thinking about how they could do the job better. As the world shifts around them, companies should be planning how best to ride these dynamics to add value.

Rule Number Seven: Treat Customers, Suppliers, Workers, and Communities Fairly

Companies need to effectively manage their relationships with their customers, suppliers, employees, and others with a legitimate interest in the company's activities. Companies should behave ethically, having regard for their impact on the environment and on society as a whole.

Well-managed companies cannot ignore their impact on the wider society. Even from a selfish point of view, it would be foolish to do so. Insensitive actions are likely to lead to failure in the marketplace, to encourage government regulation, and to create other tensions between the company's culture and that of the wider world.

But the diversified universal owners' requirements go much deeper. New capitalists need the entire economic system, not just a single company in which they are invested, to be successful over the long run. They can reap no advantage from private profit made from social cost, because they suffer from the latter just as they benefit from the former.

This does not mean that companies have limitless social obligations. Their purpose is to generate a surplus for their owners. It makes no sense, though, for companies to ignore the social costs of their activities. If they do, their new capitalist owners will object that they are just robbing Peter to pay Paul.

Nor does it mean that companies should give special benefit to one particular interest, such as the workforce or the consumer, as might the stakeholder model we discussed earlier. If they are to serve the demands of their shareowners, however, it does mean that corporate managers need to understand the position of those whom their actions affect, and to deal with them fairly. That is because, in aggregate, shareowner and stakeholder interests often overlap. In chapter 9 we suggest some actions that can help achieve this goal.

Rule Number Eight: Seek Appropriate Regulations

Companies should support voluntary and statutory measures that minimize externalization of costs to the detriment of society at large or allow an unfair and opaque competitive marketplace.

In discussing rule number seven, we ignored the difficulties that many companies have in being successful *and* being fair. It is all very well to say that companies should not pollute. But what do you do if your competitors take advantage of your socially conscious behavior to push you out of business? How can we reconcile competitive markets with social responsibility?

As this chapter has demonstrated, companies can find many ways to do this: through markets, regulations, incentives, cultures. If competitors engage in antisocial behavior, companies should, on behalf of their citizen owners, seek regulations or incentives that will modify competitive rules to ensure that rivals don't create collateral damage. Ideally, such rules should be voluntary and as flexible as possible. But where this is impractical, it is appropriate to encourage statutory regulation.

Rule Number Nine: Stay Clear of Partisan Politics

Companies are creations of the law. They should not seek to use their economic power for partisan political advantage to change the law in their favor.

The limited-liability company is a wonderful mechanism for organizing capital productively. It serves best if it operates in competitive markets, under the watchful gaze of its owners, with rules established by independent regulators. If it seeks to influence the regulator for private gain, without reference to public costs, it undermines not only the demands of its new capitalist owners but also the superstructure of democratic civil society. It can rarely make sense for companies to finance partisan politics. Should they propose to do so, they should undertake it only with their shareowners' explicit permission.

Rule Number Ten: Communicate and Be Accountable

Companies should seek an open and honest dialogue with their shareowners and others affected by their plans. They should be clearly accountable for their actions.

There are two important reasons why new capitalists require companies to be transparent. The first is that efficient markets, particularly efficient capital markets, depend on information. The second, and even more important, reason is that if companies are to be accountable to citizen investors, such owners need the information necessary to make accountability work.

Accountability lies at the heart of the civil economy. Like all other institutions, it must be possible to call companies to account for their actions, good or bad. Markets, regulators, and society may constrain companies, but only the owner can create a comprehensive framework of accountability.

Earning Confidence

If companies behave according to the ten rules of this capitalist manifesto, we would have a new model for free enterprise among publicly listed corporations.

Added atop traditional, pre–civil economy pressures on corporations is the oversight of new citizen investors. Because of their broad interests, they compel the rise of a different kind of corporation. The civil economy corporation is channeled by market forces to operate for social as well as private value precisely because it is focused on the long-term needs of its new capitalist owners.

Today, many public companies go a long way toward following the capitalist manifesto. But conventional theory has gotten sharply out of sync with reality. In theory, as we noted at the beginning of the chapter, companies might act as if they were wearing the ring of Gyges—allowing shareowners to profit, conscience-free, from their unfettered activities. In practice, companies have been constrained by external forces, including the market, regulators, and society. Increasingly, too, they are being both driven and constrained by civil owners and a widening infrastructure of civil economy institutions.

As these pressures grow, companies will be able—indeed, they will be required—to perform even better. If they succeed, they will earn the confidence of citizen investors even as they help generate sustainable prosperity. The question for the next chapter is, then, whether investing institutions are playing their part to make the circle of accountability function.

TAKEAWAYS

- For much of the twentieth century, world political and economic thinkers argued over who—private individuals or the state—should own and control productive resources to best protect society. Some worried that corporations that are singularly focused on generating maximum profit for shareowners might trample on social interests.

- Three forces constrain business from harming society: the operation of markets (the "invisible hand"); regulation; and the need for business culture to reflect the values of the society in which it operates.

- Now there is a new driving force. The owner revolution has given rise to new capitalists who hold stakes in many companies and who represent millions of citizen investors. They amount to a proxy for society as a whole. As new capitalists exert increasing influence in boardrooms, worries about companies causing social harm fall away.

- New capitalist funds have little interest in supporting action that benefits one company by damaging other parts of the economic system. They do not profit when a company dumps costs on society at large, because their citizen investor constituents will have to pay those costs too.

- By taking the point of view of the diversified universal investor, we can derive the ten most important business policies that most companies should be following. These policies, or rules, constitute what we call the *new capitalist manifesto*.

- The manifesto asserts that corporate executives can best align their performance with new capitalist owners if they pursue profit efficiently; grow where they can create value; link executive pay to real long-term performance; ensure that they don't waste capital; focus where their skills are strongest; renew the organization; treat customers, employees, and others fairly; seek appropriate regulations; stay clear of politics; and communicate enough to allow accountability.

4

Institutional Investors

Mobilizing Ownership

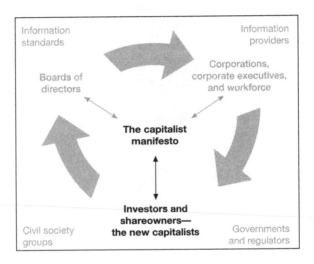

Savers entrust their money to mammoth financial institutions. This chapter describes the way these bodies have performed their charge as stewards of new capitalists' savings. And it identifies the toxic conflicts and accountability gaps that have led to the loss of billions. Step by step, these flaws are being repaired, opening channels for citizen investors to put pressure on business management.

"In the history of the world, no one has ever washed a rented car," former Harvard University President Lawrence Summers has observed.[1] By contrast, we pamper what we own, whether cars or trucks, houses or condos. Just look at the number of home improvement, do-it-yourself, and auto parts stores, or the popularity of television shows that "make over" autos and homes. If we own it, we maintain it, fix it, and improve it. Right?

Wrong—at least when we're talking about investments. Historically, millions of investors have acted like renters of corporate shareholdings rather than fractional owners of actual companies. Even worse, so do many of the mutual funds, retirement systems, and other fiduciaries to which citizen investors have entrusted their assets. Things go deeply amiss when investor passivity is chronic. Companies underperform and misbehave. Pensioners lose cash they need for retirement. Nations fail to create jobs and wealth.

But what are these collective savings vehicles? Who are the "institutional investors?" They populate a complicated landscape and go by jargon-laden terms such as separate account money managers, unit trusts, mutual funds, and hedge funds. Those investing vehicles, in turn, live in an equally jargon-filled landscape comprising defined-benefit and defined-contribution pension funds, superannuation schemes, variable and fixed annuities, and savings vehicles such as IRAs in the United States, and ISAs in the United Kingdom.

No one should be fooled by bloodless terms or complexity, however. What these entities represent are the combined retirement, savings, and investments of tens of millions of working people.[2] Together, these funds have amassed assets, deployed assets, and sold assets more effectively, for more people, than any other investment plans in history. For the circle of accountability to function, however, they need to view themselves as real fiduciaries for the new capitalists.

Many do. The mutual fund scandals in the United States and the split-capital trust debacles in the United Kingdom were newsworthy precisely because they represented behavior contrary to acceptable standards. What was scary about those misadventures, however, was that they weren't isolated incidents; they were relatively widespread and symptomatic of systemic failings. Structural flaws continue to plague markets, allowing too many of us to act like renters—or, in the vernacular of the capital markets, "traders"—rather than long-term owners. Their existence is prima facie evidence of a system in need of repair.

First we need to identify weak links in the circle of accountability. Then we can see how wholesale fixes now underway are pushing the conduct of those institutions into line with citizen investors' interests.

Whom Can We Trust?

Would you entrust your life savings to a financial adviser known as "inarticulate, apathetic, lethargic, conflicted"? Probably not, but that is the description of the fund management industry offered by . . . well, a fund manager. David Cohen of Connecticut-based Iridian Asset Management was speaking in October 2004 to the U.S. National Council on Teacher Retirement. "Institutional investors," he warned a roomful of educators anxious about pension security, are "hemmed in by a system of compliance more quick to respond to the interests of the investment organizations they represent than the beneficiaries of the funds they invest."[3]

That's not quite the image these institutions—charged with safeguarding the savings of working citizens—seek to present. Their logos and marketing messages—think Prudential's stylized Rock of Gibraltar, Allstate's "good hands," the very words *Fidelity* and *Trust* so prominent in so many money managers' names—are pitched to convey know-how, confidence, caution, and solidity. "We make our money the old-fashioned way," sniffed actor John Houseman in a memorable television ad for Smith Barney. "We earn it."

Puffery aside, though, how many funds are really best configured to take good care of your money? Let us briefly examine two of the biggest domains of capital: the asset management industry, which oversees mutual funds, unit trusts, and the like; and pension funds.

First Weak Link: The Asset Management Industry

Carly Fiorina, the high-profile, former chief executive of Hewlett-Packard, was desperate to reel in the last big blocks of votes behind her firm's controversial $19 billion merger with Compaq. It was early 2002, and her advisers were nervous. Dissident director Walter Hewlett, scion of founder William Hewlett, had gained traction in his efforts to snuff out the deal because it would destroy shareowner value. The vote was looking too close for comfort. Then Fiorina got wind of a potential disaster. Deutsche Bank's fund management arm—which controlled 17 million shares—had cast all its votes against the merger. In-house analysts had concluded that the merger would be a sour deal for their investor clients. DB's megaholdings seemed enough to tip the balance.

Fiorina swiftly phoned Robert Wayman, her chief financial officer, and left a voice mail message that later resurfaced in a lawsuit. "We may have to do something extraordinary to bring [Deutsche Bank] over the line here," she advised. Wayman contacted the bank about changing its vote as the final deadline loomed. Executives received the message loud and clear: HP would cause millions of dollars in potential investing banking business to disappear if Deutsche stuck to its no vote. Fiorina herself minced no words. Deutsche Bank's vote was of "great importance to our ongoing relationship," she asserted in a conference call with bank officials. Bank executives dutifully summoned their fund managers to an emergency meeting and told them of the risk to the firm's "enormous banking relationship with Hewlett-Packard."

The fund managers could have told the executives to stuff it. They had, after all, carefully considered their vote, and the only new information senior management had given them had nothing to do with the benefits (or lack thereof) of the HP/Compaq merger to client investors, and everything to do with the benefits HP brought to DB. Instead, fund managers switched their vote just minutes before Fiorina gaveled the crucial HP shareowner meeting to order. The merger squeaked through, with the contested DB block vote accounting for the vast majority of the victory margin.[4]

As the HP incident suggests, portfolio managers are neither evil nor corrupt nor stupid. Left to their own devices, they had reached an independent, defensible position on how to vote their shares. The problem is that economic and structural impediments within the asset management industry throw roadblocks in the way of even well-intentioned managers. Many asset management companies are subsidiaries of mammoth corporations with commercial interests that might be quite different from those of their client shareowners. Conflicts may surface in which the best interests of one division (asset management) are trumped by those of another business line (investment banking), as in the HP/Compaq merger deal. But divergent commercial interests also affect day-to-day management of shareowner money. "Ordinary investors aren't priority No. 1," *Pensions & Investments* magazine wrote in an editorial about the mutual fund industry.[5]

While some fund managers may have conflicts of interest, new capitalist investors and the asset management industry that supposedly serves them are misaligned in three other fundamental ways:

1. How fund management companies get paid

2. How investment success is calculated

3. Over what time frame success is measured

Paying for Asset Gathering, Not Asset Management

Fund management companies generally are paid on a percentage-of-assets basis. In other words, their fees are based on how much money they manage, not how well they manage it. Again, this is well known. But stop and consider for a moment: the economic model of the entire industry is designed to support world-class asset *gathering*, rather than world-class asset *management*. Indeed, the fact that many asset managers really care about doing a good job is testament more to their personal attributes than to the incentives of the industry. Certainly, being good at managing money should (and often does) lead to getting more money to manage. But advertising, paying for distribution, and a host of other activities can trump investment skill when it comes to gathering assets.

Even if the fund manager has good intentions, the structure of the industry makes it more attractive to perform well by trading shares than by acting as a good owner. Consider the following example:

Say a fund management company invests $50 billion in shares of the biggest companies in the United States. The fund managers have chosen two hundred companies from the S&P 500 in which to place their client's money. That means that they own about 1 percent of each company in their portfolio and will be one of the largest share-owners of every company in which they have invested their client's money.[6] They charge clients 0.25 percent a year to manage their portfolios.

After a time, one of the fund management firm's bright young analysts spots a company that is simply not performing as well as it should. Executives are mismanaging and unmonitored. Related-party transactions transfer wealth from owners to insiders. Pet projects are approved, though they can't possibly earn back their cost of capital. Indeed, the abuse is so great that the analyst reckons that the company, currently valued at $10 billion, would be worth $15 billion if only it were governed properly. The analyst is naturally very excited; he goes to see the senior portfolio manager.

"Look," the analyst contends, "the shareowners of this company can make a cool $5 billion if they were just to use their ownership rights to stop it from being mismanaged."

The portfolio manager looks at the analysis and is impressed. "Sure," she replies. After a pause, she continues. "But to bring about that change would require resources and expertise, a lot of which we don't have in-house. Lawyers and management experts. It might cost a million or more before we see things turn around. It's obviously not worth it."

"What do you mean not worth it?" responds the analyst. "A million dollars is peanuts. There's $5 billion to be made."

"Yes," says the boss. "But not by us. Our clients own only 1 percent of this company."

"Sure, but 1 percent of $5 billion is still $50 million," replies the analyst, somewhat sheepishly. "We can make our clients $50 million!"

"And then we get 0.25 percent of that in fees. That's $125,000. As I said, not worth it."

So the analyst retreats to his desk. The portfolio manager, convinced by the analyst of how bad management is, and by the economics that it's not worth it to get involved, sells the shares. And the company continues to underperform, steadily casting off more jobs and more value.

That's why most fund managers do not act as involved owners. It's not because they don't care. It's because they act *economically rationally* in selling their shares, rather than choosing to engage a poorly performing company. No wonder virtually every manager's marketing materials explain *buy* discipline and *sell* discipline, but not *ownership* discipline.

Mismeasured Success

The second misalignment of interest is the very metric that measures investment skill. Traditional managers are judged on relative, not absolute, return—how well they do compared with other mutual funds and with benchmarks such as the S&P 500, the CAC 40, or the FTSE 350—not on the total return a fund achieves for its investors.[7]

What does this have to do with new capitalists? Though alert and engaged owners can prevent some corporate failures, the benefit of that vigilance accrues to all investors. Assume, for the sake of this argument, that the senior portfolio manager in the preceding dialogue said, sure, go ahead and hire the lawyers, and that the intervention was successful. The fact is that most of the fund's competitors will have owned shares in the same company—and would gain value as a free rider, without having spent any of the resources or risking the kind of backlash Carly Fiorina sparked at Deutsche Bank.

Tom Jones, Citigroup's former top asset manager, was brutally honest about the situation. "I want to do what I get paid for," he said. "And shareholder activism isn't what I get paid for . . . If we spend money to do shareholder activism, Citigroup asset management shareholders bear the expense but don't get a benefit that is distinct from other shareholders."[8]

Of course, even that analysis assumes that the fund manager wants a portfolio company to succeed. Some fund managers don't. Short sellers— fund managers who sell shares today hoping to buy them back more cheaply tomorrow—are an obvious example. But the race for *relative,* rather than *absolute*, performance can create a perverse incentive for traditional fund managers to wish companies ill. They may deploy citizen investors' savings in ways that harm even successful companies.

Here's how that works. To control risk, most fund managers invest in scores, if not hundreds, of companies. For the companies they like, they hold proportionately more stock than would the average manager or the benchmark (e.g., the S&P 500). For companies they don't like, they often own some shares, but less than their average market holding. In the jargon, they are "underweight." So, for example, if GE stock accounts for 3 percent of the S&P, a manager bullish on that index might put 4 percent of its capital in GE; a bearish manager might put 2 percent. But few managers wouldn't own GE at all; it represents too large a percentage of the index, and not owning it at all would increase risk versus the benchmark to levels that would make most managers uncomfortable. [9]

So what will happen to a manager's performance record if a company in which it is underweight does poorly? Well, the outcome will wind up costing the client money, of course. But *proportionately,* the fund manager will have lost *less* money than its competition. It will have beaten the market and its relative performance will improve. So although its clients will have lost cash, the fund manager will think it has done well.

Short-Term Speculation

The third structural mismatch is the time frame. Looking at the long term is important to new capitalists saving for retirement or home ownership, but it's rarely acceptable to fund managers, who find themselves measured on relative performance over relatively short time frames. Fund ratings are compiled by calendar quarters and usually focus on one- and three-year records. Bonuses for individual portfolio managers and analysts are often computed based on quarterly or yearly relative return performance. The natural result is that they focus on lucrative short-term trading rather than on vigilant long-term owning.

"We used to be in the business of long-term investing," bemoans Vanguard founder Jack Bogle, "and now we're in the business of short-term speculation."[10] Today, the average annual turnover at mutual funds is no less than 110 percent. And the industry wastes an estimated $100 billion in investor money each year on excessive commissions, unnecessary trading, and badly executed trades, according to Liquidnet.[11] That, in turn, creates the financial market equivalent of Larry Summers's car renter's mentality. Why engage management over, say, a flawed acquisition strategy if you're not going to own the company in a few weeks?

Trading and ownership involve different skills. Indeed, many fund managers segregate the job of "owning" a company (that is, voting proxies, engaging corporate management when necessary) from the job of trading its stock. Many pigeonhole ownership as an exercise of compliance with laws and regulations, rather than a value-creating activity. So they assign the task to junior analysts, who tend to vote mechanically for one type of resolution and against another, with little or no cross-pollination of ideas or strategy with the portfolio managers who are buying and selling shares.

Portfolio managers, therefore, feel unburdened by the need to explore beyond conventional hard-number analyses to "softer" issues such as board quality, which might have more long-term predictive ability, though less relevance to next quarter's results.[12] Too often information falls between these "trading" and "ownership" silos. No wonder corporate executives frequently complain that a fund's investment analysts rarely raise governance concerns in road shows and private sessions— only to have another of the same fund's agents vote against management at an annual meeting.

Secrecy enables the mishandling of stewardship. Citizen investors in the United States, for instance, could not even discover how their funds voted shares at portfolio company annual meetings. The data was confidential until 2004, when regulators there (and later in Canada and France) forced annual disclosure of ballot records. The mutual fund industry fought the measures tooth and nail but lost. Good thing. Before the U.S. vote disclosure system was in place, mutual funds routinely backed virtually all managements on virtually all resolutions, even if shareowner interest might have dictated more critical oversight. Vanguard, for instance, voted yes at 90 percent of director elections in 2002. But guessing that votes would have to be made public, it stiffened guidelines and voted a straight yes at just 29 percent of companies one year later, a sevenfold increase in the number of companies at which it rejected management voting advice.[13]

Mutual funds' temptation to just vote yes is driven by a time-tested commercial imperative: don't bite the hand that feeds you. Each fund craves lucrative investment business from corporations it is also voting on. Consider Fidelity and Enron. "While Fidelity should have had an interest in protecting its equities in Enron from meltdown, it also sold to Enron its management of 401(k) plans for Enron employees," scholars Jim Hawley, Andrew Williams, and John Cioffi have written. But the authors assert that Fidelity may have feared that "even a modest form of monitoring of Enron would endanger its fee income from these plans."[14] For investors, though, even "modest" monitoring of corporations they co-own represents cavalier treatment of their ownership rights. With vote disclosure, that became obvious.

Mutual fund boards of directors are supposed to be a bulwark for new capitalist investors—but often they aren't. It's not hard to see why. Fund companies, not shareowners, effectively pick directors. TIAA-CREF is the only mutual fund in the United States whose investors regularly vote on board candidates; it's no accident that TIAA-CREF is considered among the most activist mutual funds. Then there is the impossible scope of the job. Directors often sit on dozens, sometimes hundreds, of mutual fund boards within a single fund company. Each Fidelity board member, for instance, was responsible for overseeing 277 funds in 2003. While there is certainly overlap in how those funds are managed, leading to efficiencies, vigilance on individual funds can crumble in the face of such volume.

The U.S. Securities and Exchange Commission mandates that a majority of fund directors be independent of the parent company so they can be free to make tough decisions that are best for shareowners. But, as *BusinessWeek* has observed, "many routinely approve management contracts at fees that are twice what pension funds pay for stock-picking services. And they are slow to insist that investment advisers cut loose portfolio managers with lousy records."[15]

With all these structural impediments and conflicts of interest, it is no surprise that the asset management industry has, generally but not unanimously, behaved as inattentive and inactive owners.

Second Weak Link: Pension Funds

It should be a bedrock assumption that pension plans represent their members' interests. The law spells that out in most countries. So do pension fund charters and contracts. But the truth is that most funds simply don't.

A fundamental lesson of civil society is that no institution will automatically look after a particular constituency unless that constituency has a voice in decision making. "No taxation without representation" was famously the rallying cry in the American Revolution. But many pension funds around the world operate with no representation at all from the very members they are supposed to benefit. Almost all corporate pension funds in the United States and Japan, for instance, are run exclusively by company officials, with no such thing as a trustee board with seats for current or retired employees. In 2002, draft legislation was introduced to require half of the governing body of U.S. corporate 401(k) plans to represent plan members.[16] The measure was hardly radical; laws in Australia, Britain, South Africa, and other countries mandate 50 percent member representation on trustee boards. Even in the United States, Taft-Hartley funds—which run across industries rather than service single companies—feature boards where half the trustees are selected by members. But the draft legislation quickly succumbed to intense business and White House lobbying.

Keeping pension plans captive gives corporate managers distinct advantages—some of which directly conflict with the interests of retirement fund members. Corporate officials can and do hire fund managers affiliated with financial-sector companies vitally interested in staying on the CEO's good side for fear of losing other lucrative business, such as underwriting. Such fund managers have almost no incentive to exert vigorous ownership on behalf of pension plan members—and every motivation to cater to the corporate sponsor, as we saw in the story of the HP/Compaq merger.

Conflicts don't have to be that dramatic. Many companies offer employees the option of investing in their company's own stock.[17] But they don't get rights to vote those shares. Generally an agent appointed by the corporate management casts ballots. The agent, in turn, is commonly predisposed to vote with management, either directly at the company's own annual meetings or at the annual meetings of fellow firms, which may be suppliers, customers, or competitors. Captive pension fund capital effectively can become a hip-pocket means of entrenchment.

Piggy Bank

Occasionally, management goes overboard, moving from influence to outright expropriation of the pension fund assets. Willie Sutton said he robbed banks because that was where the money was. Britain's Robert Maxwell figured out that banks were mere piggy banks compared with the company pension fund. Out of sight of any independent watchers, the publishing baron was able to raid the retirement plans of £440 million. In 1991 Maxwell drowned mysteriously near his yacht off the Canary Islands. His Mirror Group soon collapsed in financial crisis—and thirty-two thousand employees discovered to their horror that there was almost nothing in the till to fulfill pension promises.[18]

The Maxwell disaster triggered massive investigations in Britain to find out why those charged with protecting the pension savings of tens of thousands of Mirror Group Newspapers staff were somehow looking elsewhere while the company CEO was looting the till. The Goode Committee produced a welter of new rules, many of which found their way into the Pensions Act of 1995. The measures helped. Thanks to the reforms, Enron's U.K. employees found their pensions intact when the company folded—even as their U.S. counterparts lost almost every penny.

Roughly a decade later, analysts at the U.S. Government Accountability Office (GAO) also spotlighted the risks and conflicts of corporate pension plans. In a damning September 2004 report, the GAO found that the only barrier protecting pension plan member interests was the fraying Employee Retirement Income Security Act of 1974 (ERISA), which requires managers to act solely in member interests.[19] But writing rules down on paper is one thing. Making sure they get implemented is something else entirely. The federal Department of Labor has mounted no enforcement of ERISA's share-voting rules since 1996, as the GAO observed, leaving company managers free to claim whatever interpretations they desire of "best interests."

Stepped-up enforcement and increased disclosure were the GAO's antidotes. But it missed the most obvious new capitalist solution: ensuring that pension plan members have some voice in the stewardship of their retirement savings. That would at least guarantee that those most at risk have a seat at the table when investment decisions are made that could affect their future. That kind of guarantee would clear obstacles in the circle of accountability.

If you doubt that accountability would increase the likelihood of pension funds acting as owners rather than renters, consider this: as of 2006, in more than thirty years of investor activism in the United States, just a single corporate-run pension fund had sponsored or cosponsored a dissident shareowner resolution at a listed company. By contrast, other investors introduced more than a thousand resolutions in 2003 alone.[20] An unbroken three-decade record of near universal docility is hard to justify on investment grounds. Not every company in pension portfolios has been so trouble-free that they deserved owner silence. By contrast, the most active fund proponents of such resolutions are civil service and Taft-Hartley pension plans, which usually have representatives of employees sitting on their boards. Unlike the Deutsche Bank functionaries who changed their vote at HP, such trustees have unobstructed accountability to savers.

Report Card

Of course, even a seat at the investment committee table does not, by itself, usher in a civil economy of capital responsive to citizen investors. Why? Well, most trustee boards are a throwback: they look like corporate boards did in the early 1990s. Members are generally, untrained, and appointed through obscure nomination processes. Some are chosen or dismissed by the sponsor, not the members, so their loyalties are divided. They have few if any independent resources to deploy, so that they are almost completely dependent on advice brought to them by portfolio professionals and plan executives. Trustees have little guidance on how to assert control and challenge conventional, short-term thinking among money managers—such as why their pay usually rewards short-term performance. In the end, trustees often exercise little independence in their most basic power: hiring, monitoring, and firing money managers.

In 2003 and 2004 Britain's Department of Work and Pensions released devastating report cards on trustee boards that quantified the problem. The litany of failures illustrated just how vulnerable employee savings are to abuse—just how much pension money is managed like a rented car. The survey found the following:

- Trustees spend fewer than four hours a year, on average, dealing with investment matters in board meetings.

- Only 25 percent of funds ask trustees to undertake training.

- Trustees only rarely challenge or review the performance of investment consultants.

- Less than 40 percent of trustee boards have spent time developing a policy on shareowner activism.

- Just 22 percent of pension funds disclose to members how they comply with governance principles—and why, if they don't.

- Only 18 percent of funds have policies on social investment risks.[21]

"The result is largely absentee ownership with managements exercising powers in default that properly belong to owners," concluded former Consolidated Gold Fields managing director Allen Sykes.[22] "No trustee seems to own [the scheme]," blasted ex-Gartmore chief and U.K. corporate governance factotum Paul Myners in a 2005 speech. "No one has really got a grip."[23]

Now consider that U.K. pension funds are some of the best managed in the world, and you can see why the circle of accountability that should link new capitalists with their savings is too often broken.

Yet it can also self-repair. Seeds of new ideas are taking root, finding nourishment in the cracks and crevices of those very structural imperfections of the asset management and pension industries. Fresh practices will either coexist with traditional methods or replace them. Let's now explore how those ideas, pressed by new capitalists, are reshaping the investment landscape into a civil economy.

Repairing the Circle of Accountability: Owners Awake

It was 1987, and the corporate world was populated by a nightmarish collection of sharks, raiders, and greenmailers. Management, for its part, was bent on stopping raiders by introducing entrenching devices such as "shark repellents" and "poison pills." The one thing they seemed to have in common was the ability to make money by taking advantage of ordinary shareowners.[24]

High above Third Avenue on New York's East Side, one investor was fed up. TIAA-CREF was a unique hybrid: part pension plan for college and university faculty and part mutual fund manager, with representatives of the investors and beneficiaries on its board. What wasn't unique was the situation it was facing. International Paper's management was trying to install a rash of takeover defenses that, in TIAA-CREF's opinion, threatened to depress the value of the fund's shares. TIAA-CREF's chief investment officer approached Peter Clapman, chief counsel, for assistance. Together they brainstormed, stretching for novel ways to protect their investment. "Well, we could always file a shareholder resolution," Clapman finally said. He was proposing a tactic—a petition to management placed on the agenda of the corporate annual general meeting—that had been used before only by shareowners focused on social issues, such as divesting from South Africa. "Could we really do that?" asked the chief investment officer.

They could. They did. TIAA-CREF's proposal targeting International Paper's poison-pill takeover defense became the first dissident shareowner resolution on corporate governance put to a vote in the United States. It lost, but by garnering 27.7 percent of the votes at a time when most resolutions were getting single-digit approval, it marked a milestone in new capitalist activism.

Petitioned resolutions are merely one barometer of investor wakefulness. But glance at the state of the market today to see how much things have changed since Clapman floated his seemingly far-fetched idea less than a generation ago. In 2003 shareowners introduced no fewer than 1,077 proposals for votes at U.S. companies.[25] Once considered alien, such challenges are also now common in Britain, Canada, France, Germany, Australia, and other countries.

Shareowner resolutions have existed in the United States for generations, and they were used extensively by social campaigners during the fight against apartheid in South Africa. In 1973, shareowners, led by faith-based investors, submitted forty dissident resolutions to annual meetings.[26]

A decade later, institutional investors were discovering a startling truth: this style of shareowner activism was proving effective. Some companies were pulling out of South Africa to avoid the nastiness of boycotts and investor insurgency. Others were engaging in dialogue with the proposals' sponsors. So, when faced with the value-destroying mechanisms that later motivated Clapman, funds started asking themselves a simple question: why not apply similar pressure on boards to achieve objectives mainstream investors care about—namely, growing value, or at least preventing the misappropriation of created value?

Building Guardrails

So thought Jesse Unruh, the legendary California state treasurer. Unruh woke one morning in 1984 to discover that Texaco, under threat of a takeover attempt, had paid a corporate raider $138 million in "greenmail" to go away. Unruh was furious. That money, he reasoned, had been taken from all the owners, including the California state pension funds, and given away to one, just to insulate management. Unruh wanted national action to flag this type of abuse. In 1985 he joined with New York City comptroller Harrison "Jay" Goldin and Roland Machold, head of New Jersey's pension funds, to found the groundbreaking Council of Institutional Investors (CII), expressly to preserve shareowners' rights.[27] It was the right idea at the right time. Today the CII has 140 pension fund members, with $3 trillion in aggregate assets.

Three years later, an unlikely source turbocharged the idea that investors should be stewards of their portfolio companies, rather than just traders: the Reagan administration's Department of Labor. With Robert A. G. Monks behind the scenes, the department issued the so-called Avon letter, which declared votes at the annual meeting to be important assets of a fund. That effectively made voting at U.S. companies a fiduciary requirement for many pension funds.[28]

Until then, few investing institutions had bothered to vote shares in any market, preferring, for reasons outlined earlier, to rely on short-term trading rather than on ownership. Even a few years after the order, U.S. funds reported casting just 24 percent of their non-U.S. ballots, mainly because agents were systematically failing to deliver proxy documents on time, or else charging high fees to vote.[29] In 1994 the Clinton administration expanded the reach of the regulation to include votes at holdings outside the United States. Today, voting is routine, online, and nearly universal (though still fraught with glitches) among U.S. funds.

Proxy Vote Pushers

In Europe, investor voting and activism was slower to take off. Given the size of most European nations, many funds were diversified internationally far earlier and to a far greater extent than were U.S. funds. Yet even as late as 1996, none of the big European institutions voted more than 10 percent of shares held beyond their national market.[30] Today, voting across Europe's internal frontiers is still complicated but improved; an EU draft directive to trim barriers further surfaced in 2006. Voting is now expected rather than an exception. For example, voting in the United Kingdom zoomed from 20 percent in 1990 to 55.9 percent in 2002.[31] The Organisation for Economic Co-operation and Development (OECD) corporate governance principles now define voting as a fiduciary obligation.

When European funds, like U.S. funds, began acting like owners, they started to demand fiduciary stewardship from the managers of their portfolio companies. To its shock, the U.K. firm Hanson PLC proved one of the debut targets. In 1993 the conglomerate introduced what would once have been treated as garden-variety limits on shareowners' rights. But PIRC, the investor advocacy firm, spotted an opening and rallied unprecedented transatlantic fund opposition. "Hanson's draconian counter-measures are the equivalent of a military coup in the world of shareholder democracy," thundered the *Times* of London.[32] Facing the prospect of defeat, Hanson withdrew the measures.

Three years later, France's Eramet showed that multinational investor activism was not a one-off event, nor limited to so-called Anglo-American markets. In 1997 the French government, a 55 percent owner of the mining company, sought to advance its foreign policy at the expense of Eramet's minority owners by stripping the firm of a key South

Pacific mining license. The government assumed that the funds would stay complacent as usual. Instead, a feisty coalition of French and foreign institutions rebelled, saying simply that if this was how the French government treated owners, it could forget its ambitious plans to privatize France Telecom. That forced Paris to back down.[33]

Different Paths to Investor Power

As those examples indicate, some funds have awakened to owner responsibility not only through filing dissident resolutions and voting shares routinely, but through a wide range of engagement tactics, including coalition building, publicity, and legal action. Some are highly public. Others decidedly are not.

CII has released a focus list of poor U.S. corporate performers since 1992. By creating critical mass for corporate governance reform at those laggards, CII has helped new capitalist investors replace poor managements and challenge flawed strategic plans. As a result, activism at those targeted companies helped to create an abnormal gain to investors of 11.6 percent, or the creation of $39.7 billion in excess market value.[34] That "found money" would have stayed hidden had owners remained quiescent.

CalPERS compiles and releases an annual list of U.S. corporations with stubbornly bad governance, and it focuses outreach on each of them. New York City's funds, too, have created "focus lists." Britain's National Association of Pension Funds (NAPF) runs "case committees," confidential task forces of major investors that collaborate on behind-the-scenes dialogue with companies deemed to undermine shareowner value. Collective investor groups have been critical because they pool financial muscle.[35] But when quiet, joint engagement fails, one or more funds lead public attacks on wayward boards in efforts to fix the problem.

Since the mid-1990s, institutional activism has reached across borders. In March 1995, forty-nine people from around the world gathered at Washington's Watergate Hotel to found the International Corporate Governance Network. It is now the preeminent voice of global institutional investors, representing more than $11 trillion in assets. Soon other investors began to appreciate that global capital flows require global alliances. Trade unions created the Committee on Workers' Capital. Individual investors gave birth to the Euroshareholders organization.

Cracking the Code to Civil Ownership

The single powerful feature common to the first generation of activist institutions is that they boast governing bodies at least partially answerable to the people whose money they manage. Public funds such as CalPERS, Ontario Teachers' Pension Plan, and Australia's UniSuper, or corporate plans such as the BT Pension Scheme, are at the vanguard of new capitalist ownership in each of their markets. Each has governors or trustees elected directly or with member participation. Leaders know they are being watched and judged. They also know that if they act in ways that fail to align with member interests, they can be censured—or, in the extreme, ejected. In short, they avoid many of the structural issues that normally impair the circle of accountability. Strengthening the circle is the key to funds' behaving as if they really own citizen capital rather than merely renting it.

Drivers of Change

There has been remarkable progress in strengthening that circle of accountability. For most observers, the connections between developments have seemed unrelated. However, when you find the clues, they fit together to show a global phenomenon at work. For a brisk hunt, the three places to search are in new public policies, investment fund initiatives, and innovative market tools.

Policy Push

Change is stressful. Global capitalism has caused whole swaths of economic power to slip from familiar families or the state itself into the hands of inscrutable strangers at home and abroad. Public anxiety worsens when scandals afflict capital markets. Franz Müntefering, ex-head of Germany's socialist party, famously branded certain non-German investment funds "locusts" for pressing restructuring plans on iconic domestic companies.[36]

But thankfully, perhaps surprisingly, most of the new regulations policy makers have woven seem to create transparency and project integrity, rather than mandate a particular course of action. These measures increase institutional accountability, helping build a civil economy. Thus, whether intended or not, some of these policy measures are making it possible for new capitalist activists to take over what was once the province of prescriptive government dictates.

Recent changes in British law, for instance, aim to produce an entirely new species of retirement fund trustee. The Labour government introduced two catalysts. First, it crafted statutes requiring a minimum 50 percent employee representation on trustee boards. Then it passed the landmark 2004 Pensions Act, which set skill and disclosure standards for pension boards. Under it, trustees for the first time must be able to demonstrate to regulators and plan members that they are actually qualified to oversee investment funds.

Notably, the Pensions Act does *not* spell out what those qualities may be. Instead, it has allowed the market to fill the vacuum with a cascade of programs. Many involve trustee orientation, credentialing, and continuing-education and are springing up from the likes of the National Association of Pension Funds, the UK Society of Investment Professionals, the Pensions Management Institute, and the Trades Union Congress. Wholly new bodies such as the Independent Pension Trustee Group are helping make trustees more professional. Civil society groups have initiated programs to raise trustee awareness of broader investment issues. The Just Pensions project, with U.K. government funding assistance, launched an authoritative toolkit for trustees. So did the Carbon Trust, explaining its business case for environmental stewardship. Where before there was a deafening silence, now many voices are arguing about what it means to be a responsible trustee. It's a classic market for ideas.

Britain's focus on trustee responsibility is echoed in other markets. In March 2005 a South African company started publishing *Today's Trustee*, a periodical devoted to the field. Both SHARE, the Canadian labor think tank, and the U.S. National Labor College sponsor extensive trustee training programs. Cortex Applied Research, based in Toronto, Independent Fiduciary Services, headquartered in Washington, D.C., and Penfida Partners in London are just three of the commercial firms now offering independent services to trustees. Keith Ambachtsheer's K.P.A. Advisory helps funds modernize their governance. A glossy U.S.

trade publication, *Plan Sponsor*, features a monthly column about the fiduciary obligations of pension trustees while a blog, www.pensionrisk matters.com, opened in 2006 to spotlight pension governance.

New Capitalist Activism

No longer are fund governing bodies mere rubber stamps for sponsoring companies and fund managers. Skilled, fully informed boards, with member representation, represent real change with sweeping consequences that are only just beginning to surface. WH Smith's retirement fund trustees even scuttled a private-equity firm's bid for the company because the offer failed to make up the company's £250 million pension deficit. Think how much better protected pensioners at Enron or United Airlines would have been had they been able to rely on a well-advised trustee board. It is only prudent to expect that active trustee boards will demand far more responsive and responsible fund management—whether in safeguarding assets from pillage or monitoring portfolio companies for maximum long-term value.

Across the Atlantic, regulators are requiring deep-seated changes bound to alter the way mutual funds behave as civil owners. In the teeth of fierce industry resistance, the SEC adopted measures it said would address trading scandals unearthed by New York Attorney General Eliot Spitzer. It required not only that 75 percent of directors be independent of the parent investment company but also that the board chair be independent. The industry is suing to overturn that mandate. Nonetheless, such boards are evolving into more professional and critical bodies. As they come under the scrutiny of citizen investors, they are more likely to align their actions with the interests of new capitalists.

Policy makers elsewhere have taken a leaf from the SEC's book. Brazil, France, and Thailand, for instance, have adopted rules compelling institutional investors to vote shares and reveal their decisions. Transparency, in their view, hands citizens just the watchdog tool they need to ensure that their agents safeguard investor interests.

The savviest politicians have understood that the most fertile public policy empowers investors to take up the cudgel but doesn't dictate outcomes. What do we mean? British headlines scream regularly about "fat cat" pay among CEOs. Such attention used to prompt political pressure on the government to curb it somehow. But instead of intervening bluntly in the market to manipulate remuneration, Patricia Hewitt, then minister for industry, introduced a requirement for annual shareowner votes on corporate pay practices. It cost the Treasury nothing. With the measure, though, shareowners now have a tool they need to correct out-of-control pay, or to decide that the tabloids are making much ado about nothing, and do nothing. The political onus is no longer on the British government—or on the Australian government, which followed with similar legislation.

Fund Initiatives

The second set of clues pointing to the presence of a proto-civil economy may be found in the voluntary actions of funds themselves. It seemed almost like spontaneous combustion when the United Kingdom's Myners Report in 2001 triggered a sudden international outburst of investor codes of practice. In fact, the fuel had long been accumulating as lonely voices called for such initiatives.[37] Still, there is no doubt that, in Europe at least, the Myners Report was a catalyst.

Paul Myners, then chairman of Gartmore Investment Management, spent a year ferreting about the pension world at the behest of U.K. Chancellor of the Exchequer Gordon Brown, and then issued a withering assessment. Most pension trustees, he found, were ill trained, had sparse resources, and were paid nothing. They failed to press money managers to challenge even failing companies in portfolios. Myners's remedy was a new "culture of fund governance." His centerpiece: a *voluntary* code. Pension funds, mutual funds, and insurers should send members an annual report disclosing if they comply with the code and, if they do not, why not.[38] The report should "become a forum for decision-makers to explain and justify their approach, and for stakeholders to exercise oversight of the decisions made on their behalf."[39] Among the code's points was that each fund should have a strategy on shareowner intervention and how to measure its effect.

Before long, the key bodies of U.K. fund management—through the Institutional Shareholders Committee—jumped on the bandwagon with a new code of practice. Each effort is helping produce an architecture of fund governance that embodies, for the first time, real accountability to citizen investors and, as an inevitable consequence, real oversight of fund managers so that their performance is aligned with new capitalist beneficiaries.

The Myners approach is cropping up around the world, too. Share-owner groups in Canada, France, and the Netherlands, for instance, have recently developed homegrown codes of investor governance.[40] And at the multinational level, the International Corporate Governance Network in 2006 issued first bedrock transparency and accountability guidelines for funds. Further, investors have helped shape fund governance and responsibility guidelines newly framed by the OECD, the United Nations, and the World Economic Forum.

Milestones in the Owner Revolution

The flurry of attention to fund governance is bound to spread farther, becoming a potent new factor in the global marketplace. The domino effect will be far-reaching and long term. Look at what some key energized trustee boards have wrought even in these early days of the civil economy:

- In 2002 three U.S. state pension funds took steps to squeeze conflicts and misalignments out of the investment chain. The "Investment Protection Principles" commit funds to require money managers to report on conflicts, how they pay their portfolio managers, and what they do to act as real owners of citizen capital. Funds are now to include these factors when they hire, supervise, and fire portfolio agents.

- In October 2004 a group of big European funds founded the Enhanced Analytics Initiative (EAI), which commits each member to steer 5 percent of broker commission fees to stock research firms that analyze extra-financial factors affecting corporations. The program is a breakthrough because it puts real money behind civil economy–style investing. Member funds can now assess corporations by examining what factors produce long-term, sustainable value instead of narrow, short-term growth spurts. "Better research for better investment" is EAI's motto. By early 2006 EAI had attracted funds with more nearly $1 trillion in assets.[41]

- Coalitions of funds are forming within and across national frontiers to address overlooked long-term investment risks. Forums in the United Kingdom, North America, Australia, and New Zealand now focus on climate change as a portfolio issue.[42] Others have begun collaborating with corporations to examine risks peculiar to the pharmaceutical industry.[43]

A Sea Change in Fund Management

Finally, and perhaps most important, the fund management industry itself has begun to awaken to the power of engaged ownership. It has even begun to shift the economic paradigms by which it has been run for half a century.

First, a philosophic sea change has enveloped the field. Until recently, one-stop shopping was the industry's mantra, wherein financial institutions tried to gain "share of wallet" by seeking to control a customer's retail and commercial banking, asset management, insurance, and even investment banking. Little by little, the inherent conflicts and difficulties of that approach have become manifest. Today, there is a different thrust, toward focused core competencies that do not conflict with each other. Thus, Citicorp and Legg Mason have agreed to exchange Legg's brokerage and investment banking divisions for Citi's asset management group, allowing Legg to become a pure-play asset manager and Citi to focus on banking.[44]

More dramatically, fund managers have built an entirely new category of investments that seeks through activism to extract hidden value from companies. Somewhat counterintuitively, such corporate governance funds deliberately sink cash into underperforming, misgoverned firms and then get to work persuading boards to improve their ways.

Hermes is the largest practitioner of such methods in Europe—and has a virtual army of fifty specialists to carry it off. Its alliance partner, San Diego–based Relational Investors, is the biggest in North America. Together they manage nearly $10 billion in investments.

Activist funds are limited in what they can do alone. Without support from large institutional pools of share capital, they can fall short of mustering enough leverage to bring change to boards of directors who resist it. But if an activist fund is prepared to pick up the tab and lead the charge, others are often happy to fall in behind.

Reinventing Incentives

How is it that leaders with deep pockets even exist? Didn't we observe earlier that the economics of fund management are stacked against being an active owner and towards being a trader? How have activist funds managed not only to survive in a competitive environment but to thrive?

The answer is that they use fee structures that foster ownership. Relational and Hermes and many other activist funds don't just charge a fixed fee for the funds they manage, but also a performance fee. Typically this might be 20 percent of the outperformance of their portfolio.

Then there are the new kids on the activist block: hedge funds. They also navigate by compensation incentives that differ from the mainstream. But hedge funds are little understood and often feared. There are more than ten thousand of them, and they are far from monolithic. Some hedge funds invest in equities, some in currency, some in fixed income. Most are independent, but some are affiliated with larger banks or fund managers. Some invest in exotic derivatives that do require a knowledge of rocket science (or at least some heavy math), and others invest only in large, liquid, listed stocks.

Indeed, most hedge funds have only a few things in common. For one, they are supposed to seek absolute return rather than gains compared to a benchmark. Second, like the activist funds, they charge performance fees based on how well the portfolios turn out.

Free from the need to compete for relative performance, hedge funds don't have to invest the way everyone else does. In fact, that's the one thing they *shouldn't* do.

Some hedge funds act like ultimate renters, engaging in extremely short-term trading, sometimes based on rumors or even inside information. They may weaken or destroy companies to achieve their aims. They may act like raiders do, leaving companies worse off than before. For example, a greenmailer will extort a payment in return for simply going away. Such behavior merely transfers assets out of a company and away from new capitalist owners. But others build outsize positions in troubled companies and try to fix them.

Let's revisit that hypothetical conversation between the analyst and his boss from earlier in the chapter. Except this time, let's change the location from a traditional asset manager to a fund paid by performance fees—say, a dedicated activist fund or a relational-style hedge fund. To set the stage, we'll decrease the fund's assets by 98 percent, from $50 billion to $1 billion, a more realistic number for this type of fund. But, remember, managers are now free to invest in many fewer, "high-conviction" companies. So let's assume this fund has uniform 5 percent positions: $50 million each in twenty companies. Now let's rejoin the scene.

> One of the fund's bright young analysts spots a company that is simply not performing as well as it should. Executives are mismanaging and unmonitored. Related-party transactions transfer wealth from owners to insiders. Pet projects are approved, though they can't possibly earn back their cost of capital. Indeed, the abuse is so great that the analyst reckons that the company, currently valued at $10 billion, would be worth $15 billion if only it were governed properly. The analyst is naturally very excited; he goes to see the senior portfolio manager.
>
> "Look," the analyst contends, "the shareowners of this company can make a cool $5 billion if they were just to use their ownership rights to stop it from being mismanaged."
>
> The portfolio manager looks at the analysis and is impressed. "Sure," she replies. After a pause, she continues. "But to bring about that change would require resources and expertise, a lot of which we don't have in-house. Lawyers and management experts. It might cost a million or more before we see things turn around. Go get me a budget to make it happen."

"Really? You want to spend a million to fix this company?" responds the analyst incredulously.

"Sure," says the boss. "It's obviously worth it. We've got $50 million invested. If we can really improve the value by 50 percent that's a $25 million increase in value. And we get 20 percent of that. That's a cool $5 million, or $4 million net, right into our pockets. I'll spend a million to make five."

So the analyst bounds back to his desk, double-checks his analysis, and begins to try to fix the company.

Certainly not all situations end happily ever after. Funds can be mistaken in their analysis. Even if the analysis is right, it may not be doable. Even if right and doable, management can resist, and sometimes win, resulting only in extra cost. But the point is that the new economics makes active ownership economically rational. No wonder there were ninety known, dedicated activist funds by the end of 2005, according to Bloomberg.

These funds are having a real-world effect on both sides of the Atlantic. In 2005, hedge funds led by TCI, and with the support of mainstream fund managers such as Fidelity and Capital International, derailed Deutsche Börse's ill-managed bid for the London Stock Exchange.[45] But perhaps the best-known instance of activist intervention by hedge funds was when ESL, a Connecticut fund, saw value in Kmart when few others did.[46] Indeed, Kmart was bankrupt. ESL bought control of the company, took over the board, and reworked the company to the extent that it could then buy Sears, its older, larger competitor. Today, ESL's management is involved with every major decision made at Sears and Kmart. Eddie Lampert, ESL's chairman and CEO, is chair of the Sears board. William Crowley, an employee of ESL, is the company's chief financial officer and chief administrative officer. Two other officers, the vice president of business development and the senior vice president of real estate, are also ESL employees.[47] That is active ownership.

Not everyone benefits from active ownership, at least in the short term. When owners reassert their prerogatives, results can be unsettling and painful. Management changes, layoffs, and even wholesale plant closings sometimes flow from interventions. Yet new capitalists typically back such radical steps when companies have declined beyond repair, when *avoiding* change may be lethal.

The civil economy and proponents of "stakeholder capitalism" may diverge in such cases. Stakeholder advocates want all parties affected by a company to participate in key decisions. But stakeholder claims may sometimes be the *cause* of a business's infirmity. Managers may be unfairly enriched. Labor arrangements may be unsustainable in a changing market. Suppliers may gain from overgenerous contracts. Each of these stakeholders might block needed change because they benefit in the short term—while bleeding the company over time. New capitalist investors must choose best options for the company's long-term welfare. They will want to proactively install boards that shepherd productive relations with stakeholders and avoid crisis. But if a board fails and the company falls into a desperate condition, civil owners may have no choice but to back bitter medicine today.[48]

The point, then, isn't that all activism is "good" in the sense that outcomes are always congenial for all concerned. Rather, it is that for capitalism to be dynamic and healthy, for "creative destruction" to work its messy magic, owners need to be engaged and empowered to act.

Market Tools

There could be no bigger clue to the existence of a civil economy than the fact that grassroots investor demand has given rise to an entirely new industry: the ownership business.

Many of the services entering commerce supply energized pension funds and money managers with means to exercise their rights as owners. At least three global and a host of local ratings agencies have begun to compare corporations' governance profiles. Monitoring products have been developed that screen corporate boards for actions and conflicts that threaten shareowner value. Activism-for-hire vendors offer professional engagement with errant corporations. Web sites provide forums for investors to discuss joint action on troubled portfolio companies. Most of these options were unknown to even late-twentieth-century capitalism, but are taking root now in a twenty-first century characterized by engaged ownership. We cover them more thoroughly in chapter 6.

But one arm of the ownership business concerns us here because it is both a catalyst and a reflection of the civil market: the new watchdogs of mutual fund and pension fund accountability. These entities complete the circle of accountability by allowing citizen investors to judge the quality of stewardship among those to whom they have entrusted their money.

Log onto the Web site of financial data house Morningstar and, if you are a subscriber, you can see how two thousand U.S. mutual funds rate as stewards of client capital. Launched in 2004, Morningstar's "Fiduciary Grade" was the first commercial service to put mutual fund responsibility under the microscope. It tests board independence and assesses whether manager pay aligns with fund performance—and then ranks funds on a scale of A to F.

There will be much more benchmarking of mutual funds now that the United States and Canada require investment companies to release records of how they vote client shares. In effect, votes are a proxy for how funds behave as owners. Groups are using the data dump to craft products that allow new capitalists to judge mutual funds from a range of perspectives. Some are academic; Baruch College's Center for Financial Integrity has produced a database of mutual fund votes. Others are designed to generate investor pressure on mutual funds to act more in line with their clients' interests. Hong Kong's influential Webb-site.com is using the new data to "name and shame" U.S. funds that fail to back investor initiatives in the territory. Ceres, the environmental coalition, commissioned an analysis of mutual fund voting on climate change issues. The AFL-CIO has done similar scoring of mutual funds in respect to labor issues.

These new services join existing, but still young, online watchdogs such as Fund Democracy, founded as an advocate of investors in mutual funds. As monitors gain traction, they will compel fund companies to be far more responsive to citizen investor clients—or risk losing market share.

Pick Your Microscope

Even established analytical services have gotten into the act, sensing that accountability was an overlooked dimension to asset management.

Fitch, the rating agency, pioneered the concept of grading fund managers for quality based in part on their performance as owners. Launched in 2001, the product at first used feeble indicators. But three years later, London-based adviser Lintstock, anticipating the U.K. government's spotlight on fund behavior, unveiled Institutional Investor Profiles ("ii-Profiles"), a commercial service that monitors money managers' voting practices. Pension trustees use it to check which managers act in concert with their fund board's governance principles.

Then, in 2005, Mercer—one of the world's largest consultants—began a service that rates fund managers around the world on share voting habits, engagement practices, and the extent to which they incorporate environmental, social, and governance (ESG) analysis in portfolio selection. Clients can see Mercer's stewardship scores alongside traditional financial ratings of managers.

Matching these commercial services is a growing community of online blogs, investor advocacy tools, and civil society groups focused on monitoring the stewardship performance of funds and money managers. James McRitchie's CorpGov.net set the pattern, tracking CalPERS actions. The FairPensions project, launched in 2005, aims to mobilize new capitalist oversight of U.K. pension fund boards. And labor federations in the United States, Canada, and Britain have produced annual "key votes" surveys that hold fund managers to account for their votes at corporate annual meetings. Reports also allow pension plan members to test if their own trustees are doing their job monitoring financial agents.

Doing It Right

Let's end this chapter with a real-world example that shows how engaged ownership is supposed to work.

On the investor side was Hermes, the fund manager wholly owned by the BT Pension Scheme. On the company side was Premier Oil, then a particular concern for those interested in governance and in corporate social responsibility. Its share price was languishing; it appeared unable to deliver performance.

It was 2000, and Hermes had already relayed concerns to the company's board. Directors seemed prone to meeting the demand of two major shareowners—Amerada Hess, a U.S. company, and PETRONAS, the Malaysian National Oil Company—and not those of minority investors, including Hermes. In addition, the company was in a strategic hole. It was neither large enough to compete with the emerging supermajor oil companies nor adequately fleet of foot to seize exploration opportunities. Premier's freedom of action was further limited by the company's high level of debt. And, to top off the troubles, the firm was leading development of the Yetagun gas field in Myanmar. Ruled by a brutal military dictatorship, the country (formerly known as Burma) was a pariah state subject to international boycott. Premier had exposed itself to major ethical and reputational risks; it also had unnecessarily limited its financing options.

Hermes had little confidence that the board understood Premier's dilemmas or could craft solutions. But rather than sell its stake, leaving the company to decline at the expense of other investors, the fund set a course of shareowner engagement.

At the same time, trade union pension trustees, including those of the BT Pension Scheme, which owns Hermes, suggested that Hermes might pressure Premier to quit Myanmar. David Pitt-Watson, a Hermes executive and one of our authors, explained to them that the fund manager could not support trade union campaigns based on a "special interest," and certainly could not support a plan of action that called for forfeiting a major corporate asset. But he also noted that Hermes was eager to engage a company that failed to address risks that threatened long-term shareowner value. Premier was one such case.

Hermes also met with the Burma Campaign UK and Amnesty International and volunteered to lead a group of concerned asset managers. The fund argued against proposing a dissident shareowner resolution but pledged a range of other engagement options.

Hermes requested a meeting with Premier chairman Sir David John, which took place in January 2001. "While Sir David may not have agreed with everything we said," Pitt-Watson later commented in a Hermes report, "he was willing to help ensure that shareowner concerns were put before the board and, where appropriate, resolved." Sir David promised governance reforms and agreed personally for the first time to meet representatives of the Burma Campaign UK.

In March, Premier added another fully independent nonexecutive to the board. The balance of decision making was slowly beginning to bring minority investor interests to the fore. In October, the company began to clarify its strategic position by selling some assets in Indonesia and restructuring its position in Pakistan. But progress was slow, which Hermes attributed to the two major shareowners.

Hermes sent Sir David a "forthright" letter expressing impatience. The fund offered to warn other global investing institutions if Premier Oil's Amerada and PETRONAS directors were to block moves which were in public shareowners' interests. The fund hoped such a tactic would alert those companies to the importance of treating all shareowners equally, otherwise they would find it more difficult to raise capital on the market, and thus make them more favorable to a deal on Premier. Hermes raised the stakes higher. It hinted that Amerada's statements—that its directors did not participate in any discussions on the company's involvement in Myanmar—was out of line with the fiduciary duties of directors under U.K. company law.

Premier got the message. On March 13, 2002, management announced a roadmap to solve its problems: it would shed mature assets in return for the exit of the major shareowners, and for turning the company into a focused, nimble exploration enterprise once again. The deal was done in September. Premier Oil said that it was to swap assets for shares, with PETRONAS taking the Myanmar operation and a piece of Premier's Indonesian activities, and Amerada a further segment of the Indonesian interest. PETRONAS also would make a substantial cash payment, its 25 percent holdings would be canceled, and it would lose the right to appoint directors.

Thus, in one blow, Premier resolved its shareowning and governance issues and improved its balance sheet. By the same action, it reduced its oil and gas production activities and morphed into an agile exploration company. In addition, it had extricated itself from Myanmar in a way that was fully acceptable to the trustees of the BT Pension Scheme, the Burma Campaign UK, and other human rights lobbies—and fully economically rational.

But for the BT plan's citizen investors, perhaps the most critical outcome was the dramatic boost in Premier Oil's share price. The stock price doubled relative to the oil and gas sector during the period of Hermes's engagement, netting an excess return to Hermes clients of over £1 million, and more than fifty times that sum to other minority shareowners.

Of course these changes at Premier were not wrought by Hermes alone. Hermes may have catalyzed the change. But it was the corporation's board of directors that determined and implemented the new strategy. Would Hermes have acted if it hadn't been approached by campaign groups, or if it had had no support from other fund managers? We can't tell. What we can say is that many parts of the ecosystem of the civil economy were at work, as we'll see in later chapters.

TAKEAWAYS

- Traditional asset managers and pension plans have amassed and deployed more capital than ever before in history. But they harbor systemic flaws when it comes to aligning interests with new capitalist investors.

- Fund managers face three weaknesses. First, they are paid on a percentage of funds being managed, rather than on the *quality* of management. That leads to an emphasis on asset gathering rather than on ownership. Second, the industry's emphasis on relative, rather than absolute, performance measures makes it difficult for traditional managers to be paid adequately for engaging as owners. Third, measuring relative performance on a short-term basis leads to a reliance on trading, which encourages a renter's mentality.

- Pension plan flaws often occur because plan members tend to have little or no representation in the governance of funds. Worse, secrecy makes it difficult for citizen investors to monitor what is being done in their name.

- Despite those flaws, a minority of pension plans and asset managers have begun to engage as civil owners. That engagement has been led by pension plans, in which citizen savers have a material say in governance.

- Public policy makers—particularly in Europe—have responded both to the underlying demographics of the investor class and to various scandals. Instead of prescribing corporate behavior, they have strengthened the circle of accountability and given new capitalist owners tools to monitor agents, who act on their behalf.

- Some specialist asset managers, including a number of hedge funds, have reengineered incentives to make engaged ownership pay. There are nearly one hundred dedicated activist funds as of this writing.

5

Boards of Directors:

A New Accountability

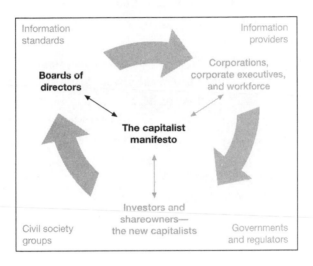

A board of directors oversees publicly traded corporations—and is accountable to shareowners. In the past, directors often served as little more than ornaments, thereby breaking the circle of accountability. But as this chapter shows, boards are becoming active, professional, and aligned with new capitalists, forcing radical change on corporate executives.

One chilly midnight in 1968, the directors of the Pennsylvania and New York railways looked on as the ribbon was cut, symbolizing the merger of their two competing companies into Penn Central, the biggest railroad in the United States and the nation's sixth largest company. Two years later, however, Penn Central was bankrupt, taking with it the cash of one hundred thousand creditors and the savings of one hundred and thirteen thousand shareowners.[1]

Creative destruction may be the norm for dynamic capitalism, but the repetitive nature of such corporate disasters across markets and decades begs a question: what is it that has allowed boards of directors to look on as corporate scandal, greed, and incompetence have engulfed their companies?

In every corporate scandal, directors have failed to protect the shareowners. Yet these directors individually were not all corrupt or inept. Indeed, on paper, some seemed to be among the most skilled and upright people in the business and academic worlds.[2] But as boards they were dysfunctional. Why? Was it just a case of serial bad apples, or bad architecture? Has there been some systemic flaw that encourages, or at least allows, such failure?

In a word, yes. In this chapter we try to identify that flaw, and also to show how new capitalist changes in corporate accountability promise to supply the cure.

The Three I's

Peter Drucker, the management guru, was clear about the problem. "There is one thing all boards have in common," he said. "They do not function." The decline in the board, he contended, was a global phenomenon. And one of the key reasons for it was the development of the large, publicly held corporation. "The original board, whether American, English, French or German, was conceived as representing the owners . . . Each board member had a sizeable stake in the enterprise . . . But large companies in advanced countries are no longer owned by a small group. Their legal ownership is held by thousands of 'investors,' the board no longer represents the owners, or indeed anyone in particular."[3]

This, then, is the great structural anomaly at the heart of today's corporation. On paper, directors are legally and ethically responsible to the owners. To them, shareowners give the power to appoint the chief executive, to determine strategy, to approve capital expenditure and dividends. Even though new capitalists may own the corporation, their influence will not be felt unless boards of directors respond to them. Yet the truth is that in widely owned companies, directors rarely know or hear from the owners or feel that their job is likely to depend on the owners' support. In companies with a controlling investor, directors often have little connection with minority shareowners.

The result has been a break in the circle of accountability. Imagine legislators who speak only with government ministers or cabinet secretaries rather than the public, or lawmakers who appoint themselves rather than being subject to periodic votes. In politics, it's called being beholden to special interests. In social work, it's called being captured by the client. In yesterday's corporate world, it was deemed normal.

The abrogation of accountability between directors and owners has been a cancer at the center of corporate legitimacy. Fortunately, it is a cancer that is beginning to yield to treatment. Slowly, board accountability is being restored, providing evidence again of a rising civil economy. First, let us look at why boards have proved so impotent. Three "I's"— insufficient *information*, improper *influence*, and *incompetence*—have conspired too often to corrode board performance.

The First I: Information

Louis Cabot was well qualified to be the director of a large company. Indeed, he had been a director of several, and would go on to be a director of the Federal Reserve Bank of Boston and a trustee of Northeastern University. Yet he was one of the directors who oversaw the collapse of the Penn Central Railroad. Here is how he described the conduct of board meetings during his one-year tenure:

At each of the Penn Central directors' meetings, which lasted only one and a half hours, we were presented with long lists of relatively small capital expenditures to approve, we were shown sketchy financial reports which were rarely discussed in any detail. The reports were not designed to be revealing, and we were asked not to take them away from the meeting. We always had an oral report by the chief executive promising better results next month.[4]

What information gets to a board, and when, helps determine how well a board functions. No matter how well motivated, an uninformed board member cannot properly perform the oversight and stewardship investors expect.

But you might ask, if the directors at Penn Central—or another company—found themselves cut off from the information they needed, why would they not simply demand it? One reason is that outside directors too often are plied with incentives to merely go along, discouraged from asking questions, and ostracized as troublemakers if they are merely being diligent.

The Second I: Influence

CEOs have influence—lots of influence—with their boards. While most welcome board input, some chief executives chafe under any constraints, even polite boardroom questioning, and use their weight to short-circuit effective oversight.

Consider the steps that CEO Ross Johnson took to make sure that he, and not the shareowners of RJR Nabisco, was the object of the directors' affection, as told by Bryan Burrough and John Helyar in *Barbarians at the Gate*, their exposé of that company. Here they describe how he kept the board compliant following the removal of board chairman Paul Sticht:

> [T]he directors found that all their needs were now attended to in detail. Bill Anderson of NCR slid into Sticht's chairmanship of the International Advisory Board and was slipped an $80,000 contract for his services. Johnson disbanded RJR Nabisco's shareholder services department and contracted its work out to John Medlin's Wachovia Bank. Juanita Kreps was given $2 million to endow two chairs at Duke, one of them named after herself. For another $2 million, Duke's business school named a wing of a new building "Horrigan Hall." (Johnson was named a Duke trustee.) . . .

At the same time, the number of board meetings was slashed, and directors' fees were boosted to $50,000 . . . Johnson encouraged them to use the RJR Air Force anytime, anywhere, at no charge. "I sometimes feel like the director of transportation," he once sighed after arranging yet another director's flight. "But I know if I'm there for them they'll be there for me."[5]

Nor was Johnson and RJR Nabisco an isolated case. The lesson he preached—that the way to compromising a board member's heart is through his or her wallet—was learned well by the next generation of CEOs. Bernie Ebbers, founder and former CEO of WorldCom (who has been convicted of fraud and conspiracy), once agreed to let director Stiles Kellett use a WorldCom airplane for $1 per month. Kellett was chair of the board's compensation committee, which in turn approved $400 million in personal loans from WorldCom to Ebbers. Kellett was surely "there" for Ebbers. When American Express had its troubles, it turned out that the corporation headed by former CEO Jimmy Robinson was paying board member Henry Kissinger a consulting fee. Of course, that called into question whether Kellett and Kissinger could be there for the owners of the company.

The Third I: Incompetence

Finally, the third I, incompetence. Boards are made up of individuals. Control who those individuals are and you likely control the board. Create a boardroom populated by social climbers, celebrity directors with little experience in business, people with irrelevant skills, or people with special relationships to the CEO or controlling shareowner, and effective oversight fades to myth.

Here is a case in point. In 1911, the inquiry into the collapse of the Brazilian Rubber Plantation and Estates Ltd suggested that the board in charge was so incompetent that they seemed to have stepped out of a P. G. Wodehouse novel: "Sir Arthur Alymer was absolutely ignorant of business . . . H. W. Tugwell was . . . seventy-five years of age and very deaf . . . Barber was a rubber broker and was told that all he would have to do would be to give an opinion as to the value of rubber when it arrived in England."[6]

More than two generations later, boardroom culture was not much improved. One veteran director, Lord Boothby, described the board member's burden, circa 1962: "No effort of any kind is called for. You go to a meeting once a month in a car supplied by the company. You look both grave and sage and, on two occasions, say 'I agree,' say 'I don't think so' once and, if all goes well, you get £5,500 a year."[7]

That situation is less common today, but it's far from extinct. Recent celebrity directors in the United States have included B-list celebrities (Priscilla Presley), athletes (former Los Angeles Dodger manager Tommy Lasorda, boxer Laila Ali), politicians of both Democratic and Republican stripes, and a host of others selected for their names as much as for their abilities. In the United Kingdom, a 2003 report by Sir Derek Higgs discovered that only 4 percent of directors had gone through the sort of hiring process that would be considered mandatory for all other grades of staff. In effect, the process for appointing and training a burger flipper at McDonald's was significantly more rigorous than that for someone overseeing a global multibillion-dollar enterprise.

So the three I's—lack of information, improper influence, and incompetence—too often create conditions that make boards systemically less effective than they would be otherwise.

Gravity-Defying CEO Compensation

Let's look at one vivid example where boards seem to have been asleep. Nothing has commanded so much media attention, or so sharply demonstrated the diversion of board loyalty from owners to CEOs, as the extraordinary excesses in executive pay awarded by directors, particularly at U.S. companies. Chief executives, of course, have long enjoyed comfortable lives, sumptuous offices, fine entertaining, private jets, and other perks. But in the 1990s, boards began to allow CEOs to cash in big time. Ironically, they did so on the grounds that it was necessary to help create shareowner value.

Essentially, CEOs argued that in order for them to care about shareowner interests, they should receive rewards when shareowners did. The preferred mechanism was the share option, which granted top executives the right to buy company stock in the future, but at today's price. Unlike similar options bought or sold in the public markets, these were given to CEOs for free. The argument was that if the share price rose, that was good for shareowners and for executives. Boards were soon handing CEOs thousands, and in some cases millions, of stock options. If shareowners suffered when prices declined, however, CEOs didn't. CEOs told boards that they had to be paid "competitive" rates to be retained. In other words, the variable compensation ratcheted only one way. Up.

Stock prices at many companies soared through the 1990s not solely because of CEO leadership but because of a cyclical rise in market prices fueled by a lowering of interest rates, which made all stocks more attractive. Even executives who had done nothing to create value benefited. But boards were often too beholden to management to rethink the money drain. They were too ill informed to fully understand the ramifications of Byzantine remuneration schemes, and too docile to stand up to compensation consultants (often hired by the CEO), who always seemed to argue that, as in the mythical Lake Wobegon, the company chief executive was above average and so should have an above-average pay package. In one singularly embarrassing example, the head of the compensation committee at the New York Stock Exchange (admittedly not a public company at the time, but a quasi-regulator of thousands of them) said he never knew that the various components of former chief Richard Grasso's package would total a staggering $187 million.[8]

So U.S. CEO pay went through the roof. Then through the stratosphere. Then out of the solar system. And boards of directors let it happen. The consulting firm MVC Associates International found that sixty companies at the bottom of the Russell 3000 index lost $769 billion in market value and destroyed $475 billion in economic value over five years ending in 2004 while their boards paid the top five executives at each firm more than $12 billion.[9] In 1992, the average compensation package for a CEO at one of the top 500 firms in the United States was $2.7 million (using 2002 constant dollars)—and that did not include pensions, perks, and sundry "stealth compensation." By 2000, the average was $14 million, a 500 percent increase.[10] In eight years, *just the inflation* in compensation among the top five hundred CEOs cost companies and their shareowners $5.6 billion per annum, the equivalent of half the country's foreign aid budget.[11]

First Class

Many CEOs may have earned their packages, performing admirably. Their boards truly understood obligations to shareowners and oversaw companies that built lasting value. But others were paid to stupefying excess despite poor relative performance by their companies or, worse, for fraudulent performance. In fact, stock options may have contributed to the fraud, as executives were motivated to talk up the value of their shares to increase still further the value of their options. In their book *Remuneration*, Michael Jensen, Kevin Murphy, and Erick Wruck describe the effect of options as "organizational heroin," as executives become addicted to feeding good news to shareowners in order to preserve option values.[12]

Boards looked the other way as greed overwhelmed owners' interests, sometimes breaching ludicrous frontiers. Directors at Global Crossing famously lavished Robert Annunziata with a 4,000-word employment contract that required the company to buy the CEO a specific Mercedes-Benz (500 SL) and pay for monthly first-class air tickets for his wife, children, and mother to visit him. That was on top of a $10 million signing bonus and two million stock options priced below market. "It seems to us that anyone who gets the equivalent of $30 million just for showing up can pay for his own airfare and Mercedes," commented The Corporate Library's Nell Minow, which gave the board low marks for responsiveness to shareowners. Global Crossing, of course, subsequently went bankrupt.[13]

In a biting commentary on director passivity, economist John Kenneth Galbraith once observed, "The salary of the chief executive of the large corporation is not a market award for achievement. It is frequently in the nature of a warm personal gesture by the individual to himself."[14] But the example of excess executive pay is relevant not just because it creates great headlines. The point is this: the epic transfer of wealth to chief executives regardless of performance happened because boards of directors did not feel responsible to owners. They failed to demand the right information, were readily captured by the CEO's influence, or were simply incompetent in overseeing their duties.

But now the situation is changing. As new capitalist investing institutions awake, they are increasingly raising questions about the board's role and responsibilities, reinvigorating the circle of accountability. They are framing what amounts to an unheralded new constitution for the modern corporation.

"Non-Performing Assets"

Let's look at one early effort by citizen investors to improve board accountability. Sears, Roebuck and Co. was an icon of the U.S. economy. Its mail-order catalog had domesticated the American West. It furnished suburbia to the requirements of returning soldiers following World War II. But by the mid-1980s, its storied history seemed ancient history. While new entrants, such as Wal-Mart, the Gap, and Circuit City, saw revenues increase, Sears suffered earnings declines year after year. It responded by running in all directions at once, getting nowhere fast. Management sold the landmark Sears tower in Chicago. It diversified into financial services, buying insurance (Allstate), brokerage (Dean Witter) and real estate (Coldwell Banker) companies, even while trying to be a mass merchant. Mixing socks and stocks proved a dismal failure.

In 1991, Robert A. G. Monks, a former U.S. Department of Labor official overseeing pension funds, the founder of proxy adviser Institutional Shareholder Services, and the leading shareowner activist in North America, took aim at Sears's board of directors. He did something both obvious and radical: he ran for election to the board as an independent.

Sears management spared no expense to defeat Monks. He was outspent and outlawyered. The company sued him in an action that seemed designed to intimidate him with the threat of personal bankruptcy. The company even shrank the size of the board to reduce the risk that dissident investors would eke out a victory.

Monks lost the battle, but he came back again the following year. This time he blasted chronic failures of the entire board to carry out their fiduciary duties to owners. He placed an ad in the *Wall Street Journal*, which was brilliant in its simplicity, effective in its message, and laser-focused on the board. The ad depicted a silhouette of the board of directors, adapted from their portrait in Sears's annual report. It carried the tag line "Non-Performing Assets?"

Monks's ad focused the financial community on these supposed fiduciaries, who until then had been nameless. The financial press began asking individual directors what they were doing for the owners they represented. Soon thereafter, Sears announced a plan to spin off Dean Witter, sell Coldwell Banker, and begin to dispose of Allstate. The company gained more than $1 billion in market value in a day. In a year, the return to shareowners was higher than 36 percent—after the stock had languished for years.[15] Perhaps more important, the Monks campaign reforged the link between Sears's board and the company's shareowners. Directors were compelled to rediscover their accountability for the performance of the company and their accountability to investors.

Fixing the Board

The civil economy was crystallizing. Crystals, of course, need a "seed" around which to form. Institutional investors found that seed by following the advice of Ira Millstein, the white-haired, common-sense-talking senior partner at law firm Weil, Gotshal & Manges. Millstein, later one of the "wise men" who guided the creation of the OECD's Principles of Corporate Governance, spoke at a forum of the Council of Institutional Investors, urging pension funds to focus on laggards in their portfolios. Soon poor performers—like Sears—became the seed around which the crystals formed.

Funds began concentrating on dismantling impediments to accountability. They pressed for requirements that board members be outsiders who were truly independent of management or controlling owners, calculating that directors free of conflicts would be better able to serve as fiduciaries for investors. Soon regulators and legislators took up the call. Today, independence has been enshrined in listing standards at various stock exchanges and governance codes worldwide.

Next, investors took on the issue of information. Best-practice codes called for key committees of the board to be able to hire experts directly, without going through management. Some got even more specific, declaring that directors receive board documents a fixed number of days before each meeting, or that directors be able to directly access anyone within the corporation so as to open information channels that did not flow through the CEO. The Sarbanes-Oxley Act in the United States requires that at least some audit committee members boast accounting and financial market expertise. Simultaneously, lawyers began advising boards that they need to be fully aware of what they are deciding in order to escape liability as well as to perform their function.

Finally, there is an increasing focus on who the directors are, in an effort to weed out incompetents and dead wood. Firms including The Corporate Library, GovernanceMetrics International, Institutional Shareholder Services, and BoardEx gave investors an easily accessible, robust database of corporate directors, complete with an analysis of how well they represent owners.

So cross the three "I's" off the table. Problem solved?

Well, not quite. Removing impediments to accountability is a necessary condition, but perhaps not a sufficient one. Lucian Bebchuk and Jesse Fried put it best, saying we need boards to be not so much independent of management as "dependent on shareholders."[16] Directors still need to be relinked to the owners they represent. Let's begin examining how to do that by asking a very basic question. "What are boards for?"

What Are Boards For?

The board of directors is the supreme executive authority of the corporation. Specifically, corporation law says that "the business and affairs of every corporation . . . shall be managed by or under the direction of a board of directors."[17] Different countries have adopted different models for top boards. Germany splits governance between a nonexecutive supervisory board and a management board charged with the day-to-day running of the company. Traditionally, Japanese boards have been large, sometimes with thirty or more members, and dominated by executives, though that is changing. In the United States, boards are smaller and overwhelmingly made up of outsiders. In Britain, boards have a mix of insiders and outsiders. In some countries, the board is prescribed by law, in others by custom. But in all countries, it is the board that is ultimately responsible for the conduct of the company. Only the board can govern the company, just as only lawmakers in Congress or Parliament, not citizens directly, may govern a country.

Given this charge, what should a new capitalist expect of an effective board?

First and foremost, the task of any board is to ensure proper entrepreneurial *leadership* of the organization. The corporation's mission is to generate a profit for its shareowners. This will happen only if it has the proper leadership and drive to do so. Here some observers disagree about recent reforms, such as the U.S. Sarbanes-Oxley Act. Overprescription threatens to so expand potential legal liabilities that board directors may shun risk and hence reward, so that the cost of compliance outweighs the benefits. If this proves true over time, reform will prove self-defeating. In an entrepreneurial market economy, governance is not truly about directors heeling to political correctness or ticking the compliance boxes. Directorship is not police work. It is instead about generating value.

The second task of any board is to be able to form judgments about what is best for all shareowners, independent of executive management or a controlling owner. The board must ensure that managers put their shareowners—and not themselves—first. Directors must be willing and able to remove the CEO, if such a step becomes necessary. That is the ultimate test of their independence of management.

And that brings us to the third task of boards: applying expertise. If directors are to make good decisions, they must tap and utilize specialized know-how, particularly in companies whose operations are technically complex. Sometimes directors have to look outside the company for such services to get an unbiased eye on affairs.

On paper, all these charges are clear enough. In the real world, though, the path to value-creating leadership is fraught with conflicts and difficulties. Put yourself in a director's shoes. On behalf of shareowners, whom you rarely, if ever, meet, and who have provided little guidance on your duties, you must hire and support a chief executive and a top management team. You must properly motivate them and give them incentives, and cajole and encourage them to develop and implement new value-creating strategies, all within ethical and legal bounds. You will take full common responsibility for the policies adopted while at the same time knowing that, should the CEO and her or his team prove a failure, you will have to replace them. And all this you will have to do in the blaze of exposure, disclosure, and regulation that surrounds most public companies.

Those are daunting assignments. Yet quiet milestones bring them within reach as never before. We are beginning to see the emergence of a new architecture for accountability.

The Constitutional Company

It is worth reflecting just how far we have come in reconstructing boards. As we saw in chapter 2, the early days of the company were pretty lawless and speculative. Over the years, most countries' laws, regulations, and cultures have powerfully circumscribed the ability to abuse shareowners. Of course, this is not true everywhere; absent constraint, directors can wreak havoc with investors. This was apparent in Russia in the 1990s, following the success of the government in privatizing former state-owned enterprises but before shareowner protections came into force. Directors would sell the output of their enterprises at low prices to companies that they controlled, tidily keeping the bulk of profit for themselves. If minority shareowners objected, the directors would simply issue more shares at low prices to themselves and their friends. Sometimes they skipped the middle step, simply "erasing" names from the legal register of those holding shares, thereby granting themselves even more of the company.

In most of the world, these excessive abuses are illegal, and have been for some time. And in most developed markets, there has been a rigorous spring cleaning to ensure that directors are not able to abuse their positions.

As recently as the mid-1980s, "insider trading" was not illegal in many of major Western markets. An unscrupulous director could buy shares before announcing good news about company performance, or sell before bad news, profiting at the expense of the shareowner. In France, such practices were legal until 1970 and in Germany until 1994.[18] Today legislators are taking pains to ensure that improper behavior of this nature is difficult to undertake. In May 2005, the Spanish stock market sent a frisson of concern throughout the corporate community by demanding that boards declare any transaction between a company and "persons with whom directors hold . . . affectionate bonds." Directors protested, fearing what was dubbed a "lover's guide to boardrooms."[19]

A second, crucial reform has been the separation of powers between different groups of directors. For many years, German companies have operated a two-tier board system in which a supervisory board oversees the activities of the executive board. In countries with a single-tier board, reformers have sought to identify issues about which the chief executive's judgment is bound to be conflicted. These include his or her own appointment, dismissal, and remuneration; the nomination of new directors; and the response to the report of the auditors. Such issues are taken out of the executive directors' hands and given to committees that comprise only independent directors. Special roles for independent directors are now inscribed into such diverse building blocks of corporate infrastructure as the listing standards of the New York Stock Exchange, the Combined Code in the United Kingdom, SEBI rules in India, and directives of the China Securities Regulatory Commission.

Dependence on Shareowners

Many countries have gone farther, requiring the separation of the role of chairman of the board from that of chief executive. The chairman is explicitly responsible for ensuring the proper functioning of the board, including guaranteeing oversight of the CEO. Within this framework of oversight, the CEO has license to run the company but is not in a position to be his or her own boss.

These reforms advance the separation of powers within the board, marking major progress in constitutionalizing the corporation. They represent efforts to expunge negative, improper influences that might divert the board's obligations away from shareowners. The tougher and newer work is in defining affirmative obligations directors face, not just to be independent of the executive but to be "dependent on sharehold-ers," as Bebchuck and Fried say. These are critical advances in creating a civil economy.

Perhaps the most crucial is the spreading consensus that directors should be appointed by and removed by owners, much the way mem-bers of a Parliament or Congress are chosen, and removed, by citizens. You might think we do that now, but we don't—at least not everywhere. True, the appearance of such a right of owners is pervasive: we say di-rectors are "elected," and there are proxy "votes" and independent in-spectors of "elections." Yet the reality is somewhat messier.

There were, and indeed still are, many devices that managers and controlling shareowners have used to avoid accountability to investors. For example, they issue preference shares that had equal rights to ordi-nary shares, but no votes. They form pyramids of holding companies, where one company controls 51 percent of the next, allowing control to be maintained even as the economic interest is diluted. They make it difficult for shareowners to vote, for example, by requiring physical at-tendance at the annual meeting, or requiring original signatures on proxies (rather than allowing facsimiles or Internet voting), or insisting that shares cannot be sold during a voting period.

Bit by bit these abuses are being swept away. Just twenty years ago, "one share one vote" was the rallying cry that led to the formation of the Council of Institutional Investors, the trailblazing organization of pension plans that banded together to improve corporate governance. Today, it is accepted best practice in many nations. This is not to pre-tend that it has been universally adopted; far from it. But in most Eng-lish speaking countries, preference shares and dual voting rights are increasingly rare. In continental Europe, such practices are diminish-ing. In Brazil, which had previously allowed two-thirds of share capital to be issued as preference shares, this has now been reduced to 50 per-cent, and "Novo Mercado" companies adhere to "one share one vote" as a matter of course.[20]

Shareowner activists are attacking pyramid-holding structures. In some jurisdictions—for example, Norway, Sweden, and Finland—in order to ensure they are protected, shareowners are granted specific rights to nominate directors. In Italy, laws are currently being put in place that will allow minority shareowners to elect their own slate of directors to the board to ensure that the management does not abuse its power.

Soviet-Style Board Elections in the United States

All these reforms encourage investors to assume their fiduciary responsibilities. Levels of voting are rising everywhere. In Britain, as we noted in chapter 4, funds voted only 20 percent of shares at a typical company back in 1990. Today the average turnout is 55.9 percent. Indeed, voting analysis is a big-time business, as we will see in chapter 6. Institutional Shareholder Services, the largest voting-advisory service, has 550 employees, and now advises more than thirteen hundred clients globally. Twenty years ago, its finances were so fragile that survival was in doubt.

Of course, voting makes little sense unless a process exists to identify and nominate competent candidates. Usually the corporate board itself puts forward candidates. Historically, this often meant that the chief executive or a controlling shareowner hand-picked the slate. But today, separate nomination committees, composed primarily of independent directors, are becoming standard best practice in many large markets. In some, such as the United Kingdom, codes mandate that there must be a proper procedure to find nominees who are appropriately qualified before they go to the shareowners for approval. Indeed, a thriving director-search business has emerged.

Surprisingly, the laggard is the United States. There, the mechanisms available to owners to mount nominations seem either futile or overly confrontational. On the one hand, owners may suggest nominees to the board, but boards are free to ignore such suggestions and usually do. Of course, owners may wage an expensive proxy battle (as Monks did at Sears). But the expense and the confrontational nature of the situation (it is even legally defined as a "contested" election, as if elections by right should be unanimous) means that few shareowners engage in such battles. Indeed, the tactic is more usually used as part of a hostile takeover. What is missing is the middle ground that exists in some other countries: the ability for shareowners to consider director nominees that a subset of owners puts forward, in a less confrontational, more routine manner.

Making matters worse, directors in the United States and Canada reach office through the peculiar plurality voting method. Investors cannot vote against any candidate; they may only vote yes or indicate that they want to withhold their ballot. The ludicrous bottom line is that in a typical, "uncontested" election, an entire slate of directors may be elected on the yes vote of a single share. Even if every other share is withheld, the directors win. Monks and Minnow characterize the situation simply: "The election is just a formality."[21] Even mainstream judges agree; most U.S. director elections are "an irrelevancy," asserted Delaware justices William Chandler III and Leo Strine Jr. in a landmark 2003 paper.[22] Other critics have been still more blunt, terming the system "soviet-style."

But change is coming. A switch to forms of majority rule is likely, thanks to intense new capitalist pressure. The International Corporate Governance Network, Council of Institutional Investors, and Canadian Coalition for Good Governance (CCGG) have made majority voting a key reform in their agendas. Even the staid American Bar Association has opened the door, if only a crack, to ways elections can be changed to enhance directors' accountability to shareowners.

Increasing numbers of U.S. corporations, seeing the dawn of civil economy accountability standards, have already begun to move in that direction. In 2005, Pfizer, long a corporate governance leader, announced that it would require a director to resign if a majority of shares were withheld for his or her election, though technically the board could still choose to keep the member. Pfizer's innovation, soon followed by Disney and others, promises finally to make the election process close to meaningful. Intense CCGG pressure convinced every major bank in Canada to take the same course within a matter of months.

Rush of Change

Overall, the turn to accountability has been so global and so comprehensive that criticisms made in the early 1990s already seem out of date. That is not to say that the struggle for the "constitutional company" is over—far from it. But enormous progress has been made.

In the single decade from 1994 to 2004, more than fifty countries introduced new codes of corporate governance that strengthen the circle of accountability.[23] It took hundreds of years for nations to establish a system of political accountability. In just two decades, corporations around the world have undergone reform in their levels of accountability at many times the speed. In some countries, modernization has amounted to the corporate equivalent of a revolution. New frameworks of board performance, competence, and accountability mark commercial developments equivalent to the development of a bill of rights or a constitution in the political sphere.

Have these constitutional changes made a difference? You bet they have. Let's take just one example. Booz Allen Hamilton, the consulting firm, has been monitoring the hiring and firing of CEOs of the world's top twenty-five hundred companies over the past ten years. In 1995, boards removed less than one in ninety CEOs following a period of poor performance. Essentially the CEO had a job for life. By 2004, however, the study detected four times the numbers of dismissals for poor performance. The authors concluded: "The trend is undeniable, and the implications profound. Dissatisfied large shareowners and other corporate constituents have wrested the power from imperial chief executives in all the world's major economies . . . [B]oards and management need to adapt their organizations and processes to an environment where executive leadership is no longer dominant by default."[24]

The Booz Allen Hamilton study raised another pointed observation. Poor performance, not personal ethics, illegality, or power struggles, triggered most CEO departures. And more board performance reviews are likely to cost more CEO jobs in the future. Independent directors were found increasingly to be warming to their new role in scrutinizing management.

Board Police?

In short, the long era of rubber-stamp boards outlined at the start of this chapter is, year by year, being replaced by a framework of board responsibility and accountability. Much work remains, particularly in enhancing director dependence on civil owners. But what has already occurred represents an enormous strengthening in the accountability of the corporation, through its board, to its owners.

Still, a few argue that new capitalists' fixation on accountability is a fad that fails to recognize the entrepreneurial purpose of the business, which is to profit by offering customers a better service at lower cost than the competition. If we focus too much on the accountability of boards, critics ask, won't we end up diluting their prime function, which is to provide entrepreneurial leadership to the organization?

Certainly there are real dangers if, in the cause of good governance, we become overly legalistic about processes and procedures. The aim of greater accountability is to increase value for shareowners. Legal makework, by contrast, is aimed at reducing liability without regard to whether the cost of that risk reduction is worthwhile. But there the problem lies not in the principle of reform but in how it is enacted.

It is difficult to see how, in principle, an unaccountable system could deliver greater value than an accountable one. Indeed, history shows that—whether in corporations or countries—a lack of accountability and imperial leadership are associated with economic decline rather than a general economic upturn. It is true in every era and in every geography. Think of monarchist France, communist Soviet Union, or today's totalitarian North Korea. Lack of accountability and imperial CEOs did not work at corporations such as Maxwell Communications, WorldCom, or Sunbeam. Even when it appeared to function, as at AIG, it seems a matter of time before the lack of accountability raises risks of a major problem, scandal, or both.

Lack of accountability seems to encourage corruption at the top levels, not value creation for the whole. But the converse now appears to be true. As discussed earlier, study after study show that as companies become better managed, more accountable, and more constitutional in nature, they become worth more. As Deutsche Bank found in 2005, "Companies with improving governance outperformed those with deteriorating performance."[25]

That, then, begs several key questions: How do we know when a company is being accountable? How do we know when it is being well managed? Indeed, given the recent scandals rife with fraudulent accounting, how do we even know if a company is profitable? Answers hinge on the work of packs of little-understood external agencies responsible for monitoring companies. As we'll see in part 2, they are part of an ecosystem of the civil economy. Their epic transition needs to be decoded too.

TAKEAWAYS

- The board of directors is the critical link through which a company's operations are made accountable to shareowners.

- Too often in the past, directors have not had the independence, the information, or the competence to serve as effective governors of companies.

- Since the mid-1980s, we have seen a revolutionary change in the construction of the board, aimed at increasing its independence and accountability. This is a global phenomenon of profound consequence.

- Board reforms include drawing clear distinctions between board and CEO functions, creating special roles for independent board members, and giving the board access to the expertise it needs.

- Improvements in both shareowner voting percentages and in how shareowners may nominate and elect board members have the potential to further increase the accountability of the board, making it not only independent from management but *dependent* on shareowners.

- Board reform offers the promise of companies that are truly focused on delivering the long-term needs of new capitalists.

PART THREE

The New Capitalist Ecosystem

Monitoring the Market

The Information Moguls

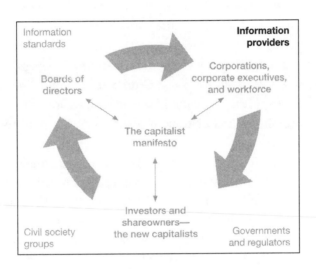

Information is the lifeblood of markets—but what happens when there is a general breakdown in the integrity of information? This chapter spotlights conflicts of interest among brokers, auditors, market analysts, and credit raters. It then describes how new capitalists are compelling such information moguls to make companies more transparent and funds more vigilant.

Kristen Campbell could have been basking in the prospect that her Merrill Lynch bonus would hit another record the next month. Instead, she was at the breaking point. It was November 2000, when the Internet bubble was at its crest, and the high-tech stocks she was supposed to be analyzing were getting junkier by the day. But she could say nothing about that to the millions of retail investors who relied on her for objective judgments. Merrill's investment bankers were hungry for the millions in fees they could reap by managing the stock sales of Internet startups. So the message from the top was clear, if unstated. Analysts' jobs were to fuel the investment banking business by pumping out reliably sunny ratings, no matter how poor the stock.

For Campbell, Goto.com was the last straw. Todd Tappin, its chief financial officer, was dangling investment banking business for Merrill, but he wanted Campbell to brand Goto a solid "buy." She had pored through the prospectus—and could see no good grounds for such a rating. Steaming, she sat at her desk and snapped an e-mail to her boss, Henry Blodgett.

"I don't want to be a whore for f---ing management. If a rating means that we are putting half of Merrill retail into this stock because they are out accumulating it, then I don't think that's the right thing to do. We are losing people money and I don't like it. John and Mary Smith are losing their retirement because we don't want Todd to be mad at us." In conclusion, Campbell loosed some blunt words that would resurface seventeen months later at the heart of a New York State prosecution case against Merrill Lynch: "The whole idea that we are independent from banking is a big lie."[1]

Campbell was right. A commonplace of Wall Street was that investment research, branded as fiercely impartial, was in fact secretly skewed to generate investment banking business. The scale of deception was breathtaking. On the cusp of market collapse, for instance, Salomon issued not one "sell" recommendation on 1,179 stocks it was rating. "We support pigs," proclaimed Citicorp analyst Jack Grubman in an e-mail.[2]

Conflicts twisting Wall Street research did indeed steer untold numbers of John and Mary Smiths to sink scarce savings into junk stock. But analysts are only one cohort in a vast but surprisingly little-known army of mandarins who make markets work.

These intermediaries form a critical part of the ecosystem that either blocks or enables corporate accountability to new capitalists. Auditors opine on the financial health of the company. Agencies analyze the propriety of the directors who sit on company boards. Advisers to pension funds recommend types of securities and countries in which those funds should invest, and the asset managers through which they should invest. Credit-rating agencies determine if bonds are appropriate investments. And brokers and analysts, such as Kristen Campbell, advise on the buying and selling of stock.

Without these intermediaries, and without an assurance of their integrity, the capital markets would seize up. Citizens around the world more freely entrust their savings to capital markets when they have confidence that these information intermediaries play fair.

Even with best intentions, however, these agents too often don't play fair, largely because of chronic conflicts of interest. Economists would say these distortions undermine the efficient allocation of capital, holding back potential for growth. Organizational theorists term the situation a principal-agency problem. Retirees victimized by deception might instead say the system is a racket.

Seen through civil economy eyes, intermediaries hijacked by a host of pressures obstruct the circle of accountability that should bind new capitalists to enterprises. Ruptures block effective oversight by investors. In addition, without such monitoring, corporations too often receive the wrong signals about whose interests they are there to maximize.

Scandals such as the one that prompted Kristen Campbell's damning e-mail have not only exposed dysfunctions among information moguls. They have also unleashed a torrent of remedial measures in countries around the world. Their objective is straightforward: to dredge the clutter of conflicts so that stock analysts, credit raters, auditors, and other intermediaries align their work directly with investors' interests. Clearing channels of accountability, a defining objective of citizen shareowners in a civil economy, already promises to alter the way companies are run. But few yet appreciate how profound are the changes that are coming.

Toxic Lullaby

What went wrong to begin with? For decades, the economic culture surrounding corporations seemed to be singing a lullaby that softly rocked investors, regulators, and much of the world to sleep. Even the most sophisticated financial institutions paid scant attention to auditors, credit raters, brokers, and the like. They were important cogs in the market's machine, to be sure. They seemed to work. As a result, funds failed to muster the enthusiasm to unravel the web of money, standards, contracts, and practices that framed the world of middlemen.

Mass somnambulating proved a dangerous mistake. The truism is indeed true: information is power. The intermediaries between corporations and the rest of the world control information and, with it, the ability to control the fortunes, even the fate of the world's top corporations themselves. They are the information moguls.

While shareowners were asleep, power players were able to avoid the spotlight. That twilight, in turn, was at least partially responsible for the Enron disaster, allowing the auditing firm Arthur Andersen to certify that Enron's books met U.S. accounting standards, even while the energy trader was imploding. Averted eyes allowed credit-rating agencies to mark WorldCom's bonds as investment grade—and therefore safe enough for the proverbial widows' and orphans' savings accounts—just months before WorldCom filed for bankruptcy in the biggest fraud in the history of commerce.[3]

At the core of all of these scandals was a single potent toxin: conflict of interest. Services ostensibly designed to benefit investors were paid for, or subsidized by, parties whose interests may have been different from, or even damaging to, those of the very investors the services were supposed to benefit. Because corporations usually paid the bill, professional agents who should have served the owners instead danced to management's tune. Think of it this way: a free press is a vital pillar of civil society. Imagine what would happen if you couldn't count on objective news, if reports were replaced by advertising, paid for by the very people and institutions journalists were supposed to cover. In a way, that's what happened to markets. The information intermediaries on whom the civil economy relies were conflicted. As a result, the watch-dogs did not bark.

Broken Brokers

Of all intermediaries, perhaps it is the brokers who have the greatest temptation to stray from the straight and narrow. Brokers are rewarded by the amount of shares they trade. Therefore, rather like tabloid jour-nalists, they are eager to create a "story" that will encourage people to buy or sell shares. Canny investors, just like canny newspaper readers, understand that these are the rules of the game, and they weigh broker-age advice accordingly. What is much more insidious is if brokers are placed in a position where they feel other conflicts of loyalty.

Consider Citicorp's Jack Grubman, perhaps the poster child for abuses. Though hired, like Kristen Campbell, to offer impartial advice to investors, he behaved as if his clients were actually the telecommuni-cations corporations he was supposed to monitor. Grubman served, for instance, as a key adviser to ex-WorldCom boss Bernie Ebbers in the company's takeover of rival MCI—even as he was supposed to be pro-viding objective advice to shareowners on the deal. When asked whether he was bothered that his firm was reaping investment banking fees re-lated to his activities while he was advising investors, Grubman didn't just step over the line. He erased it. "What used to be a conflict is now a synergy," he asserted. "Objective? The other word for it is uninformed."[4]

Grubman was as abysmal a judge of talent as he was of ethics. In ad-dition to acting as consigliere to Ebbers, he bonded with another chief executive, Joseph Nacchio of Qwest. In a moment of exquisite karma, Nacchio was charged with securities fraud within twenty-four hours of Ebbers's conviction for the same crime.[5] Thus Grubman, who called the rest of us "uninformed," turned out to have advised two telecom CEOs who between them committed, or failed to detect, more than $13 billion in accounting fraud. That is equivalent to somehow misplacing the entire gross domestic product of Nicaragua, Botswana, and Estonia combined.[6]

It wasn't that the information moguls of the late twentieth century were uniquely crooked. There was something embedded in the corporate ecosystem that encouraged—or at least allowed—ethical lapses to be tolerated, or even described as brilliance.

In the case of brokerage-sponsored research, financial firms commonly offered research as loss-leading bait to lure investment banking fees. Grubman at Citicorp and Henry Blodget at Merrill Lynch may have been extreme examples of conflicts of interest. But the fact that they were their companies' brightest stars demonstrates just how skewed the Wall Street culture had become.

Shoots of the civil economy, however, sprouted among the rubble of the scandals. New York State attorney general Eliot Spitzer joined with the SEC to force injunctions on many financial powerhouses: Bear Stearns, Credit Suisse First Boston, Goldman Sachs, Lehman Brothers, JPMorgan, Merrill Lynch, Morgan Stanley, Citigroup, UBS Warburg, and Piper Jaffray. The settlement barred the firms from breaking the law, of course, and extracted among the highest civil penalties ever paid. But it also imposed a key Spitzer idea: that research on stocks should be unbiased and investor-centric, so that John and Mary Smith can make truly informed judgments on where to invest their savings. Firms had to pry their research arms away from their investment banking arms.[7]

Dedication to objective information—a mission followed only by minor players before the Spitzer settlements—quickly spawned a new independent stock research movement. The lure of money helped. The global settlement with investment companies created a $450 million kitty for independent research. A troika of U.S. state pension funds—North Carolina, New York, and California—gave it a further push by adopting "Investment Protection Principles" designed to purge conflicts from analysis.[8]

The first-ever professional association for independent research, Investorside, got off the ground in 2002. Investorside makes no bones about what are, in effect, its civil economy credentials. Its Web site describes the group's raison d'être as "[r]estoring trust in the U.S. capital markets by promoting investment research that is financially aligned with investor interests." The idea proved so powerful that Investorside amassed seventy member firms—including major houses such as Sanford C. Bernstein and Argus Research—in its first three years. In Europe, a coalition of funds called the Independent Research Think Tank moved in 2005 to promote parallel market and EU support for independent research.[9]

The Enhanced Analytics Initiative has gone farther. A cooperative venture among new capitalist–oriented pension funds, it directs brokerage fees *not* to those agencies that encourage them to trade shares, but to those that investigate the long-term health of companies, including their environmental, social, and governance risks. Armed with such analysis, owners can better carry out their duties as stewards. By early 2006, as we noted earlier, EAI had attracted funds with nearly one trillion dollars in assets.

Stock research, though its scandals and remedies made the biggest headlines, represented only one of the arteries that urgently needed clearing in the push for an accountable economy. Others lay just out of sight.

Where Are the Auditors?

The most essential intermediaries of all are the accountants. They are pivotal to ensuring that capitalism has integrity, or, in the parlance of the trade, a "presumption of regularity"—the underlying belief that you can believe what you are being told about the financial position of the company in which you are investing. When that presumption is exposed as faulty, the system seizes up. For accounting information on the world's largest companies, we have to look to one of the "Big 4" sprawling partnerships, each employing around one hundred thousand people globally, with scores of offices in most countries in the world: Pricewaterhouse-Coopers, Deloitte, KPMG, and Ernst & Young. (Arthur Andersen, which used to be a fifth, famously imploded after the collapse of Enron.)

When financial statements begin to lose credibility, it is an expensive business. The Brookings Institution quantified the cost to the U.S. economy of the 2001–2002 corporate governance scandals as the equivalent of a $10-per-barrel increase in the price of imported oil. That $35 billion hit to the country's GDP came about largely because of decreased faith in the capital markets.[10]

That wasn't counting the direct cost to citizen savers of the Enron and WorldCom scandals: about a quarter of a trillion dollars in market capitalization. To put that number in context, $250 billion could fund the budget for the United Kingdom's entire defense, housing, and environment budgets, as well as fund the U.S. Department of Homeland Security and NASA for a year, plus erase the entire budget deficit for Italy—with enough left over to fund the Vatican until the year 2193. Follow-on effects were also severe. For example, New York State comptroller Alan G. Hevesi estimated that New York State and City lost about $1.25 billion in tax revenue because of the scandals.[11]

Understandably, then, "where were the auditors?" became the citizen investors' lament in the Enron, WorldCom, Adelphia, Maxwell, HIH, Ahold, Parmalat, and other scandals. Wall Street and Main Street felt equally betrayed by the accountants' failure to detect and warn of fraud. Auditors were supposed to be the investors' eyes and ears. Partners at Arthur Andersen, implicated in the Enron fraud, were rightly vilified for neglecting the firm's public purpose. But as the scandals continued to unfold, it became obvious that systemic failures—not just a few bad apples—lay at the heart of the problems.

By the 1990s, auditors had built substantial capabilities for management consulting, and they had taken huge side projects, with large price tags, from their very own audit clients. Under those conditions, it was a brave auditor who would be willing to stand up and reveal uncomfortable truths about the clients' books—particularly when the auditor's company acted as a consultant to that client. In addition, there were underlying legal structural problems, particularly in the United States. Unlike information moguls in other countries, U.S. auditors operate against the background of a unique but ill-understood market flaw that leaves them particularly susceptible to letting shareowners down.

Blind Spot

There is legally no such thing as a "U.S. corporation." There are Delaware corporations, California corporations, New York corporations, and Nevada corporations, but no American ones. The individual states, not Washington, D.C., grant corporate status and regulate day-to-day corporate behavior. That matters to citizen-investors because where state law prescribes what the public company can do, an entirely separate phalanx of federal statutes dictates the auditors' functions. In fact, believe it or not, many states do not even require public financial reports, not even Delaware, the leading state in which large public firms incorporate.[12]

In many other countries, the twin issues of company law and disclosure to the marketplace are naturally entwined in national legislation. When they are on different tracks, though, the potential for gaps between them can open the way to misdirected audits, which can in turn lead to corporate governance disasters. In a best-case civil economy, the annual auditor's report would judge whether the entire governance structure of a public company—board and management—is properly performing its role as steward of shareowner capital. In an uncivil economy, by contrast, the auditor's report focuses narrowly on the technicalities of whether the company is complying with detailed accounting rules, which may or may not protect investors. Forests can be missed for the trees.

Why? We have to turn the clock back nearly a century for the answer. As many as 30 percent of companies listed on the New York Stock Exchange didn't bother to produce annual reports for investors in the decade leading up to the stock market crash of 1929. Of course, even when they did, the accounts were hardly lucid, or even honest. "The . . . reports [are] all obfuscated and darkened over with fuliginous matter," sniffed Harvard Professor William Z. Ripley in a 1926 *Atlantic Monthly* article. "To the uninitiated . . . they may tell too much that is not so, or too little of what they ought to tell."[13]

Then came Black Friday and the Great Depression and widespread poverty and hunger—and a national hue and cry for reform. The best minds in the nation agreed to national, uniform regulation of corporations, including financial reporting, basing much of the new concepts on existing British law. There was, however, one major obstacle. Under the Constitution, the federal government had no power to demand audited financial reports, while the states, beholden at the time to the corporations, were not about to mandate them. Franklin Roosevelt's administration soon devised a creative way around the problem.

Washington did have unquestioned authority over interstate commerce, including stock markets. So in the Securities Act of 1933 Congress claimed standing to regulate audits not based on *shareowners'* need for information, but on *traders'* need for information. As British account-ing expert Tim Bush notes, "To this day, the US 1933 Act is still trying to do two entirely different things in a rather inelegant way: to regulate the sale of securities and as an indirect way of governing companies."[14]

The solution was brilliant, but circuitous and bursting with unin-tended consequences. For one thing, the federal law made auditors ac-countable to the corporation, not the shareowners. So CEOs and boards were empowered to hire their own scrutineers—hardly a recipe to guar-antee disinterested reviews. The 2002 Sarbanes-Oxley Act improved mat-ters by handing an independent board audit committee the power to hire and fire the outside auditors. That, however, is still a step removed from direct accountability to shareowners, as is the case in most of the world. No wonder accounting firms saw no conflict in selling tax shel-ters, management consulting services, information technology imple-mentation, and a host of other nonaudit services to corporations, or even directly to chief executives, CFOs, and other senior managers for their personal enrichment. They, not the shareowners, were the clients. During the five years ended in 2003, sixty-one *Fortune* 500 companies bought $3.4 billion worth of tax shelters from the very same auditors hired to provide independent opinions on the integrity of those schemes. Executives at seventeen of those companies arranged with the auditors to benefit personally from those shelters.[15]

Share Versus Fair

Ernst & Young's tax advice to Sprint highlights just how far share-owner and management's interests can diverge, and how outrageous re-sults can be. During the first half of 2000, Sprint was in public merger negotiations with WorldCom. Seeing sure money on the table, top offi-cials at Sprint borrowed millions of dollars to exercise stock options, creating a major personal tax obligation for CEO William Esrey and other senior executives. When the merger fell apart, however, the price of the stock went into free fall, plunging from $67 to $36 in just two months. That wiped out millions in value from the executives' hold-ings, but not their tax debt.

Ernst & Young, supplying both tax counseling and an outside audit, went to work. It recommended that Sprint simply take back the options the executives had exercised, a plan that would have saved the executives taxes due on more than $300 million in paper profits—but cost shareowners by denying the corporation $148 million in tax benefits. To its credit, Sprint decided against the plan. But the fact that an *auditing* firm even suggested it illuminates how much damage investors can suffer when the law cuts the link between citizen investors and the agents they rely on to be watchdogs. As Pat McGurn of ISS has observed, "That is the most bald-faced conflict you could have." [16] But at one level, it should not have been surprising. That year, Sprint paid Ernst & Young a total of some $65 million in fees. The big money was in consulting. Only $3.5 million, or 5.4 percent, was for audit work. [17]

The Sprint case aside, most accountants were ethical and dealt fairly. In fact, the greater wonder is not that scandals broke so regularly, but why so many companies and auditors behaved honorably when U.S. federal law on audits, until the Sarbanes-Oxley Act was passed, required no effective allegiance to shareowners.

Because here is the crux of the problem. U.S. law on audits, constitutionally benchmarked to market price rather than shareowner stewardship, rests on a great, hidden assumption: that the corporation is trying to maximize its value to shareowners. Sometimes, though, it isn't. For instance, management may expropriate value to benefit itself or controlling shareowners via related-party transactions. If, as occurred at Tyco, the chief executive pays for his wife's lavish $2 million birthday party from the corporate till and the action falls short of technical fraud, the auditors will not necessarily let shareowners know about it. Such profligacy may well indicate that a company's management and board are cavalier about shareowner stewardship. But that is no business of the auditors, under U.S. law.

Compare these practices to the British system, from whose laws entire sections of the 1933 Act were plagiarized. The Companies Act makes it clear that auditors are appointed by, and accountable to, shareowners— not the board and not management. Crucially, rather than police fair trading of shares on exchanges, auditors in Britain must annually assess how well directors and executives safeguard shareowner capital. This responsibility was spotlighted in a landmark 1990 U.K. case, *Caparo* v. *Dickman*, wherein Lord Justice Oliver opined that "it is the auditors' function . . . to provide shareholders with reliable intelligence for the purpose of enabling them to scrutinize the conduct of the company's affairs and to exercise their collective powers to reward or control or remove those to whom that conduct has been confided."[18] That is a very broad mandate indeed.

As Tim Bush points out, this has created a problem. The original U.K. practice, which the United States sought to emulate, demanded that an adequate audit present a "true and fair" view of a company's state of affairs, avoiding obfuscation and spin. That mandate mutated into something different in its voyage across the Atlantic. Court decision after court decision in the United States has allowed corporate managers to withhold damaging, but not fraudulent, information, under the so-called business judgment rule. Courts have even given a green light to executives to use "puffery and spin" that may readily mislead investors, as long as it falls short of breaching technical accounting rules. In other words, auditors can legally allow companies to conceal from shareowners issues relating to the competence of management, waste, and business misjudgment.

Audits for New Capitalists

While hamstrung by the federal/state split, U.S. regulators and lawmakers moved to improve audits in the wake of scandals. Government prosecutors effectively forced Arthur Andersen out of business, and Congress created the independent Public Company Accounting Oversight Board as part of the Sarbanes-Oxley Act. The PCAOB issued a slew of regulatory standards designed to make accountants enforce fair standards. The problem is that those rules place a bigger burden on business. The list of Generally Accepted Accounting Principles in the United States is now four times as long as the list in the United Kingdom, as U.S. regulators have tried to microprescribe how capital markets should manage an issue that is, at root, one of governance and stewardship.

For its part, PCAOB increased its policing resources. In 2005 it boasted a budget of more than $137 million and had a staff of 450 people overseeing the 1,623 firms auditing U.S. public companies.[19] The European Commission is planning to create a similar body. And the global accounting profession—through its International Federation of

Accountants (IFAC)—established an independent Public Interest Oversight Board in 2005 to monitor audit ethics worldwide.

Perhaps more important, the private sector itself—animated by the rise of new capitalists—is now busy creating an investor-centric, civil economy model for audit oversight to replace the one discredited by conflicts.

Institutional investors around the world once rubber-stamped any auditor that management proposed. Now they routinely object when accounting firms make more money from consulting than from auditing.[20] When a simple objection is not enough, they have set about suing accountants who fail in their obligations to investors. Witness the record $65 million Arthur Andersen agreed to pay to settle a lawsuit alleging that it should have detected and alerted shareowners to the WorldCom fraud.[21] It is no accident that the plaintiff in the Andersen case was New York State comptroller Alan Hevesi, sole trustee of New York's $120-plus billion pension fund and a former cochair of the Council of Institutional Investors, the U.S. trade group that has pioneered much in the way of corporate governance activism. Hevesi contends that information moguls corrupt civil society and poison capitalism when they let conflicts negate their fiduciary responsibility.

New information moguls are springing up to service new capitalist needs. Howard Schilit's Center for Financial Research and Analysis (CFRA), for instance, scrutinizes the adequacy of public audit reports. In the years since its founding in 1994, CFRA has garnered some four thousand investors and regulators who rely on its daily reports. Think about that for a moment: this new capitalist institution has flourished precisely because of the inadequacies of traditional information moguls. And Schilit intuitively understands the difference. CFRA prominently displays the logo of Investorside on its Web site, certifying "no investment banking conflicts."[22]

All this has caused accounting firms to pay attention.

Just Say No

Lisle, Illinois, is a small town west of Chicago that wraps itself in bucolic symbolism. Lisle bills itself as "the Arboretum Village," and its Chamber of Commerce sponsors an annual Smile Days celebration. For those in search of the civil economy, it is also the unlikely site of a landmark event.

The year was 2004, and the site was the Lisle headquarters of Molex, a diversified electronics manufacturer. Deloitte & Touche, the firm's auditor, demanded that it correct 2004 financial statements to remove a bookkeeping error that had inflated Molex's stated earnings. CEO J. Joseph King refused, and the board backed him up.

End of story? It would have been a few years before, but not anymore. Here is how *BusinessWeek* summarized what happened next: "Then Deloitte did something unexpected: It quit. Two weeks later the firm wrote a blistering and detailed account of the affair for public disclosure at the SEC. That virtually assured that no auditor would work for Molex again as long as King was in charge. Within ten days, the directors had eaten crow: They ousted King, promised to hire a new director with financial expertise for their audit committee, and agreed to take training classes in proper financial reporting."[23] Now that is how a civil economy information mogul is supposed to work.

Re-imagining the Shareowner's Watchdog

Federal watch dogging is having a salutary affect on U.S. accounting firms. And because the U.S. market is so large, the safeguards enacted have forced changes at accounting firms worldwide—even though legal terrains are entirely different. Arguably, in fact, it might be a wiser course for shareowner interests to base global best practices not on Washington standards alone but on a smorgasbord of regimes.

French regulations, for instance, require a public company to hire not one but two accounting firms to conduct an outside audit. This duplication may be more costly, but it builds in quality control and lessens the chance that the audit can become a captive of management. The duo must jointly perform the work and cosign the audit reports, producing checks and balances unknown in English-speaking markets.

The crisis at Vivendi proved the system's worth. In 2001–2002, chief executive Jean-Marie Messier tried to slip in a complex off-balance-sheet stock sale to inflate Vivendi's profits by $1.4 billion. Co-auditor Arthur Andersen was ready to allow the transaction. But the second co-auditor, Salustro-Reydel, cried foul, and the Commission des Opérations de Bourse (then the chief market regulator) agreed. Had Vivendi been listed elsewhere, the Arthur Andersen opinion might have prevailed—giving shareowners a warped portrait of the firm's underlying finances. Might a dual audit system have caught accounting fraud at Enron before the company collapsed, costing new capitalist owners billions in savings?

Active and alert civil owners, independent monitors, and new regulation have together helped propel necessary overhauls in the culture of auditing. Still, fundamental questions about alignment of interests remain. Can citizen investors really trust audits to safeguard their interests when services are paid by the same corporations they audit? Are shareowners best served when the number of global audit firms has shrunk to just four? Forward-looking investors are digging even deeper to find structural ways either to mitigate potential conflicts or to prevent them altogether.

Pierre-Henri Leroy, head of the Paris-based adviser Proxinvest, contends that universal adoption of the French dual audit standard would infuse new blood into today's oligopoly of multinational accounting giants. Peter Butler, the former chief of Hermes engagement funds and co-founder of Governance for Owners, argues for a more radical, "new-style audit" solution to benefit investors. Butler proposes that long-term shareowners take part ownership of an alternative industry of audit service providers.[24]

Or what about yet another break from tradition: allowing shareowners to elect a special committee of investors with exclusive power to appoint an auditor? Morley, the fund management group, suggested that plan in comments to the U.K. Ministry of Trade and Industry.[25] Australian activist Shann Turnbull has long taken a similar view. Swedish corporations already follow such practices.

Whatever solution is ultimately adopted, the accounting profession is center stage in the civil economy debate. Companies can become accountable to citizen owners only if their actions are independently measured and reported.

Free and Fair Elections

In the thickest jungles of the capital market dwells another breed of information mogul even less understood than accountants: enterprises that help advise shareowners how to vote at corporate annual meetings. Judgments by these "proxy advisers" have grown so influential that they can make or break a CEO's reign, cement or scuttle mergers and acquisitions, and accelerate or stall a company's embrace of socially responsible behavior. Citizen investors need to be able to count on proxy advisers to represent their best interests. Can they?

Maybe you've received proxy voting documents in the mail. If so, you know the packets often contain dozens of dull, dense pages. Now imagine you're a large institutional investor with scores, hundreds, or even thousands of stocks in your portfolio, and an obligation to vote on between two and forty resolutions at every one of those companies. On behalf of their clients, many such funds outsource the work to a specialist who has the time and expertise to analyze the independence of board members or the propriety of remuneration packages. The leading company in this field is Institutional Shareholder Services (ISS), one of the most important information moguls and one many individual savers may never have heard of.

Headquartered near Washington, D.C., ISS advises pension funds, banks, money managers, and mutual funds on how to vote their shares at thousands of corporate annual meetings. For years, ISS had the U.S. market virtually to itself. By 2000, it was estimated to influence as much as 20 percent of all shares voted at U.S. corporations. And given its expansion into Britain through a joint venture with the National Association of Pension Funds and acquisition of Brussels-based Deminor Rating, ISS has achieved status as a power behind voting results at company meetings globally. During the 1990s and early twenty-first century, numerous stock option plans, mergers, and proxy battles succeeded or foundered based on ISS's recommendations.

ISS's power has stemmed from its central positioning as a civil economy institution: it works on behalf of investors and is paid by investors. That model is part of its heritage, established firmly in the early years, when ISS founder and renowned shareowner activist Robert A. G. Monks and associates Nell Minow and Howard Sherman were struggling with fewer than forty clients and little revenue. In fact, they turned out to be midwives to a new template for civil economy intermediaries.

In 1989 Monks took a phone call from legendary financiers Richard Rainwater and Eddie Lampert. The two had a proposal. They had invested heavily in Honeywell, once an icon of U.S. engineering prowess, which had lost nearly half a billion dollars the year before. In Rainwater and Lampert's opinion, Honeywell management was handling the crisis poorly. Rather than try to fix the problem by improving the company, executives were circling the wagons. Management proposed a bristling arsenal of anti-takeover defenses, including staggering director terms so that CEO-friendly incumbents would always dominate.

At the time, only corporate raiders were fearless enough to fight such proposals, and none were in sight at Honeywell. Lampert and Rainwater, however, were a different species of investor. They did not want control of Honeywell. Rather, they planned to exert shareowner pressure on management to change its ways, thus boosting the stock price. But they couldn't do that if executives were locked away in a protective cocoon. So they proposed that Monks and ISS lead a battle against the takeover defense resolutions. There was no substantive conflict—what Rainwater and Lampert were proposing was what ISS had been preaching. In addition, ISS could use the cash and the visibility. Nonetheless, ISS decided that the best way to avoid any appearance of conflict was to do the Honeywell project free of charge. That way, it would be clear that ISS was working for its clients, not for Rainwater and Lampert, though they did coordinate activities. "The proposition of not being paid by Richard was important to us," recalled Monks a decade later. "To this day, we have never been paid by anybody but the stockholders for anything."[26]

Times have changed, a lot. Today proxy advice is no longer a bootstrap business led by proselytizers, but a sophisticated pool of financially savvy firms skirmishing for shares of a market worth some $400 million worldwide.[27] ISS itself, after changes in ownership and leadership, still finds core earnings in the provision of proxy analysis, voting, record keeping, and governance ratings to institutional investors. But it also boasts a corporate service, advising executives on the very issues it analyzes for investors. It offers corporate managements tools for how to present a resolution so that it can pass ISS's own screens—for example, how to craft an executive compensation plan so the level of dilution (increasing shares granted to employees, at the expense of shareowners) will not trigger analysts at ISS to recommend a no vote.

As credit-rating firms have done, ISS has "erected a firewall between its institutional and corporate activities in order to maintain the highest level of objectivity in research and integrity in voting recommendations," and taken other steps designed to mitigate the perceived conflict.[28] On one hand, the fact that corporations want and seek its advice is evidence of the new influence of active owners. On the other, the fact that it has a corporate consulting service has opened the door for doubt. Perceived conflicts at ISS have been the subject of prominent stories in the *Washington Post, New York Times, Financial Times, Wall Street Journal*, and other publications, as well as the subject of pointed criticism by governance guru Ira Millstein.[29]

Antidotes to Conflict

As the top information mogul, serving as a key hired voice for tens of millions of civil owners—more than any other firm—ISS has been under pressure to be open and transparent. Regulators may even sniff an opportunity for intervention to protect shareowners. The U.S. SEC made just such a start in 2004, issuing an unequivocal warning to funds to screen outsourced proxy advisers for any conflicts.[30]

Regulation is not the only solution here; robust competition may represent a cure. Investors dissatisfied with one provider may select another. Sure enough, stirrings of an investor-focused economy have given rise to multiple vendors. In the United States, ISS now competes for business with Egan-Jones Proxy Services, a subsidiary of the bond rater Glass Lewis and Proxy Governance. Other services operate in different markets and across borders—for instance, PIRC, the Association of British Insurers, IVIS, and Manifest in the UK; Proxinvest in Paris; Corporate Governance International in Sydney and ISS Proxy Australia in Melbourne; and Korea Corporate Governance Service and the Center for Good Corporate Governance in Seoul. Each of these offers investor-centric analysis, seeing singularity of mission as a key selling point in the civil economy. "The integrity of our recommendations is not clouded with the complication of also selling corporate directors and managers consulting services pertaining to these same shareholder proposals," declares one.[31]

Such developments are little appreciated in most boardrooms, yet executives would do well to decipher their meaning. Trends show that proxy-voting moguls are moving ever closer in alignment to the interests of new capitalist owners, clearing a critical obstacle on the path to accountability. "We are not trying to be popular with the CEO crowd," Greg Taxin of Glass Lewis has explained. "We aim to protect investors from risk, whether it is popular with the powerful or not."[32]

But as important as reengineering the vote may be, progress in the evolution of the civil economy will still stall unless pension funds themselves are properly advised so that fund managers can fulfill their fiduciary responsibilities.

Gatekeepers' Masters

Pension funds often hire consultants to help them navigate complex decisions—one of the biggest being which investment firms are best suited to manage their money. Such advisers have grown to become powerful gatekeepers. On their say-so, trustees send rivers of cash heading toward some fund managers and not others. The potential for conflicts to skew recommendations is enormous, especially as the fees that funds pay for pure independent advice are comparatively modest. Just as the Citicorps and Merrill Lynches permitted lucrative investment banking fees to trump objective research, some consultants succumbed to temptation. They struck deals to channel client money to fund managers that somehow paid them fees, and kept arrangements secret from pension funds that trusted them for objective advice.

Again, the worst abuses cropped up first in the United States. That is not because the law was imprecise on conflicts. In fact, the Investment Advisers Act of 1940 is unequivocal that consultants must tell their clients openly about any potential conflicts and provide disinterested advice. But with 1,742 advisers registered as of 2004, the U.S. Securities and Exchange Commission had too small a staff and too little interest in policing the obscure industry to deter the tangle of conflicts that tainted key middlemen in the 1980s and 1990s. In fact, enforcement was so dependably dormant that regulators in 2005 were forced to concede an embarrassing finding. "Many consultants believe they do not have any fiduciary relationships with their advisory clients," wrote staff in a 2005 report, "and ignore or are not aware of their fiduciary obligations under the Advisers Act."[33]

That same belated SEC probe uncovered what is almost surely the tip of an ugly iceberg. Staff experts took a microscope to twenty-four sample consultants and sifted through the way the gatekeepers did business. They unearthed case after case of cozy relationships between consultants and money managers, most of them kept well hidden. "Pension consultants typically do not disclose to current and prospective pension plan clients that they receive compensation in various forms from the same money managers that the consultant may recommend to the client," the survey concluded. [34]

Consultants ran conferences for pension trustees and charged investment managers high fees to attend. Managers willingly paid in order to stay in the consultants' good graces. They also willingly wrote checks to consultants for as much as $70,000 a year for financial software, for the same reason. Some advisers drove pension fund assets to money managers that secretly agreed to use the consultants' affiliated brokerage services. Others advised both money managers and investors, or even ran investment funds themselves.

Consultants justified deals as a way of subsidizing the cost of services provided to pension funds, endowments, foundations, and other institutional investors. As a consequence, potentially conflicting activities were going on for years.[35] Observers suspect similar concealed breakdowns have occurred in Europe and elsewhere, because the financial temptation to shoulder conflict for hefty earnings appears to be the same, regardless of the market.

Independence Day

Still, even in this dusky corner of the market, regulators and funds responsive to new capitalists are pressing fitfully for a switch to civil economy practices. "My hope is that trustees will ask more questions, and the consultants will provide more information about their conflicts, and those two things will really improve behavior," declared Lori Richard, director of the SEC's Office of Compliance Inspections and Examinations, who released the 2005 report.[36] Institutional investors are indeed probing consultants about business they conduct with money managers. Mercer, one of the largest consultants, is ending its sponsored conferences. And pension funds are hiring consultants advertising themselves for the first time as conflict-free.[37]

Ennis Knupp, a Chicago-based adviser, is one such consultant. Its philosophy does not mince words. "You hire an investment adviser for an independent perspective," says founder Richard Ennis. "Make sure you get one." Here is the pitch from the firm's Web site: "Our sole line of business is providing consulting services to institutional clients. We have no affiliations with brokerage, investment management, or investment banking firms, nor do we sell information or services to these entities. Our firm, and therefore our advice, is completely and unequivocally unbiased."[38] The firm's reputation for keeping its interest aligned with its clients is winning business as the move toward civil economy institutions accelerates. Ennis Knupp was the thirteenth-largest consultant in the United States in 2001, advising on slightly more than $250 billion in assets. By 2003, the firm had leapfrogged to sixth place on the competitive charts, and was advising on nearly $435 billion.[39]

As funds shed conflicted counselors, citizen investors will likely find their equity savings more skillfully advised. There is, however, one last information mogul that deserves attention: advisers on bond investments.

Dis-credited?

Pension consultants deal with large, sophisticated clients. What about the retail, citizen owner investors at the other end of the spectrum? Guardians of the proverbial widows and orphans, bond-rating agencies define the border between securities they label "investment grade" and those they mark as "junk." How much interest companies pay to borrow capital hinges on the upgrades or downgrades they receive from the dominant global trio of Standard & Poor's, Moody's, and Fitch. The better the grade, the less they pay. Thus corporations have a powerful incentive to push their score higher. At the same time, though, regulators have long relied on rating agencies—even granting them an officially blessed oligopoly—to give the most vulnerable investors a fair way to measure risk when they decide what bonds to buy or sell for their nest eggs. Is that confidence justified?

The big three regard themselves as beyond reproach, trusted by all. Yet there is an obvious elephant in the room. It is a well-behaved elephant, sitting quietly in the corner and trying—with considerable success—to be ignored by everyone. But it is still a very large elephant.

The truth of the matter is that corporations, not investors, buy and pay for those ratings. Can S&P, Moody's, and Fitch impartially assess a company when they rely on the same firm for payment? That the three key ratings services are still trusted is evidence that they value their franchise, and that they have instituted procedures to manage conflicts. But investment banks had also supposedly engineered "Chinese Walls" to manage conflicts. Mechanisms designed to overcome so fundamental a conflict may turn out to be unsustainable over time. Indeed, S&P and Moody's faced harsh criticism in 2001 for giving Enron and WorldCom stocks investment-grade ratings almost up until the moment each corporation imploded, even though the agencies had enjoyed privileged access to internal financial data. Were the raters swayed by revenues from the firms? Or were they merely deceived? In any event, the fact that these questions can be raised is evidence of the damage that can be done to investors' confidence because of the structure of the payments.

Another problem is that agencies face constant temptation to sell their client corporations both consulting services and ratings. As much as Chinese Walls may interlace a rating company, to onlookers and companies alike such business begins to look like a racket. In 2004, for instance, S&P started marking down companies in credit reports for poor corporate governance practices at the same time that another arm of S&P advertised its readiness to offer governance consulting services. S&P was sensitive to the obvious potential for conflict. It barred its governance unit from seeking business from any company credit analysts tagged for additional governance assessments.[40] Yet how long before such practices start to decay the trust civil owners place in bond ratings? Perhaps years or decades. But then again maybe a week from Wednesday. Trust tends to unravel quickly once it begins to fray.

In an economy characterized by choice, competition could be an antidote. But that is far from easy in the credit-rating business. The big three agencies have avoided major competition until now, partly on grounds of quality, but they have had a colossal assist from U.S. regulation. In an antiquated bid to assure rating integrity, the SEC long ago created an artificial oligopoly. Regulators bestowed on S&P, Moody's, and Fitch, the title of Nationally Recognized Statistical Rating Organization (NRSRO). This obscure gong means that NRSRO ratings, and *only* those ratings, can affect which bonds are certified "investment grade" and thus which are legally acceptable for the most vulnerable investor portfolios. Because the U.S. market is so overwhelming, the SEC rules have made the big three dominant players all around the world. Upstart rating agencies have not succeeded in getting the SEC to grant them NRSRO status. But the civil economy is far ahead of regulators. Here, too, new capitalists' compulsion to clear obstacles to investor-centered intermediaries is yielding results.

Rating Trust

The credit-rating market is fragmenting. For one, major fund managers such as PIMCo, Western Asset Management, and Prudential have fine-tuned their in-house analyst units so thoroughly that each can often profile changes in corporation's creditworthiness before the big three. And, by definition, these firms' interests are entirely aligned with those of portfolio managers, not the companies they review.

How viable is that competition? While he was deputy comptroller of New York City, Jon Lukomnik, one of our authors, once interviewed investment firms jockeying for a contract to manage a high-yield portfolio for employee pension funds. One specialist bond manager after another would come in to demonstrate how slow the traditional rating agencies were in raising or lowering ratings, and how lags created opportunities for the portfolio managers who did their own research. The firms offered preprinted charts showing the number of upgrades and downgrades their research had anticipated or missed; the charts of the bond prices showing how much money they had made when the rating agencies finally came around; and how many disasters they had anticipated in advance of the raters—or, worse, which meltdowns the raters had missed. After about ten of these presentations, the New York pension fund staff was left wondering why anyone paid any attention at all to S&P and Moody's. The answer, of course, was that the independent credit analysis they had been privileged to see over the past six hours was bundled in with money management services, and not available as a freestanding product. This meant that those prescient analyses remained internal to a particular bond manager, unavailable to the general public.

Until now. Independent ratings firms such as Egan-Jones and Credit-Sights have sprung up and gained traction in the marketplace. Those ratings are available to anyone willing to pay a subscription fee. The firms emphasize their independence and alignment with investors as a distinguishing factor in their analyses, charging the big three with running a business model that is structurally conflicted. CreditSights, for example, notes, "Our only vested interest is in helping investors make money and limit risk."[41] Does being investor-focused make for better analysis? It is, of course, an open question. But Egan-Jones did downgrade WorldCom a full 227 days before Moody's or Standard & Poor's, and it warned its client investors prior to the big three about Enron, AT&T Canada, Deutsche Telecom, Ford, Comdisco, and other situations.[42]

Transformation and Evolution

Enron touched off scandals in the new capitalist ecosystem akin to a forest fire. Destruction to the savings of citizen investors and whole markets was staggering. But the firestorm exposed conflicts long ignored, upending the worst offenders and allowing a richer, more diverse civil economy infrastructure to take root. New, nimble information moguls are being born, seeing in the altered landscape a range of commercial opportunities. Traditional ones are altering in fundamental ways because, like all creatures faced with a rapid change in the environment, they face a stark choice: adapt or die. Some will thrive and some will fail, just as some of the new regulatory reforms affecting intermediaries will succeed and others prove wrongheaded. But the fresh dynamism of the system presents the possibility of a more robust capitalism: managers effectively monitored for optimum performance, and new capitalist investors empowered to ensure that their savings produce optimum value.

Something else fundamental has happened that makes a civil economy possible. Shareowners have learned to focus on the quality and competence of the information moguls on whom they rely, and which before they had taken for granted.

Perhaps inevitably, if new capitalists now pay attention to *who* provides them information and *how*, they inevitably next want to know *what* information they really need to fulfill their ownership responsibilities and grow value.

That is an overwhelming question with profound implications. If we do, indeed, manage what we measure, then new civil economy data points would have the potential to radically remake how executives manage corporations, and how citizen investors think about companies that depend on their capital. Those are the issues we explore in chapter 7.

TAKEAWAYS

- Brokers in the pre-Enron era often skewed their investment advice to serve conflicting commercial motives. Regulators forced a remedy: Independent stock research. New capitalist funds have taken change farther, fueling innovative services designed to align trading analysis with the interests of long-term citizen investors.

- Auditors too often saw themselves working for a company's management instead of watch dogging on behalf of the firm's owners. The state/federal divide in the United States exacerbated the situation. While regulation has imposed fresh safeguards, shareowners themselves have sought antidotes by scrutinizing auditors and cultivating ideas for reform.

- Proxy-voting agents are little-known intermediaries with colossal influence over the way citizen investors' interests are communicated to corporations. New capitalist demand for unconflicted, quality advice has spawned an industry of services that put companies under a governance microscope.

- Consultants form a cadre of gatekeepers that help determine how and where citizen savings are invested. Yet a network of hidden commercial relationships have tainted their advice. Funds are now driving demand for conflict-free services.

- Credit-rating agencies are touted as helping the most vulnerable citizen savers steer clear of high-risk investments. Yet they harbor a fundamental conflict: they are paid by the companies they rate, not by the investors they are supposed to protect. The big three rating firms—Standard & Poor's, Moody's, and Fitch—strain to manage potential conflict. But new capitalist funds are also seeking alternatives in smaller, conflict-free agencies.

- Shareowners have learned to focus on the quality and competence of the information moguls on whom they rely, and which they previously had taken for granted.

7

Accounting Standards
Escaping Brother Luca's Boxes

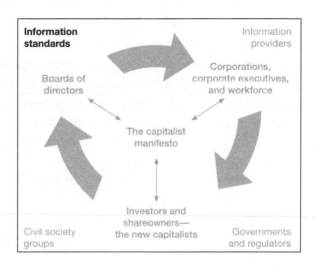

Conventional guideposts such as accounting standards have fallen badly out of date, making it tough for new capitalists and corporate executives alike to measure and manage real value. This chapter profiles the rise of innovative, civil economy metrics—and shows practical ways they are being used to align companies with the long-term interests of citizen investors.

Accounting rules were not written on two stone tablets at Mount Sinai. That's a good thing, for two reasons. First, most human beings have enough trouble following those Ten Commandments, no less the thousands of accounting opinions. More important, accounting rules haven't aged nearly as well as that other set of commandments, despite being thousands of years younger.

Still, the metrics by which we measure economic success do boast a pedigree half a millennium old, dating back to the Italian Renaissance. World commerce has of course changed rather a lot since then, yet traditional accounting methods have not kept pace. Like a doctor trying to use only an antiquated x-ray machine to examine a heart, getting a snapshot of the skeleton but no information about cardiac health, new capitalists who use only traditional accounting tools cannot see whether a modern public company boasts the financial physique to create long-term value, or harbors undetected diseases that sap or destroy its worth.

The consequences are sweeping. If we cannot accurately measure a company's state, we may routinely misjudge the performance of its directors. We may buy or sell a stock in response to highly deceptive data. Managers may hire and fire employees based on false signals. Directors may commit capital to value-destroying enterprises and starve productive ones. In short, if our measuring instruments are out of sync with real-world circumstances, everyone loses. Investors lose oversight power, corporate managers hemorrhage productivity, and economies fail to reach their potential in wealth and employment.

There is good news as well. Accurate and relevant information standards are evolving behind the scenes. They represent key machinery of the civil economy ecosystem, opening ways for investors, corporate managers, directors, and others to better weigh a business's real ability to add or destroy value. Penetrating information like that helps make the circle of accountability function.

Brother Luca's Legacy

Five hundred years ago, Franciscan friar Luca Bartolomeo Pacioli taught mathematics and perspective. A talented young student named

Leonardo da Vinci put the lessons to good use in his masterpiece *The Last Supper*. But Brother Luca was nothing if not multitalented; he is best known for his 1494 book, *Summa de Arithmetica, Geometria, Proportioni et Proportionalita*, or *Everything about Arithmetic, Geometry and Proportion*. Printed on the Gutenberg press, it had thirty-six chapters outlining a proto-accounting system. Pacioli claimed it would "give the trader, without delay, information as to his assets and liabilities."

Pacioli divided every merchant transaction into two equal and opposite parts. When a merchant bought goods, he (1) received the goods and (2) parted with money. When he sold, he (1) parted with goods and (2) received money. This was the birth of "double-entry" accounting, wherein credits (either increases in liabilities or decreases in assets) equal debits (increases in assets or decreases in liabilities). Pacioli's system worked. It has continued to form the basis for accounting for half a millennium.

But why is this important for the civil economy of the twenty-first century? Because, beginning in the nineteenth and early twentieth centuries, the increasing separation of managers from owners meant owners needed someone and something to give them assurance about the financial health of the organization in which they had made their investment. The U.S. stock market crash of 1929, and the depression that followed, created a boom industry in assurance, as owners tried to understand what their stock certificates really represented. Increasingly, they turned to accounting and accountants. Consider that the American Association of Public Accountants was founded in 1887. By 1916, it counted barely 1,000 dues payers. Today its successor, the American Institute of Certified Public Accountants, boasts 334,000 members, or roughly one out of every 900 Americans. And not every accountant in the United States is a member.[1]

By and large, that huge resource pool of traditional accounting expertise worked, and worked well. But then again, many of the basic drivers of the economy had not fundamentally changed from Pacioli's time. Until the last quarter of the twentieth century, we were still, for the most part, an economy based on *things*, things that were bought and sold. Yes, whale oil gave way to electricity, and horses lost out to cars. But we were still largely an economy that made, bought, and sold tangible assets.

Trillion-Dollar Driver

Even today, balance sheets still do a good job summarizing assets such as land, factories, and cash. But those assets, combined with physical labor, are not the only creators of value—not even for über-automaker General Motors, whose crown jewel is no longer its famous assembly lines but its finance subsidiary. Yet our accounting system has not fundamentally changed to accommodate the fact that what economists call "intangibles"—brands, advertising, patents, trademarks, copyrights, financial know-how, worker knowledge, productivity techniques—drive today's economy far more than plants and equipment and steel. "It is intuitively obvious," concluded a Deloitte study in 2004, "that the balance sheet, profit-and-loss account, and cash flow statement are the results of nonfinancial drivers."[2] The amounts involved are hardly trivial. Corporations in the United States alone now spend an estimated $1 trillion each year on intangibles they consider necessary to power growth.[3] "An intangible asset is—if it is successfully managed—a claim to a future benefit that does not have a physical or financial embodiment. When that claim is legally secured, as with a patent or a copyright, we generally call that asset 'intellectual property,'" explains Professor Baruch Lev of New York University, an expert on the subject.[4]

Today, a shrewd investor tries to reckon a company's worth by estimating its future cash flows from both intangible and tangible assets. That reckoning is tricky; the classic Paciolian paradigm is effectively blind to intellectual capital. Anything that lacks a "physical or financial embodiment" is merely a ghost in traditional accounting.

To illustrate the perverse outcomes of conventional accounting, let's consider a hypothetical situation. If at the height of his creativity Microsoft founder Bill Gates had jumped from Microsoft to German software giant SAP, you can bet Microsoft stock would have slumped and SAP stock would have zoomed. Gates's skills would have been an asset, in the colloquial sense that you and I understand that word, and in the sense that the stock market uses Professor Lev's definition. Yet nowhere on Microsoft's balance sheet would we find Gates listed as an asset. Indeed, we would find him mentioned only for his compensation, on the expense side of the income statement (and perhaps also on the liability side of the balance sheet, where we might see compensation that he had earned but not yet been paid).

Now expand that example to the entire information economy. Is it logical that the creators of value—the bankers at Goldman Sachs, the industrial designers at Samsung, the reporters at Agence France-Presse, the engineers at Embraer, the iPod programmers at Apple—be considered liabilities rather than productive assets that can continue to create value in the future?

Things are just as skewed on the other side of the balance sheet. Today's most menacing threats to corporations—reputation risk, competitive pressures, contingent liabilities based on environmental or other regulatory issues, even the basic sustainability of the business model itself—are rarely reflected until and unless the threat becomes so acute that managers set aside special reserves to pay for it. By then, it is often too late for the investor to sell, or for a manager to do much to mitigate the problem.

"Wait a minute," you might say. "The financial statements work. They never were supposed to reflect all knowledge about a company, and certainly not all forward-looking information."

Exactly. Yet isn't that precisely what a new capitalist—or director, or corporate manager, or any other link in the accountability chain—would like to know? We need tools to measure the past but also to forecast what is likely to happen in the future, and how prepared the company is to meet challenges. Key assets such as management capability or corporate reputation, or liability risks such as the effect of climate change or corruption, are hard to value—but if we don't try to measure them, we would be capitulating to the old and familiar and allowing best to be the enemy of better.

Two experts spotted warps caused by accounting gaps decades ago. In their 1987 book *Relevance Lost*, Thomas Johnson and Robert Kaplan, professors of management accounting, said bluntly, "Today's management accounting systems provide a misleading target for management attention and fail to provide the relevant set of measures that appropriately reflect the technology, the products, the processes, and the competitive environment in which the organization operates." They went on to say that "[w]here an ineffective management accounting system prevails, the best outcome occurs when managers . . . bypass it by developing their own information systems."[5]

Taking Control of the Numbers

No modern managers run their companies relying only on traditional accounting measures. Corporate managers have found innovative ways to track real value drivers such as order flows, pricing pressures, patents or copyrights or other intellectual property and the license fee trends attributable to them, the percentage of revenue created by new products, regulatory risks, customer satisfaction, and workforce contentment. Executives give their management team both formal and informal evaluations. They monitor the competition.

The trick, in other words, is to find meaningful benchmarks beyond the legally required numbers. Here is how Thomas Johnson put it in his 1992 book, *Relevance Regained*: "The financial score is like the score in a tennis match. As tennis players know, it is necessary while playing to keep one's eye on the ball, not on the scorecard. But non-financial measures of operating performance, unlike traditional cost measures, often *are* the ball, not just the score. Controlling processes in order to improve many non-financial measures undoubtedly will improve a company's competitive position. But manipulating processes in order to achieve accounting cost targets is not likely to improve competitiveness at all."[6]

If good corporate managers keep their eye on the ball of nontraditional accounting metrics, so too do good investors. As a result, our system has degenerated into a Kabuki farce. Companies devote months of effort and millions in expenses to re-tailor operating results to fit into a standard accounting format for public release. Despite all that effort, the first thing most analysts do when an earnings announcement appears on their screens is try to "reverse-engineer" it back into the operating reports by which the company management actually runs the place. Only then do analysts think they can truly understand what is going on.

Fortunately, new information tools are being developed, supplementing traditional accounting methods that are no longer sufficient for today's new-capitalist investors. Executives are hearing the message: approximately 72 percent told the Economist Intelligence Unit in a poll that "investors are placing greater emphasis on sustainable, long-term growth."[7] The emerging information ecosystem is among the telltale indicators that a civil economy is rising.

Who Owns Information?

In traditional accounting, the relationship between a corporation and outsiders—owners, suppliers, customers, workers, or society at large—was simple and linear. It was defined by their transactions with the company. And corporations claimed nearly exclusive control over the details. Shareowners were effectively in an information ghetto, unable to discover from independent sources what companies were really doing. Governments, to be sure, established some minimal disclosure standards. But companies maintained a firm grip on what the market could learn, suppressing some measures that would have benefited other parts of the civil economic ecosystem. Think, for example, of the battle over accounting for stock options in the United States. For years, corporations fought successfully to avoid charging stock options as expenses, even though they clearly shifted value to management, and even though the vast majority of owners wanted options to be counted as expenses.

Today, though, as we have seen, shareowners are gaining muscle to upend old power relationships. Consumers, unions, and community groups find they can now negotiate not only with their traditional CEO interlocutors but with big citizen-owner funds that can make their voice heard in corporate boardrooms. It is a newly multipolar world. More funds insist that information standards promise meaningful corporate insight, not just fodder for compliance. In a civil economy, information increasingly is demand-pulled by new capitalist owners, not supply-pushed by corporations, as it once was.

For example, take environmental issues. At one time they weren't even seen as inside the corporate orbit—but now pollution and climate change are mainstream issues to varying degrees around the world. Some three-quarters of European institutional investors think environmental sustainability is a core investment concern, and about 20 percent of U.S. investors do.[8]

Let's consider a real-world example of environmental reporting. Should General Electric report to shareowners on progress in cleaning up PCBs (a type of heavy pollutant) it dumped into New York's Hudson River many years ago? Yesteryear, that would have been an issue of concern only to GE and its regulators. Environmental advocates would have been marginalized, resorting either to pressing regulators as part of the community, or mobilizing consumer boycotts, which are often ineffective. Now, however, new capitalists and environmentalists overlap—though imperfectly—through investments in collective investment funds. And some institutional shareowners have an appetite for information on environmental risks. So for several years funds have petitioned formal resolutions at GE's annual meeting, asking management for a report on the PCB cleanup.[9] The initiative has forced the directors, as representatives of shareowners, to explain their position, and has encouraged other shareowners to share anxieties about the PCB issue with GE. The company, in turn, considers information disclosure an ownership issue, rather than an issue that "special interests" have foisted on it. It engages in dialogue, using the proxy statement to describe its "significant" environmental program, including its "voluntary agreements with government on remediation of virtually all sites." This example spotlights the increasing complexity of relationships among the various constituencies—and the growing need for more, and different types of, information.

Avoiding Hijack

All this complexity leads to a question: what information should citizen owners pay attention to? How do they know what is material? Are special interests hijacking funds when they align with environmental advocates to demand more corporate disclosure? Or are shareowners being prudent fiduciaries in seeking nontraditional information that is key to investing wisely in today's capital markets?

One test to determine an issue's legitimacy is to view it through the lens of the capitalist manifesto outlined in chapter 3:

1. Be profitable and create value.

2. Grow only where you can create value.

3. Pay people fairly to do the right things.

4. Don't waste capital.

5. Focus where your skills are strongest.

6. Renew the organization.

7. Treat customers, suppliers, workers, and communities fairly.

8. Seek regulations that ensure your operations do not cause collateral damage and your competitors do not gain unfair advantage.

9. Stay clear of partisan politics.

10. Communicate what you are doing and be accountable for it.

Many of the information metrics and reporting systems now appearing on the investment landscape are designed to measure and understand those ten "rules," since they are the requirements citizen owners make of corporations. Of course, time will prove some irrelevant, faddish, or even downright silly. Some if not most of the new metrics will fail the test of time. Others, however, will be enduring.

Measures and systems generally fall into three categories:

- *Metrics designed to measure management's ability, desire, and likelihood to create value for external owners.* Some of these, such as Economic Value Added, or EVA, are manipulations of traditional accounting measures, designed to more clearly illuminate management's true success in creating value.[10] Others, such as corporate governance ratings, are new, civil economy inventions built of indicators designed to judge shareowner friendliness and measure newly recognized risks.

- *Measures to judge the sustainability of the enterprise over long periods.* These measures often focus on contingent liability analysis. Metrics addressing environmental issues are the most advanced.

- *Enhanced disclosure focusing on real but intangible drivers of value in a company, such as intellectual property.* These extra-financial metrics are often more crucial to company value than the numbers presented in the balance sheet.

Let's look more closely at each to find the most fertile aspects of the civil economy's emerging information ecosystem.

Measuring Value Creation

New capitalist owners need to measure how effectively a company creates or destroys value for them. Manipulation of traditional accounting provides some help in solving half the problem: how effectively a corporation creates or destroys value overall. The second facet—the "for them" part—has only recently gained traction as critical. In other words, how shareowner-friendly is a particular corporation or management team? How is value apportioned among minority shareowners, management, controlling owners, and others? Together, the new metrics hand shareowners instruments designed to gauge how well a corporation meets the first four guidelines of our capitalist manifesto: a corporation's ability to create value (number 1), decide appropriately where to grow (2), align compensation policies with owners' desires (3), and conserve capital (4).[11]

Simply put, a corporation should be a value-creation factory. Inputs—whether raw materials, intellectual property, money, or anything else—enter, are transformed and enhanced and then sold, and profits emerge. That is an oversimplification, of course. All sorts of difficulties stand between the inputs and outputs. And sometimes things happen in a different order. An insurance company, for instance, sells its services before it incurs most of its costs—indeed, even before it is certain what those costs will be. By simplifying, we can home in on bedrock questions: How well does the value-added process work? How much output (profit) is created per unit of input? In other words, how effective is the corporation at creating value?

A number of academics and practitioners have manipulated traditional accounting metrics in varying ways to determine the answer. Perhaps the best known is Economic Value Added, or EVA. Stern Stewart & Co., its inventor, describes EVA as "the financial performance measure that comes closer than any other to capturing the true economic profit of an enterprise."[12]

Even discounting for marketing hyperbole, EVA does attempt to capture how effective a corporation is at adding value. That is because it factors in the cost of capital. While there are literally dozens of adjustments that can be made in a full implementation of EVA, the basic formula is fairly simple: Free Cash Flow – [Capital × Cost of Capital].[13] In other words, EVA assumes that a corporation and, by extension, an owner, has options for its capital. A shareowner can always sell his or her stake in the company and invest it in other companies, bonds, fine art, oil futures, gold coins, or whatever. If economically rational, both shareowners and companies seek the highest risk-adjusted return for capital. But what is economically rational for the owner is not always economically rational for the manager. So instead of returning surplus revenues to investors through share buybacks or dividends, corporations may hang onto capital, or go on value-destroying acquisition sprees or capital expenditure binges.

Examples abound. Think of the old-style Japanese company, which targeted increased production and market share. Such strategies may have churned out record profits as measured by traditional accounting measures—which in turn gave senior managers more prestige, power, and perquisites. After all, they were presiding over a larger domain. However, those measures could not reveal whether profits were truly value added or whether they might simply be a reflection of scale achieved through access to below-market-rate capital supplied by other members of a *keiretsu*, the conglomerate family. When one part of the *keiretsu* group had to compete in an open market, all other members of the group suffered. More penetrating metrics might have shown investors that they could have done better if they had parked their cash in a savings account. In other words, behind a veil of accounting standards that underplay the cost of capital, a company can post growth and formal profits even while destroying value. All it takes is bad capital stewardship, a mistake not limited to Japan.

EVA and related metrics seek to reveal how effective a particular corporation is in converting capital into real economic profit. By including the cost of capital in the calculation, as well as the amount of capital needed to generate profits, such metrics give an economically rational bottom line aligned with owners, not managers. After all, it is owners' capital at risk.

Value for Whom?

Still, EVA-style standards solve only half the problem. Yes, they help determine whether the corporation produces real economic profit. But even if it does, how can we be sure that managers will distribute surpluses equitably? New capitalist owners want to reap their fair share. Unfortunately, the scandals of the 1990s and 2000s, as well as continuing out-of-control executive pay, serve as brutal reminders that managers' and owners' interests are not always aligned.

Related-party transactions can skim off profits to manager-affiliated entities; at Enron, private deals transferred massive amounts of value to management. Executive remuneration can be a ticking time bomb that dilutes the existing owners' stake or simply explodes into a large cash payment some time in the future. Maurice Greenberg, the former chief executive of AIG, had accumulated $202 million—more than a fifth of a billion dollars—through a secretive compensation scheme.[14] Perquisites often are unrelated to performance. Tyco's multimillion-dollar birthday party for the ex-CEO's wife is a case in point.[15] Just because a corporation makes money does not mean shareowners will benefit. On the other hand, well-designed executive remuneration can motivate and retain senior management talent, and some perquisites can channel CEOs toward better performance.

In whose interests, then, are the managers working: their own, or those of their shareowners? How is a new capitalist to judge?

Investment-Grade Governance

To solve that problem, an international industry of corporate governance raters has developed since 2001. Led by GovernanceMetrics International (GMI) and Institutional Shareholder Services (ISS), these providers aim to quantify the characteristics of a company's governance.[16] Their purpose is to alert shareowners to comparative risks that a company will take advantage of investors. While GMI and ISS operate globally, there are many national ventures, including The Corporate Library in the United States, the Russian Institute of Directors, India's ICRA, and Thai Rating and Information Services. These rating companies' metrics go well beyond traditional yardsticks of corporate quality, testing board accountability, the relationship of executive pay to performance, controls on related party transactions, and other variables that are forward-looking in a way that traditional information standards are not.

In the United Kingdom, BoardEx keeps a register of all company directors' interests and connections. In the United States, The Corporate Library database contains similar information about board members, including data about interlocking boards of directors, and board effectiveness ratings. Given that directors are representatives of owners, it is striking that such crucial information, which now cost-effectively allows citizen owners to call boards to account, was simply not available as recently as the late 1990s.

Ratings and director evaluations allow funds to bring "governance-worthiness" into decisions about investment and activism. Of course, corporate governance is but a means to an end. The end is to create value for the owners. Early evidence suggests that it does. Studies using GMI data have consistently found that U.S. and European companies with higher-ranked corporate governance profiles outperform those with lower ratings.[17] Other researchers find the same result using ISS data. "Better-governed firms are relatively more profitable, more valuable, and pay out more cash to their shareholders," concluded Professor Lawrence D. Brown and Marcus L. Caylor of Georgia State University.[18] Similar results are surfacing from independent researchers in other markets. For instance, higher-ranked Japanese companies outperformed lower-ranked ones by 15.12 percent annually, reported scholars from the University of Maastricht and the Auckland Institute of Technology, using GMI data.[19] Deutsche Bank found that U.K. companies with the highest governance ratings far outperformed those with the lowest. The gap was 32 percent, according to five-year data released in July 2005.

"Good governance is lower equity risk which should translate into higher valuation multiples," the Deutsche Bank study concluded.[20]

As parallel findings mount, governance screening should become a commonplace tool for new capitalist investors. Along with EVA-style standards, governance data rank as the first category in the market's arsenal of new information tools. Let's move on to the second category of civil economy metrics, those designed to measure sustainability.

Measuring Sustainability

At three minutes past midnight on March 24, 1989, Captain Joseph Hazelwood was relaxing in his cabin on the *Exxon Valdez*. He had retired for the night, giving the helm over to third mate Gregory Cousins after shifting the massive tanker northward to avoid small icebergs skirting the Alaska coast. A minute later there was bedlam. Just beyond Busby Island, the top of Bligh Reef sliced open the hull of the massive tanker. Some 11 million gallons of thick oil oozed out, blackening the waters of Prince William Sound. For weeks afterward, televisions around the world pictured drowning oil-slicked seabirds, dead fish washing up on rocks, and the stained shoreline against the pristine Alaskan wilderness. Soon the environmental disaster turned into financial cataclysm: Exxon lost about $15 billion in market value as a direct result of the *Valdez* spill.[21]

By September of that year, a number of institutional investors had had enough. In a private library in midtown Manhattan, New York City comptroller Harrison J. Goldin (investment adviser for the New York City pension funds), California comptroller Gray Davis (trustee of the California Public Employees Retirement System, or CalPERS, and the California State Teachers' Retirement System), and Joan Bavaria of CERES, then a little-known Boston-based environmental group, unveiled the "Valdez Principles." What this coalition of environmentalists and investors had in common was a belief that environmental issues carry real financial risks. To the environmentalists, damage to the environment was a cost in and of itself. To Goldin, Davis, and the other new capitalist–style investors, environmental issues were deferred contingent liabilities, able to explode suddenly and rip holes in balance sheets much as the Bligh Reef had ripped open the hull of the *Valdez*. Now both groups wanted corporate America to sign onto ten principles of responsible environmental conduct.

Holding their press conference in a library seemed to foreshadow the reaction to their statement: a hushed silence. "As it turned out, large corporations were not even slightly interested in signing the principles," Bavaria recalled.[22]

So the coalition went to work. Ken Sylvester, a veteran of the South Africa anti-apartheid campaign in Goldin's office, together with Andy Smith of the Interfaith Center on Corporate Responsibility, drafted shareowner resolutions asking companies to comply with the Valdez Principles. Ceres mailed hundreds of letters to CEOs asking their companies to endorse the principles. Slowly, some smaller companies said yes. First was Smith & Hawken, a garden tool company. Then Aveda, a cosmetics company. Then Ben & Jerry's ice cream, which brought with its endorsement the company's unerring public relations skill. It pointed out that calling the guidelines the Valdez Principles was like calling the Audubon Society "the dead oily bird society."[23] Sponsors rechristened the document the CERES Principles. Shortly after, Sun Company—an oil company!—became the first *Fortune* 500 signatory to the environmental guidelines.

What set a precedent here was the last Ceres principle, which stated that signatories needed to evaluate their environmental policies and procedures annually, support the creation of environmental audit principles, and make an annual public report on how they had met the previous nine principles. The birth of environmental information standards for new capitalists was at hand.

Now fast-forward a decade, to the World Economic Forum in Davos, Switzerland, where the great and the good of global corporations gather for their annual conclave. United Nations Secretary General Kofi Annan challenged the business community to reach beyond environmental standards alone and develop sustainability principles to benefit both commerce and the broader society. That speech led to the Global Compact, a voluntary, principles-based network. In the short time since then, it has become the flagship for sustainability standards. In general, sustainability corresponds to the sixth through ninth imperatives of the capitalist manifesto—renew the organization; treat customers, suppliers, workers and communities fairly; seek regulations that ensure your operations don't cause collateral damage and your competitors don't gain unfair advantage; and steer clear of partisan politics. The Socially Responsible Investment (SRI) community calls these measures of success a "triple bottom line," with economic, environmental, and social benefits. The New Capitalist sees these as risks and opportunities to be monitored as part of a company's single bottom line of long-term value for citizen investors.

A Scrum of Standards

By early 2006, more than twenty-three hundred companies were participating voluntarily in the Global Compact. So were myriad business groups, trade unions, civil society organizations, and even some cities and stock exchanges.[24] The compact's first two principles cover human rights, the next four relate to labor standards, three are environmental guidelines, and the final principle relates to anticorruption policies.

Of course, the development of these guidelines hasn't stopped "specialist" benchmarks from developing and even thriving. To provide just a taste, here are a half dozen of the most influential organizations currently promulgating, supporting, and certifying compliance with various sustainability standards:

- AccountAbility is a London-based nonprofit that created and tends the AA1000 standards for use in assessing just how accountable organizations are to their stakeholders. The AA1000 framework is built around three core principles: stakeholder engagement, organizational responsiveness to that engagement, and self-learning and innovation.[25]

- Fairtrade Labeling Organizations International (FLO) focuses primarily on the agricultural sector in emerging markets. Created initially in the Netherlands in 1986 and now run out of Germany, FLO certifies that small farmers and laborers in emerging markets have been paid fairly for their products, and that those products have been grown under humane conditions.[26]

- The International Labour Organization (ILO), part of the United Nations system, has created various international labor standards, many of which have been voluntarily adopted by larger corporations.[27]

- The International Organization for Standardization (ISO) traces its roots back to 1946. For decades, it set industrial standards for mundane but essential items, such as nuts, bolts, and screws. Today, it is better known for ISO 9000 (quality management) and ISO 14000 (environmental management). Those standards have in turn created a thriving industry of accreditation and certification consultants operating, quite literally, from Argentina to Zimbabwe.[28]

- Social Accountability International (SAI), based in New York, focuses on labor standards. Its flagship SA8000 is designed to enable retailers and others to "maintain just and decent working conditions throughout the supply chain."[29]

- Transparency International, a Berlin-based nongovernmental organization, offers (together with SAI) "Business Principles for Countering Bribery."[30]

Clearly, the floodgates are open. That is both a blessing and a curse. To which of the thousands of new standards should new capitalists pay attention? To what metrics should a company manage? Pity the corporate manager hemmed in on one hand by traditional accounting, forced to pay attention to EVA, and now asked to incorporate hundreds of social indicators, with none of them likely to yield anything better than approximations of the corporation's capacity to deliver sustainable returns to its owners. How does a company manage to comply even if it wants to? One answer represents the third category of the new information ecosystem: a coordinated framework for disclosure of intangibles.

Reporting Ghosts, or Intangibles

Robert Massie, head of Ceres, and Allen White, senior fellow of the Tel-
lus Institute, envisioned a unified reporting system broad enough to accommodate all the emerging standards, flexible enough to be useful
and accepted worldwide by both the nonprofit and business sectors.
They found partners in the United Nations Environment Programme
and the London-based corporate responsibility consultancy Sustain-
Ability. Two years later, the new Global Reporting Initiative released its
first-draft generally accepted reporting framework to a packed audito-
rium in London. It had been ten years to the month since the *Exxon
Valdez* had run aground. In 2002, GRI became a fully independent entity headquartered in Amsterdam.

Today, GRI works with virtually every major civil sustainability
standard-setter. At the heart of a GRI report is a set of sustainability
guidelines, which outline core content generally applicable to all organizations in any industry. Technical protocols provide details, definitions,
and specifications on specific indicators such as child labor. Although
the reporting framework is designed to be flexible and applicable across
all industries, GRI provides "sector supplements" to reflect the unique
concerns of certain industries, such as mining or finance.[31]

One reason for GRI's wide acceptance has been a "multi-stake-
holder" governance structure that allows virtually every relevant party
in the market to express its viewpoint. As of 2005, GRI's board of directors included corporations (Deutsche Bank, Tata, and Anglo American);
technical experts (Association of Chartered Certified Accountants, Deloitte Touche Tohmatsu); and civil society groups (AFL-CIO, the South
African Human Rights Commission). The board, in turn, relies on a sixty-
member stakeholder council with global representation, and also on a
ten-person technical council. A still broader organizational stakeholder
council consists of nearly two hundred fifty businesses and organizations.

The point of this robust, if potentially unwieldy, governance structure is that almost any issue can be heard and vetted by relevant experts
before being incorporated into GRI-style indicators. That has had some
appeal. Nearly eight hundred global blue-chip corporations report ac-

cording to GRI standards to some extent. "The GRI is fast becoming the de facto standard defining the triple bottom line," Allan Fels has observed.[32]

For a new capitalist, though, there is a caveat. GRI is not an owner-centric institution. It is based on stakeholder interests—the notion that nonowners such as employees, government, and interest groups should enjoy separate but equal access to information to those who have their capital at risk. We touched on stakeholder issues in chapter 4, and noted that under the new capitalist model the issues stakeholders care about come to the fore through convergence with owners' interests. By contrast, under stakeholder theory, values are derived from among, and negotiated between, many constituent interests whether or not they are consistent with the owners' long-term desires.

While we need to keep that bedrock distinction in mind, the daily information needs of owners and other stakeholders often coincide. Sir David Clementi, chair of Prudential, squared this particular circle in a speech to the International Corporate Governance Network's 2005 annual meeting: "There are a number of other stakeholders to which we are accountable: our employees, the communities in which we operate, regulators and, of course, our customers. But dealing with these stakeholders, honestly and openly, represents good business. We plainly, for example, have an important responsibility to our employees; but how could we build value for our shareholders if we did not take enormous care of our human resources? So it is not difficult to see that concern for these other stakeholders is entirely consistent with our attitude that our primary responsibility is to our shareholders; and to build value in the company for them."[33]

But how does it all work in practice?

The Coloplast Experiment

In early 2003, a small army of PricewaterhouseCoopers (PwC) researchers invaded the offices of Schroders, the U.K. investment manager, to conduct an unusual experiment.[34] They came armed with two documents. One was the annual report of Coloplast, the Danish medical products company acknowledged as an innovator in the use of extra-financial data. The other was a carefully reconstructed version of the same report. It featured full financial data using conventional accounting and the front-end management narrative, but it omitted the extensive extra-financial metrics Coloplast adds. The PwC team gave different versions to different Schroders equity analysts, and asked each to produce a buy-or-sell recommendation and a two-year revenue and earnings forecast. The consultants monitored each analyst and gave each the same two hours to produce his or her forecast.

PwC's mission was simple. The firm wanted to learn how a team of investment analysts would treat the two versions. Would the more inclusive, civil economy–style report lead to more positive recommendations, implying that Coloplast could gain cheaper access to capital? Or would the analysts consider the extra-financials irrelevant bells and whistles, implying that shareowners remained unconvinced that intangibles related to value? The results were striking.

At first blush, the PwC team thought the extra-financial reporting mattered not at all, or even that the information was detrimental, as the Schroders analysts who received only the standard financial data predicted higher average revenue and earnings estimates than the analysts who were given the full report. A quick probe revealed the reasons why, however. The analysts with standard reports had given a wide range of estimates, and a few high numbers had skewed the result. By contrast, those given the full report had a much tighter range of estimates. More important, though, fully 80 percent of those given the inclusive report had rated the stock a buy; despite the higher average estimates, a majority of those given the financial-only report had rated it a sell.[35] That left the PwC task force scratching its head and asking why.

They concluded that analysts working off the full report had not only more confidence in their ability to understand Coloplast's drivers of value, but also more confidence in management's ability to keep its eyes on the ball rather than the score, to use the analogy from Johnson's *Relevance Regained*. Drawing comfort from Coloplast's detailed metrics that track intellectual property such as new products and patents, they judged the company less risky than the average stock. By contrast, analysts who had received only the standard financial reports thought Coloplast was more risky—and labeled it a sell.

PwC's findings show that credible extra-financial metrics allow shareowners to see into a corporation and determine whether it is performing in ways that match new capitalists' long-term interests. "In the absence of any supporting information," the researchers asserted, "the investor is forced to try to gain reassurance about the quality and sustainability of corporate performance from the unsubstantiated narrative of the 'front end' of the report and the accounts and the audited financial statement itself . . . Without more substantive evidence of good overall corporate performance, cynicism quickly sets in."[36]

Thus, enhanced, civil economy–style disclosure really covers the alpha and omega principles of our ten-point capitalist manifesto: create value (1) and communicate what you are doing and be accountable for it (10). Absent real drivers of value, a corporation has little to communicate; absent communication, a well-managed, value-adding corporation cannot influence the marketplace to give it a lower cost of capital going forward. Enhanced disclosure is the feedback link that creates a virtuous circle of the ten civil economy imperatives.

Beyond Numbers Alone

Two years after the Coloplast experiment, a study on the other side of the Atlantic gave statistical reinforcement to the inferences PwC derived.

Brian Rivel was born to be a market researcher. His father founded Rivel Research Group, a U.S. company helping *Fortune* 500 companies understand how institutional investors make buy-or-sell decisions. Therefore, when Rivel surveyed 306 portfolio managers and analysts in 2005, he knew what to expect: growth in earnings per share (EPS) would be the most important factor investors considered when deciding whether to purchase shares in a particular company. After all, it had been that way for a generation.

But this time Rivel found that, in fact, EPS growth failed to top the list. Instead, management credibility influenced 83 percent of all internal buy decisions, and that an effective business strategy influenced 77 percent. EPS growth, while still important, was only fourth, at 68 percent. Both tangibles and intangibles filled out the list: reliable cash flow

FIGURE 7-1

Next generation accounting

Value creating activity	Historic cash flow			Prospective cash flow indicator		
	1998	1999	2000	2001	2002	2003
Innovation						
• R&D expenditure	150	161	170	Moderate increase	Moderate increase	Steady state
• Cost of research alliances	70	72	96	Steady state	Steady state	Steady state
• Revenues from patent sales	(5)	(9)	(12)	Significant increase	Moderate increase	Steady state
• Revenues from new products introduced in last four years	(830)	(854)	(1,035)	Moderate increase	Moderate increase	Moderate increase
• Knowledge management experience	25	28	35	Steady state	Moderate increase	Moderate increase
Brand value						
• Advertising	30	31	30	Steady state	Steady state	Steady state
• Promotion	25	22	20	Steady state	Steady state	Steady state
• Marketing	30	31	31	Steady state	Steady state	Steady state
Customer value						
• Revenues (segmental analysis)	(1,277)	(1,294)	(1,501)	Moderate increase	Moderate increase	Moderate increase
• New customer reviews	(98)	(102)	(120)	Steady state	Significant decrease	Steady state
Human capital value						
• Remuneration and benefits	430	410	401	Steady state	Steady state	Steady state
• Average salary ($000)	80	85	92	Steady state	Steady state	Steady state
• Training and development expenditure	45	49	62	Significant increase	Significant increase	Significant increase
• Health and safety expenditure	5	5	6	Significant decrease	Significant decrease	Significant decrease
Supply chain efficiency						
• Cost of sales	715	720	840	Steady state	Steady state	Moderate increase
• Distribution costs	40	39	50	Moderate increase	Moderate increase	Moderate increase
• Outsourcing expenditure	5	45	60	Significant increase	Steady state	Steady state
• Systems costs	25	30	40	Moderate increase	Moderate increase	Steady state
Enviromental and social value						
• Environmental compliances and levies	5	10	12	Significant increase	Significant increase	Significant increase
• Charitable and social expenditure	2	2	3	Moderate decrease	Significant increase	Significant increase
• Net payments to government	351	361	365	Steady state	Steady state	Steady state

Legend:
- ⊕ Significant increase
- ⊘ Moderate increase
- → Steady state
- ⊕ Significant decrease
- ⊗ Moderate decrease

Risk indicators	Nonfinancial indicators	Historic trend 1998	1999	2000	Objective
• Technological obsolescence	• Patent portfolio (No.)	110	112	140	10% annual increase
• Staff retention	• Percentage of revenues from new products	65%	66%	69%	80%
• Product development cycle time	• Ideas generated	1,240	1,253	1,372	2,000 by 2002
• Fashion trends	• Brand awareness (1992–100)	127	128	131	150 by 2003
• Seasonallty					
• Price competitiveness	• Market share	20%	20.5%	22%	25% by 2003
• Fashion trends	• Market growth	4%	5%	4%	NA
• Consumable income/ savings ration	• Customer satisfaction (1998–100)	103	104	103	110 by 2003
• Product availability	• Customer retention	87%	87%	87%	90% by 2002
• Competitive remuneration	• Number of employees	5,375	4,823	4,358	
• Work/life balance	• Key employee turnover	11%	10%	10%	Less than 8%
• Personal development	• Employee satisfaction (1998–100)	104	103	101	115 by 2003
	• Sickness absence (man days)	2,956	3,003	2,905	2,000 by 2002
	• Unsolicited applications	320	300	295	400 by 2003
	• Rookie ratio (<2 years)	32%	26%	27%	20%
	• Average training hours	65	70	69	90 hours by 2003
• Political uncertainty	• Average order handling time (hours)	6	6.5	5.5	4 hours by 2003
• Unit cost inflation	• Deliveries on time (%)	90%	93%	93%	98%
• Product quality	• Complaints	537	557	590	300 by 2003
• Order fulfillment	• Product defects	265	233	207	50 by 2002
• Processing efficiency					
• Human rights in Asia	• Greenhouse gas emissions (tonnes)	15	18	17	12 by 2002
• Health and safety	• Use of packaging materials (tonnes)	5	6	7	Less than 5
• Animal welfare	• Number of actions against the company by third parties	2,350	3,100	3,025	Less than 2,000 by 2001

Source: Adapted from PricewaterhouseCoopers LLP publication entitled *ValueReporting Forecast 2001—Trends in Corporate Reporting*, 56–57. Used by permission.

was third at 72 percent; balance sheet strength, 61 percent; economic and industry trends, 48 percent; innovative products or services, 44 percent; corporate governance, 42 percent; corporate culture, 33 percent; attractive dividend, 13 percent.[37]

What's the point? As the Coloplast experiment suggests, numbers alone no longer cut it. Citizen investor funds are increasingly looking to nonstandard measures, partly because such gauges are more forward-looking than the numbers alone, and partly because they give credibility to the traditional metrics.

The Rivel research and Coloplast experiment beg a question. In an ideal world, what information would new capitalist owners want companies to disclose? What would an ideal enhanced corporate report look like? GRI may answer that question for sustainability concerns. But what about a holistic report that includes traditional metrics, sustainability metrics and forward-looking, value-creation metrics?

Civil Economy Accounting

A number of market participants have suggested formats and standards for the next generation of accounting. David Phillips, a partner at PwC in London and a leading expert on effective narrative reporting, has written one of the more thoughtful drafts. In accordance with PWC's standards (see figure 7-1), he would open a company's "value analysis" report with a double-entry format. Only this time, the columns would not be assets and liabilities or revenues and expenses, but rather "value-creating activity" and "risk indicators." Phillips's ideas of value-creating activities include innovation, brand value (recent spending on advertising, promotion, marketing), customer value (for example, revenues from new customers), human capital value (which Phillips calls a value-creating activity, not just an expense), supply chain, and environmental and social value.[38]

In each category, PwC proposes indicators and measures, both historic and forward-looking. On the value creation side of the ledger, Phillips calls for a corporation to reveal the past three years of cash flow and a projection of whether such indicators are likely to increase, decrease, or remain the same over the next three years. On the risk indication side, he suggests measures of a historic trend, as well as the objective for risk mitigation, if any. Figure 7-1 shows a summary of PwC's proposal for next-generation reporting.

Next-Generation Accounting

PwC's proposal is hardly the only possible blueprint for information standards as the architecture of the civil economy takes shape. Deloitte's "In the Dark" study marks another initiative to improve accounting.[39] It is nonetheless noteworthy that big global accounting firms are brainstorming ways for the market to move beyond the ancient boxes of Brother Luca's double-entry system.

New capitalists require fresh standards to complement traditional accounting. Their goal is to benefit from what we might call the "Coloplast effect." Relevant measurement allows investors to identify which corporations are really managing for the long-term benefit of the citizen investors who stand behind today's funds, and which corporations are geared to producing short-term, inequitably distributed profits. As the new standards improve, corporations on top get a lower cost of capital. Citizen owners can better control risk and reap more robust returns over time. And society benefits as enterprises redefine how they deal with their employees, environmental responsibility, and social factors as material assets to be cultivated. Powerful gains are to be harvested from breaking out of the information standards ghetto.

TAKEAWAYS

- Traditional accounting is a poor judge of intangible assets and their potential. That amounts to a critical shortcoming, given that knowledge assets have overtaken bricks and mortar as drivers of economic growth.

- Modern information benchmarks are needed as much by new capitalists trying to value companies as by corporate executives searching for the best means to manage their company.

- Whole new sets of civil economy metrics and reporting standards are surfacing. Not all will survive. Those with traction are likely to

  - measure a company and its management's ability, desire, and likelihood to create value for external owners (e.g., EVA and various governance ratings);

  - judge the sustainability of the enterprise over long periods of time (e.g., Global Compact and GRI); or

  - focus on real but intangible drivers of value in a company, such as intellectual property (e.g., PwC's value analysis template).

- The Coloplast experiment and Rivel's research results suggest that new capitalists value enhanced disclosure of extra-financial indicators. Civil economy owners tend to reward companies that demonstrate capacity to make good use of intangibles. Benefits may include loyalty, higher stock prices, and a lower cost of capital.

NGOs and Capital
Civil Society Meets the Civil Economy

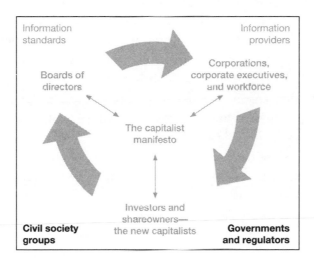

New capitalists are also consumers, employees, and citizens. This chapter reveals how grassroots civic organizations have pioneered innovative ways to use capital markets and ownership powers to influence corporate behavior and how governemments and regulators can help create a civil economy.

I t was an April day in 2000 in Washington, D.C., and a river of placard-toting protesters was flowing between the wide concrete banks of Pennsylvania Avenue, marooning an army of bankers, lobbyists, and lawyers in offices overhead. They peered out nervously through half-drawn window shades. Less than five months earlier, many of the same chanting marchers had boiled into riot in Seattle during the World Trade Organization's summit. Now, police had warned, it was the U.S. capital's turn. World Bank and International Monetary Fund officials were gathering there for spring meetings. The conclaves formed an irresistible magnet for tens of thousands of demonstrators bent on condemning what they saw as an emerging economic order dominated by multinational corporations. Suddenly one in a clutch of watching bankers spotted an enormous banner unfurled on an office building: "Join the Worldwide Movement Against Globalization!" Chuckles broke out all around. Hadn't anyone in this ragtag throng noticed the dottiness of such a message? Hey, the onlookers assured each other, maybe these guys aren't so formidable a threat after all.

Many corporate executives had long brushed off social pressure groups in much the same way, seeing them as an unnatural intrusion into business decisions. "It's of the same order as the hula hoop—a fad," once declared former Campbell Soup president W. R. Murphy.[1] The executives had a point. This was a rational judgment. Until recently, such campaigns were like pebbles cast from *outside* the marketplace tent—by religious or human rights groups focused on single issues, such as ending apartheid in South Africa or stopping sales of cigarettes to minors. Boardrooms could wait out such niggling attacks, confident that the problem or its advocates would go away. If criticism bit at the margins of a company's reputation or sales, directors could always make perfunctory public relations gestures to ward it off.

But the days of belittling protesters and critics are ending. Seattle and Washington would together prove a visible milepost along the road to a civil economy—events that ushered fringe anticapitalist dissent into a mass global audience. Citizens around the world were offended by the lawlessness of many of the protestors, but the protests reminded them of their own deep anxiety about the sweeping shifts in international commerce that have redistributed jobs, shuttered family businesses, homogenized cultures, and stolen economic clout away to distant climes. What the televised street protests did was stir this grassroots unrest into fuel for a potent new power in the marketplace: the civil economy organization focused not on relatively marginal matters but on the fundamentals of business.

Today, groups lobbying corporate behavior are a central component of the new capitalist ecosystem. Increasingly, they have learned to creep *inside* the market tent, leashing those big causes to the very real clout of new capitalist money. Their argument, made with varying consistency, is that social responsibility is good for the bottom line, as well as just plain good. Their ambition is nothing less than to redefine the bedrock notion of shareowner value to incorporate elements of corporate social responsibility as a permanent, entrenched feature for every single business entity. And, abetted by troubled citizens, in a thousand unconnected but parallel ways, such groups are relentlessly constructing a market infrastructure geared to doing just that.

What's New?

Some may yawn. After all, business has had about four hundred years to get used to public cries for social responsibility.

That's certainly true. When bankers readied the Vereenigde Oost-Indische Compagnie, the Dutch East India Company, for the world's first-ever initial public offering in 1602, they had to face down antiwar protesters. The issue was acute. The company's strategy in Asia hinged largely on the generous application of warfare, blockade, piracy, assassination, imprisonment, plunder, terror, slavery, bribery, and other standard business tactics of the day. When the VOC's directors turned to ordinary citizens for capital in the form of traded stock, Dutch religious pacifists suddenly gained a tool to voice objection. Some churchgoers, meeting by lamplight in Amsterdam homes, formed pacts to boycott shares until the company foreswore the use of violence. Others made a show before their neighbors of selling any VOC stock they had. Determined believers courted arrest as they picked their way door to door along the canals, gathering signatures for a notarized public petition broadcasting their protest.[2]

Dissenters swayed the company not an iota. Canny executives marshaled enough capital from wealthy traders and enough muscle from government to suppress the protests. But the Dutch burghers, in trying to carry values they learned on church pews into the fray of commerce, were pioneers of the civil economy. They were the first to comprehend that a public company's appetite for capital represents powerful potential leverage for civic groups—if only they could gather enough ownership stakes to make the executives care. For hundreds of years such groups couldn't. That lesson was dramatically relearned on February 7, 1970.

On that day, Ralph Nader stood at a lectern in Washington's National Press Building, facing a battery of cameras and reporters. The wiry thirty-six-year-old had already achieved fame in a dramatic consumer campaign to improve auto safety in the United States. Now, as he waited for the room to quiet, he was preparing to open a historic second front in his crusade to curb the unaccountable power of multinational companies. Nader would hitch demands for corporate social responsibility to shareowners, thus picking up where the VOC's protesters had left off in 1602. The initiative would stun both executives and investors.

"Shareholders are harmed as consumers and citizens by the very activities that they own in part," he proclaimed to the packed press conference. Nader unveiled the Project on Corporate Responsibility—and identified its first target: General Motors, the icon of U.S. enterprise. "Campaign GM" would "tame the corporate tiger," he predicted, by convincing pension funds and other big investors to join their share votes to rebel petitions filed at the firm's annual meeting. And if funds "decline to respond," Nader promised that his growing national army of activists would work the grassroots to make them do so. "The constituents of those institutions will be contacted," he warned. "The campaign will reach to the universities and their students and faculty, to the banks and their depositors and fiduciaries, to churches and their congregations, to insurance companies and their policyholders, to union and company pension funds and their membership and to other investors."[3]

The insight animating Campaign GM was simple: standing behind the veil of faceless big funds owning blocks of stock were citizen investors. Get to them, and you move the funds. And the funds, in turn, have the weight to move boardrooms. Nader, of course, was not concerned with the goal of maximizing shareowner value. But he understood the power that could come by linking his social mission to new capitalists who were.

Campaign GM proved a mighty spark. Management appealed to the SEC to block two of the first dissident investor resolutions in North America. But by just two votes to one, with two members absent, commissioners ruled that General Motors would have to submit the proposals to a shareowner ballot. On that razor-thin judgment would hang decades of subsequent shareowner activism.

Campaign GM's spark had far broader effects. Before long, as Nader rightly envisaged, civil society groups used to reaching for levers of public policy saw a new potential power in the harnessing of capital, not just communities, to their causes. That was true across the Atlantic, too. In 1977 a U.K. group called End Loans to South Africa filed an almost unheard-of dissident resolution at Midland Bank. Campaigns thus became primitive forms of civil economy organizations.

Why primitive? Compared with the groups entering the marketplace today, many of those emerging in the 1970s and 1980s were hobbled by one of two weaknesses. First, they confined themselves to a narrow constituency by focusing on a single issue. Second, few such ghettoized campaigns could tap enough capital to rustle more than the outer fringes of the average CEO's world.

For all that, Nader's political progeny drew key lessons from the experience—lessons that would help them find a way to compel CEOs' attention long after Nader himself ceased being a disciplined force.

The Wrong Battlefield

Consider the brawniest drive of the era: the campaign to force companies out of apartheid South Africa. U.S. businesses thought the battleground on sanctions was centered in the White House and Congress.

And until 1986 the antisanctions lobby could count both branches of government safely in its camp. President Ronald Reagan opposed penalties on South Africa from the beginning of his first term, in 1981, and blocked them for five years in the Senate and House of Representatives.

But business had calculated wrongly. This time, unlike any other policy contest before it, the struggle followed a new trajectory, moving onto the streets and, from there, into the investment world and then into boardrooms. Civil society had refused to take Reagan's no for an answer. Campaigners turned to capital—and led a grassroots drive that forced a new U.S. foreign policy that flowed right around an isolated White House. Randall Robinson's TransAfrica and other like-minded groups trained their sites on public employee pension funds and university endowments to produce "peoples' sanctions." Marshaling attention-grabbing demonstrations, constituent demand, and state legislation, they compelled these big investors to disinvest from companies doing business in apartheid South Africa—on grounds that companies that remained put shareowner value at risk.

Executives at first thought they could ride out the pressure. But by 1993, when newly installed President Nelson Mandela called finally for an end to global sanctions, campaigners had convinced forty of the fifty best-endowed U.S. universities, as well as pension funds of more than a hundred state and local jurisdictions in the United States, to put anti-apartheid disinvestment policies into effect.[4] Suddenly, hundreds of billions of dollars were not available to corporations with South African operations. In addition, activists supplied political cover for congressmen who finally voted to override Reagan's veto and pass the landmark Comprehensive Anti-Apartheid Act of 1986.

Chief executives took account of the new facts on the ground—and beat a rare retreat. Threats to stock price, bad publicity, and costs of defending against incessant challenge were no longer worth it. From 1985 to 1987, the apex of sanctions pressure, about a hundred and fifty U.S. corporations pulled the plug on their operations in South Africa. To be sure, the consequences of withdrawal were marginal for the companies and the South African economy alike. But anti-apartheid campaigners were positive about the change, because many of Pretoria's white supporters saw the mounting exodus as a demoralizing affirmation of international isolation.[5] They believed that the psychological impact proved one vital factor in President Frederick de Klerk's ultimate decision to negotiate a historic transition from minority rule to democracy.

For shareowner activism, though, South Africa proved a dead-end street. The single-issue campaign had nowhere to go once millions of new voters elected Nelson Mandela South Africa's president and put an end to apartheid. Coalitions disbanded, and groups that remained focused on the issue found that their support and revenues were drying up. The civil society organizations responsible for the sanctions campaigns had discovered the power of capital to sway business behavior, even against stiff resistance. But they had also stumbled upon a harsh reality. Without the fuel of broader issues and wider constituencies, campaigns tend to break up once the issue in question is resolved and must be rebuilt from scratch for each fresh concern.

Into the God Box

The sturdier path to a new ownership culture, it turned out, would be paved in an unlikely precinct of civil society: the religious community.

The building at 475 Riverside Drive in New York is a high-rise architectural monstrosity, made more noticeable by its location three miles north of the skyscrapers of midtown Manhattan and adjacent to the spires of Riverside Church. Its rectangular shape, plus the various religious groups situated in its rabbit's warren of offices, gave it its inevitable nickname: the God Box.

Galvanized by inroads into activism made by Campaign GM, leaders of six Protestant denominations gathered there in 1971 to discuss ways to tap the new tool of shareowner petitioning. They pooled resources in an organization that would soon emerge as the Interfaith Center on Corporate Responsibility, or ICCR. Engineered to coordinate shareowner campaigning by religious endowments and investment funds, ICCR grew to become the single most potent source of investor activism over two decades in the United States.

Program director Tim Smith coordinated backers, research, and publicity for dissident shareowner resolutions. In 1972, ICCR sent proposals to five puzzled corporations, asking them to curb weapons sales, close South African plants, and adopt responsible mining practices. But Smith was only just beginning. By 2000, ICCR represented as many as 275 Christian and Jewish funds with portfolios amounting to more than $110 billion. And in that year alone it oversaw 145 resolutions submitted to 112 corporations on an array of issues, including governance, third world debt, workplace discrimination, and the environment.[6]

Poetry and Proxies

Critics in boardrooms—and, indeed, from some pews—could not help but pose a question: what on earth did the lofty poetry of faith have to do with the dreary prose of corporate proxies? The answer to that is critical, because it helps us understand why any civil society organization would migrate into capital markets to carry out advocacy.

Faith groups embraced shareowner activism because they discovered that access to ownership gave them a voice, values gave them a message, and the failure of public policy to effect the changes they desired gave them a motive. "As an investor," concluded an influential 1972 analysis, "the church has a special opportunity and responsibility in defining and affecting social good which it cannot avoid without contradicting its own purposes."[7]

Religious bodies across the world traveled much the same road to discovering their identity as new capitalists. In 1973, Charles Jacob, investment chief for the U.K. Methodist Church, led an effort to establish faith-based stewardship funds—but focused on supporting ethical corporate behavior rather than agitating against laggards.[8] Friends Provident, with its Quaker traditions, had always been an advocate of socially responsible investing. Its stewardship fund is testimony to that heritage, as are the continuing efforts of F&C Fund Management, its parent, to make businesses more socially responsible.

In Toronto the Taskforce on the Churches and Corporate Responsibility opened in January 1975. Crispin White spearheaded Britain's Ecumenical Committee for Corporate Responsibility in 1988. Similar groups surfaced in France, the Netherlands, South Africa, Australia, New Zealand, and elsewhere—and not only in the Judeo-Christian sphere. In April

2005, delegates from Buddhist, Hindu, Islamic, Jain, Sikh, and Zoroastrian faiths joined in London with Christian and Jewish representatives to found an umbrella civil economy group, the International Interfaith Investment Group. Known as 3iG, its mission of building a globally coordinated network to spread religious-based influence through capital markets is the natural culmination of ICCR's unassuming launch on Riverside Drive thirty-four years earlier.

Neither 3iG nor any of the national or cross-border alliances are precise ICCR clones, of course, since laws and practices differ from place to place, dictating divergent tactics. But all share a common objective: hitching values to capital. If past experience is any guide, the key to the success of 3iG will be the group's ability to make the ownership case. Only then will it create a broad enough new capitalist coalition to influence corporate agendas. Construction of this grid has taken place almost entirely outside the headlines, and well beyond the normal scope of corporate reconnaissance.

Some market watchers may raise alarms: What happens if faith objectives trump legitimate concern for shareowner value? Could faith investors muster sufficient stock pressure on a company to stop it from selling contraceptives, for example? It seems unlikely, because what infuses religious fund coalitions with clout is diversity and breadth of membership. Those features, at the same time, make it less probable that any one campaign could hijack such broader-based investor forums for highly controversial purposes. Moreover, religious investors may form the core of the coalition, but they lack the muscle of less "values-driven" investors, such as pension funds, mutual fund companies, and other institutional investors. Faith groups often work in conjunction with such "bottom line" oriented investors, so the issues need to have business rationales, lest their partners rebel.

Ten Rules for Sustainable Engagement

In truth, though, religious investors have had their most profound influence in establishing what amounts to a prototype of a civil society organization using capital markets to influence corporate behavior. The building blocks they fashioned would later be used by trade unions, environmental activists, antipoverty lobbies, and other nongovernment groups electing to pursue their missions through capital. Lessons we can extract boil down to ten basic principles, what we might describe as the genetic code for a new-capitalist organization in a civil economy.

1. *Convert the values mission to a business mission.* The language of markets was, is, and always will be money. So the civil economy organization translates its mission into numerate terms if it aims to win friends in the boardroom or among fund managers. Each needs to make a persuasive business case for change. Pushing corporate attention to climate change risks? Express the argument based on the long-term financial welfare of the company and its owners. Absent real bottom-line effects, values-based investors will not attract enough new capitalists to affect corporate norms.

2. *Assert rights of ownership.* Perhaps the greatest achievement of religious market pioneers was their clear-cut assertion that stock carries with it the primal right to behave as an owner—to question, obtain information, engage, and—where necessary—dissent.

3. *Break out of the ghetto.* The Achilles heel of early civil economy proponents was their reliance on narrow constituencies. Such groups failed to make headway or else faded away. ICCR's inclusive approach, by contrast, promised to deliver what we call "sustainable engagement." The civil economy organization builds as broad a new capitalist coalition as possible without watering down bedrock objectives.

4. *The more capital, the louder the voice.* The mathematics of capital markets is pretty simple: the more shares you speak for in a company, the greater the chance directors will pay attention. The civil economy group seeks to gather in its silo as many funds with as much cash as possible to swell its financial presence. This also has the effect of winnowing the focus of activism to issues that can rally the broadest coalition, which usually means those that have the biggest bottom-line effects.

5. *Build investor coalitions.* For many faith-based, environmental, or other community groups, the task of standing shoulder to shoulder with bloodless money-managing institutions may hardly come naturally. Yet this skill is precisely the measure of a civil economy organization's impact. Job one is maximizing capital clout behind the mission. That demands the painstaking work of constructing bridges to other silos where the big money lies, even when such entities are not typical allies.

6. *Become a utility.* When corporate mergers work right, it is often because they figure out ways to consolidate common functions efficiently. ICCR did exactly the same, centralizing activist research so that its many individual religious fund constituents did not have to do all the grunt work themselves. The successful civil economy organization serves as a kind of "engagement utility," generating issue analysis, advocacy options, outreach and publicity assistance, and proponent recruitment.

7. *Multitask campaign issues.* Civic anxiety with the corporate world cuts across many issues, from ethical behavior in the boardroom to treatment of employees to pollution. Early civil economy groups concentrated on one issue each. Moreover, public concerns run to many companies, not just a General Motors. ICCR became adept at serving as a clearinghouse for dissident campaigns on dozens of issues at hundreds of corporations. The strategy ensured its ongoing survival and leveraged lessons learned in one campaign across others.

8. *Watch the gatekeepers.* Intermediaries, ICCR discovered over time, are largely unseen but critical players in the capital market. Investment advisers guide selection of fund managers, for instance. Fund managers in turn decide what stocks are bought and sold. Proxy agents influence voting outcomes at corporate annual meetings. A civil economy organization boosts its role by keeping close tabs on such bodies—feeding them facts, analysis, and opinion in support of its positions, and calling them to account when they are seen as going astray.

9. *Believe companies could be on your side.* Early U.S. civil economy groups, accomplished in agitprop tactics common to the political sphere, were quick to use confrontation as a first rather than last resort in pursuing shareowner campaigns. ICCR was not afraid to be aggressive, but its opening approach was to explore dialogue and negotiation with target companies. The strategy bolstered ICCR's credibility with corporations and constituents, enhancing prospects of success. Scores of companies have agreed to various suggestions, from nondiscrimination in Northern Ireland to environmental reporting.

10. *Go global.* Ideas click across frontiers as quickly as capital, making home country–only shareowner campaigns virtually obsolete. ICCR actively worked to spawn similar groups in other markets and, finally, to support the multinational, multifaith 3iG initiative pioneered by the U.K.-based Alliance of Religions and Conservation (ARC). International cooperation among mature civil economy groups can broaden the capital pool behind campaigns and cross-pollinate best engagement tactics.

These first principles proved powerful enough to fuel the quiet multiplication of civil economy bodies around the world. But it would take lessons from parallel initiatives—by trade unions, nongovernment organizations, academics, and media—to map the new capitalist organizations we see today, which are capable of reshaping enterprise.

Consorting with the Abominable

"You mean, to be an effective labor leader, I must be a capitalist? This I cannot accept!" The French trade union leader was in New York in February 1999, leading a delegation on a tour of U.S. pension funds. Her assignment: trying to understand corporate governance, and why worker-controlled plans were increasingly engaging with corporations to protect employee retirement savings. The Americans in the room looked at each other in bewilderment. Mobilizing the tools of capitalism was precisely what they were learning to do to safeguard employee assets. And they had outlined just such strategies in detail to their visiting colleagues. But the outburst was a stark reminder of how far a road they had traveled from old habits of recoiling from the world of profit seekers. The model they were now pioneering promised to shift the balance of corporate power in their direction. But it had meant crossing the Rubicon. Many unionists around the globe, not just in France, were still not prepared to accept the legitimacy and potential of the market.

Bill Patterson believed that labor's way forward indeed required leashing rather than condemning capital. Like Tim Smith in the religious community, he had had an epiphany. While working in the 1970s and 1980s at the Amalgamated Clothing and Textile Workers Union, Patterson had watched ICCR succeed, and he grew to understand how a civil society organization could vastly amplify its power by tapping the strength of pension funds. In 1992 he got his chance. Teamsters president Ron Carey hired Patterson to run an Office of Corporate Affairs to test the waters of shareowner activism. After all, labor had an enormous stake in the welfare of corporations. Jobs were at risk. But so were the retirement savings of employees. Teamsters members alone had more than $40 billion in assets in 175 pension plans. Unions had left the stewardship of their money almost exclusively to professional fund managers. Patterson, with an assist from federal judge Kimba Wood, would change that forever.

Just as the 1970 SEC decision on General Motors had opened the door to dissident shareowner proposals, so Judge Wood's pivotal April 19, 1993, ruling on Wal-Mart would clear the way for trade unions—first in the United States, then elsewhere around the world—to become civil economy organizations.

At issue was a seemingly innocuous nonbinding shareowner resolution. A joint coalition of church and union funds wanted Wal-Mart to report to investors on policies and progress in eliminating discrimination against workers on the basis of gender, race, and another factors. Wal-Mart executives scrambled to prevent the proposal from coming to a vote, and they had already won the SEC staff's backing in 1992. But proponents saw the decision as a precedent setter and challenged it in a U.S. district court.

Judge Wood pondered arguments until the very last minute, forcing Wal-Mart to hold the presses on its 1993 annual meeting notice and proxy statement.[9] Then she ruled decisively for the investors. Before her decision, shareowners had found the way blocked to virtually all attempts to petition employment-related resolutions. Regulators deemed them "ordinary business," which, under U.S. securities law, meant that the board alone had authority to address them. Wood concluded, though, that "equality and diversity in the workplace involve substantial policy considerations" beyond the mundane of daily "ordinary business."[10] The decision opened a new avenue for shareowner engagement. Labor soon designed ways to march through it.

First it framed a rising tide of shareowner resolutions. In 1997, with Patterson having moved to the AFL-CIO, its affiliated unions filed nearly eighty dissident shareowner proposals on issues ranging from equal opportunity employment to takeover defenses. Then the federation released first guidelines on share voting, distributing ten thousand copies to trustees and fund managers. It pumped eye-catching tools into the market, including a canny Web site called Paywatch.org, which allows any user to calculate the number of years it would take on a particular salary to match the annual cache awarded a given CEO. Patterson's alma mater, the Teamsters, joined the fray with "America's Least Valuable Directors," a roster of nine notorious board members. Most important, the AFL-CIO gave birth to its Key Votes Survey, which would lay the groundwork for pension fund trustee training and, in turn, systematically put pressure on money managers to vote union member assets in alignment with union member interests, as interpreted by Patterson's office.

Suddenly labor had overtaken the ICCR, becoming the single biggest source of shareowner activism in the United States. And trade unions in Canada, Britain, Australia, and continental Europe were soon to follow—first with national efforts, and later in a global collaboration called the Committee on Workers' Capital. Labor had once advanced member welfare exclusively by exercising shop-floor muscle and lobbying public policy. Now it discovered that harnessing capital could help fight job discrimination and promote healthier companies capable of generating jobs, all while fulfilling its principal fiduciary obligation of protecting the value of pension fund savings.

Mechanics and Missteps

What did labor add—or fail to add—to the canon of civil economy organizing? One profoundly accurate insight was the focus on pension fund trustees as a critical but broken link in the circle of accountability. No other group before it—but many after—understood that a new infrastructure of training, skills, information, and action was needed to convert such bodies from rubber stamps to active stewards.

Labor also proved adroit at adapting not just the language of fund management but the detailed mechanics of Wall Street. Look how the union coalition fought PetroChina's initial public offering, mounting a sophisticated investor outreach campaign that matched Goldman Sachs road show for road show, fact for fact. No civil society organization had tried that before.

Finally, labor leaders launched an innovative experiment to rally grassroots worker opinion behind their capital agenda. This was a breakthrough idea. Paywatch.org would attempt to ground shareowner activism in constituent support. The objective made sense because member enthusiasm could stir greater pressure on pension funds and money managers to raise the matter with corporate boards. That precisely captures the thrust of a civil economy. To reach its full potential, the civil economy needs to be underpinned by a working circle of accountability linking new capitalist owners to funds and companies. And what better way to test that power than on the hot-button issue of CEO remuneration?

But Paywatch.org proved to harbor the same chronic flaw seen in the anti-apartheid shareowner campaign. It rested wholly on a single issue that could fizzle or flare, depending on headlines and events. The venture had no way to evolve naturally into an engine generating the kind of durable, broad-based, multi-issue grassroots constituency for ongoing shareowner activism. Paywatch.org had two further weaknesses. It was identified solely with trade union interests, even though runaway CEO compensation was troubling to a much bigger audience. And it was under-resourced, making it look more like a public relations gimmick than a vehicle for mobilization.

The unions also stumbled over the vital importance of converting the values mission into a money mission. Get that equation wrong, and consequences can be fatal. Labor fund activism left itself open to charges that it was a stealth ally in union workplace conflicts rather than a legitimate defender of retirement plan interests. Exhibit A: the U.S. supermarket chain Safeway, where union funds in May 2004 led a shareowner drive to oust CEO Steven Burd from the board. Safeway was known for poor governance, and was a fair target for investor activism. But timing made unions' motives suspect: they acted just weeks after a bitter strike in California. And leading the charge was CalPERS, whose president, Sean Harrigan, also served as a top official in the union that led the strike. Harrigan had excused himself from the case, but that wasn't enough. The misstep handed opponents and even fund allies what seemed to be a smoking gun: evidence that union funds were seeking to wage a workplace dispute through investor activism rather than bargaining. Harrigan himself lost his CalPERS post seven months later, partly over the Safeway controversy.[11]

The lesson: civil society organizations can pursue their objectives through capital. But if they fail to translate their goals credibly into the currency of the market, they will rightly lose their legitimacy. The bottom line remains the bottom line. While citizen investors may have multiple dimensions as owners, consumers, suppliers, union members, and churchgoers, when dealing with their investments they think first as owners.

The civil economy (and the citizen owner at the base of it) binds capitalism to values. But it does not replace capitalism with theocracy or political philosophy. Making money over the long run remains the sine qua non. That is why pension funds and other investors own companies. Undermine that foundation and pension funds will have to sell their shares, undermining the very basis of a civil society organization's legitimacy.

The Big Bang

The social community that would next follow labor into shareowner activism took this teaching to heart—and built perhaps the most potent examples yet of new capitalist pressure. By 1999, the faith and trade union wings of civil society had pioneered full immersion in the capital market. But these coalitions still represented relatively narrow streams of opinion. Events on the streets of Seattle and Washington, D.C., would tap a far wider vein of public anxiety over the course that business was taking.

A funny thing happened in the wake of those protests. Bludgeoned by popular anxiety about globalization and a string of Enron-led scandals, the reputation of business in developed markets plummeted. In polls measuring whom the public trusted the most and the least, CEOs were near the bottom, just above car salesmen.[12] At the same time, public faith in citizen activist groups soared. The public relations firm Edelman surveyed fifteen hundred opinion leaders. Its "Barometer" rated them "the most trusted institutions in the United States, Europe, Latin America and much of Asia." In the United States alone, the trust rating of nongovernment organizations (NGOs) jumped from 36 percent in 2001 to 55 percent in 2005.[13]

Though some street demonstrations resembled criminal behavior more than civil disobedience, their call for a "worldwide movement against globalization" grabbed the attention of mainstream public opinion like few other events. Further, they blew open opportunities for groups advocating corporate social and environmental responsibility, once branded as gadflies, to reposition themselves as defenders of a silent majority, but defenders who understood capital markets and could obey the law. Many such organizations seized the chance to expand nascent efforts in capital markets to press their advantage. Quite independently, without knowing much of each other's activities, the groups formed a global wave of such initiatives.

By one count, some 282,851 NGOs existed around the world in 2003.[14] Only a small fraction turned to ownership issues. But among them were catalysts critical to the architecture of the civil economy. Some concentrated on stirring citizen savers to sway financial institutions in favor of socially responsible investment. Others focused directly on boards of corporations and institutional investors. Tracking the courses they followed is a shortcut to deciphering the ways business is being revolutionized.

A Case in Point: USS

Consider the Universities Superannuation Scheme (USS), the pension fund for U.K. academics and administrators in higher education and one of the largest retirement plans in Britain. Wielding more than £20 billion, it emerged in the new millennium as one of a handful of big global pension funds committed to reinventing ownership. It pushed the envelope with pace-setting ideas such as the Enhanced Analytics Initiative, wherein members committed a percentage of broker commissions to firms showing that they consider social, environmental, and governance risks when analyzing companies.

But USS had famously shunned shareowner activism as late as 1999. How had the giant fund overnight sought to become both a paragon and an evangelist of responsible stewardship? Rewind to September 1997, and focus in on a small room at the Friends Meeting House in London. There, half a dozen academics and students from the Oxford-based campaign group People & Planet joined forces to start an ambitious drive at USS.

People & Planet's new spin-off group, Ethics for USS (E-USS), adopted a single goal: recruit enough support among faculty to force the fund into "an ethical investment policy that is accountable to its members."[15] At first, E-USS ran aground. It called on USS to start selling off companies in its portfolio that E-USS deemed unethical. But at the time, all U.K. pension funds hewed to the legal guidance of the 1984 Megarry judgment, which seemed to preclude negative screening.[16] USS dismissed E-USS's appeal out of hand as both irresponsible and illegal. Evidently, disinvestment would be a cul de sac.

E-USS then took a fateful decision that rescued it from obscurity. It went back to the drawing board, dumped its screening demand, and issued a fresh, new capitalist–style agenda in a sophisticated white paper, "Meeting the Responsibilities of Ownership: Our Proposal to USS."[17] Now it wanted USS not to divest, but to be a shareowner activist—an objective tailored to achieve market legitimacy. For two years E-USS went to ground, building grassroots support among academics, university vice chancellors, union pension fund lawyers, and government ministers. Government, it turned out, was an indirect ally, crafting a rule that would mandate from July 2000 that all pension funds disclose whether they address social issues in investment. In December 1999, USS's board agreed. E-USS may not have rallied more than a vocal minority of members. But it had mustered enough support, and at the time had made a strong legal, financial, and public relations case. USS announced that it would henceforth strive for leadership in responsible investment and shareowner engagement. And it would report regularly on its work to members.

Thus was born one of Britain's first civil economy institutional investors, linking citizen owners through an accountability circle to their pension fund, and producing as a result an activist shareowner force pressing for more accountable companies and market intermediaries.

Battle over the Bottom Line

Along with four other NGOs, People & Planet is testing a cloned approach at additional pension plans—mustering member pressure to produce transformation in fund management. Called FairPensions, it represents an aggressive effort to stir accountability at retirement schemes.[18]

People & Planet is hardly alone. Other civil society groups have entered the market seeking similar conversions at financial institutions.[19] In fact, the more you look, the more you can see new civil society initiatives aimed at mobilizing grassroots civil owners. Such ventures hold potential to follow E-USS's success in stitching big money to member interests, triggering new capitalist pressures on corporate boardrooms across a broad front to alter their practices.

Don't make the mistake of assuming, though, that all such projects favor traditionally "left-wing" forms of corporate social responsibility. Accountability in the capital markets opens the door to many strains of opinion about what generates value. Look at the Free Enterprise Action Fund (FEA), opened in March 2005 and backed by a panoply of conservative NGOs. Openly ideological, it aims to outperform by investing in companies "at risk from social activism" and then pressing those firms to resist "anti-business" funds and lobbies. Corporations that uphold "the American system of free enterprise," FEA believes, will produce outsize returns. FEA's prospectus asserts that the fund reserves use of every available tool of shareowner activism to move boards against "appeasement."

FEA's appearance on the scene underscores the point that divisions evident in politics surface, often in different forms, in capital markets when they are accountable. The rise of civil economy structures only guarantees that such contests may be waged, whereas before they were suppressed to the benefit of managers or controlling owners. They do not dictate which approach, which set of civil economy organizations, will prevail at any given company or time. An NGO such as Account-Ability, for instance, is dedicated to promote "accountability for sustainable development." Others may see accountability as a route to quite different corporate ends. As in politics, outcomes hinge on which force musters the more persuasive argument for value and delivers the most powerful punch of constituents.

Civil economy organizations understand that they will have to manufacture a whole new arsenal of campaign tools that reach deeper into the constituencies served by financial institutions and sustain robust monitoring over time—not just for a one-time mission. Various groups have already made headway. For instance, "How Responsible Is Your Pension?" scored Britain's top 250 pension plans in a bid to help stimulate rank-and-file advocacy.[20] Handbooks—such as *The Campaigner's Guide to Financial Markets* or Friends of the Earth's *Guide to Shareholder Activism*—were primers to instruct activists in the arts of grassroots mobilization.[21]

The route ahead will involve tools adapted from the political world, where advocates thrive precisely by perfecting means to motivate constituents. Communication, canvassing, get-out-the-vote efforts, and Internet outreach are skills new to capital markets. But just as CEOs now require unprecedented political dexterity, so such measures are increasingly becoming central to new capitalist organizations.

Aiming for the Board

Rousing the grass roots was not the only strategy that environmental and social responsibility groups hit upon. Some chose strategies leading directly to engagement with the boards of corporations and financial institutions.

Twenty-five people converged on the Rockefeller estate's Pocantico Conference Center in New York on two cold days in January 2003 to craft one such initiative. Investors and experts from around the United States, they were invited by CERES, the environmental coalition, to brainstorm a way forward for a "sustainable governance project." CERES head Robert Massie had long warned of the looming dangers of climate change. Now he was convinced that solutions lay in the coupling of two great movements—the drive for environmental protection and the push for investor protection.[22]

Massie helped engineer a high-profile Institutional Investor Summit on Climate Risk at the United Nations. There, a core of fund leaders founded the Investor Network on Climate Risk to encourage fund collaboration on environmental shareowner activism.[23] CERES is the group's secretariat. The network parallels similar investor bodies in Britain, Australia, and New Zealand.[24]

Downing Street was the launch site of another classic example of civil society engagement in the market on issues once pigeonholed as "social" but now redefined as legitimate extra-financial risk. On December 4, 2000, a coalition of U.S. and U.K. philanthropies gathered at Prime Minister Tony Blair's office to announce the Carbon Disclosure Project. Within two years this new "secretariat" began circulating surveys to 500 top listed corporations in the world on their greenhouse gas emissions. By 2005, the group had gained endorsements from 143 funds, speaking for no less than $20 trillion.[25] Sponsors expect that data to help promote disclosure standards within companies and performance monitoring by large shareowners.

Other new capitalist groups specialized in generating briefings, manuals, and codes for pension fund trustees, corporate boards, or shareowner activists, making the business case for socially responsible corporate behavior. The UK Social Investment Forum (UKSIF), for instance, launched a project called Just Pensions, which published first ever toolkits for trustees on owner stewardship.[26]

A Brain Trust

Two other social domains have added to the ecosystem surrounding the civil economy's circle of accountability: academia and the media.

When they opened Columbia University's Institutional Investor Project in 1988, Ira Millstein and Louis Lowenstein could only have guessed that the seed they were planting would germinate into a network of global brain trusts for a new way of business. Millstein, an attorney with Weil, Gotshal & Manges, and Lowenstein, a law professor at Columbia, had sensed the need for a forum to explore a strange new phenomenon: big funds swelling to power in the marketplace. What were the implications for corporate boards, CEOs, and society at large? Would fund stewardship emerge as an antidote to the 1980s reign of corporate predators, or would conflicts and torpor choke its potential?

In May of that year, the two chaired the Institutional Investor Project's debut conference, "The American Corporation and the Institutional Investor: Are There Lessons from Abroad?" It was the first conference anywhere to probe comparisons in corporate governance between markets. There, Jonathan Charkham, then an adviser to the Bank of England, issued a prophetic call to arms. "There is a clear opportunity for institutional investors to seize the greenmailers' and raiders' clothes, dust them off and put them away. *They* have the chance to spot the upside potential and shake up boards so as to bring in new management to realize it."[27]

Bent on painting a clearer portrait of funds' profiles in the capital market, Millstein and Lowenstein commissioned quantitative studies by IIP director Carolyn Brancato. And they funded two other inquiries that would lay the groundwork for understanding the new channels of capitalism. How do institutional investors actually make portfolio decisions? How do boards actually react to their big shareowners? Michael Useem of the University of Pennsylvania published *Investor Capitalism*, a breakthrough book based on the Project's questions.[28]

Columbia's scholars and lawyers were well ahead of their time. But a global pageant of think tanks on investor-led capitalism would follow.[29] In 1988 not a single academic body focused on investor-led capitalism anywhere in the world. By 2005 dozens of such centers had emerged in nearly every corner of the globe, supplying intellectual and statistical heft to market change, and forming what in essence is a new discipline of civil economy studies. The Global Corporate Governance Academic Network, sponsored by the World Bank, made early efforts to link them into a common platform for research. But for now, no universal list exists even to identify groups coming to life each month, let alone coordinate them.

"Follow the money" was the advice "Deep Throat" gave to reporter Bob Woodward in the midst of the Watergate investigation. Academia did precisely the same. Organically, without central direction but in response to worldwide financial currents, it built an infrastructure of learning as capital flowed from traditional sources such as families, house banks, and the state into the hands of institutional investors. University centers and independent think tanks now chronicle new capitalist wealth, and train corporate directors and pension fund trustees. They illuminate gaps in legal regimes, pointing the way for national and international reform. They supply sound bytes for media correspondents grappling to understand scandals and trends. They advise boards, executives, shareowners, lawmakers, and regulators in the daily jockeying of markets. And in doing all of this, they serve as a vital circulatory system of ideas and information within and between countries. In time such centers will surely link in more formal ways. But they already are an unheralded driver of fundamental change for every major actor in the capital markets.

Freedom of the Blog

A fearless and inquisitive press is what the public expects to unearth skullduggery in the public policy sphere. How could armies of business correspondents have missed serial, ill-concealed kleptocracy at private-sector luminaries such as Adelphia, Parmalat, and HIH?

Watchful news media are a critical part of the ecosystem of an accountable economy. By probing and exposing, news hounds can serve as the eyes and ears of new capitalists when other safeguards fail. If the media are silenced or blinded, the chances of malfeasance inevitably rise. "Boards of directors are just like sub-atomic particles," says governance expert Nell Minow. "They behave differently when they are observed."[30] The same principles hold in civil society; remember that the very first amendment to the U.S. Constitution calls for freedom of the press. Uninhibited newspapers are responsible "for all the triumphs which have been gained by reason and humanity over error and oppression," President James Madison later explained.[31]

When it comes to the corporate world, though, most newspapers and broadcasters sometimes bark loudly and sometimes slumber until they stumble upon crises. They deny that. "For all of the faults, the media continues to play a watchdog role," *New York Times* business editor Lawrence Ingrassia told a conference in April 2005. "It is our responsibility to not just report the news, but to hold government and corporations accountable. You would really not want it any other way. Our job is to shine the harsh light of truth on institutions and the people who run them."[32]

In fact, it appeared to take the cataclysm of Enron to convince the *New York Times* and other U.S. media that dogged tracking of the governance of companies was worth the effort. Look at one barometer culled from LexisNexis searches. In the two years before the *Wall Street Journal* broke news of scandal at Enron in November 2001, the *New York Times* used the term *corporate governance* just 102 times, or an average of only about once each week. In the two years after, though, the phrase showed up on 476 occasions—more than once a day. That wasn't just a bubble.

Similarly, it took fallout from the Robert Maxwell scandal to get the *Financial Times* to commit to a reportorial beat covering boards of directors. During the two years prior to Maxwell's mysterious drowning on November 5, 1991, the *FT* cited the term *corporate governance* a total of 379 times. In the two years after, the number shot to 724.

Why the historic timidity in coverage? Critics cite the intense concentration of media ownership. In the United States, for instance, only twenty companies now control 70 percent of the daily newspapers in circulation.[33] And they rely heavily for advertising revenue on the same CEOs their journalists are meant to cover. Can media resist pressures to avoid critical scrutiny of corporations? If not, there the story of media's role in the civil economy ecosystem might well end—but for the Internet.

Boards Under e-Scrutiny

James McRitchie is a California state employee with a nose for shareowner activism. In 1995, he moonlighted something completely new: a free Web site, CorpGov.Net, devoted exclusively to news and analysis of corporate governance. McRitchie kept a special eye on CalPERS. "I felt the key to future corporate behavior depended on the voting behavior of pension funds and mutual funds in corporate elections," he wrote ten years later.[34] The site proved an important central clearinghouse of information, tapped regularly by investors and others seeking insights on the new field.

Stephen Davis, one of our authors, began publishing a weekly newsletter, *Global Proxy Watch*, in January 1997, first by fax and later by e-mail. The newsletter helped knit together the new industry of corporate governance and shareowner activism. By 2005 consultant-publisher Davis Global Advisors was launching the newsletter by email each Friday from Boston to subscribers in thirty-nine countries. *GPW* aimed to cross-fertilize ideas across borders—highlighting new capitalist developments in one market likely to move opinion leaders in another.

David Webb is a former investment banker and an intense computer whiz. In 1998, working out of a spare room in his rented Happy Valley flat in Hong Kong, he started a blog, Webb-site.com. It would soon shake the territory. Posting regular stories on his nonprofit site, Webb picked apart company accounts, blew the whistle on financial deception, exposed crony transactions, and proffered hard analysis of the territory's top family-owned companies unlike anything investors could find in mainstream media. None of this would have mattered, except that before long Webb-site.com drew more than 10,000 subscribers to its e-mail bulletin, or one out of every 690 people in Hong Kong. That would be the equivalent of nearly half a million readers in the United States. Local or foreign, investors with money in Hong Kong grew to rely on the site as an independent resource on business in the region. "Webb has almost single-handedly changed the terms of the corporate governance debate in Hong Kong," concluded *BusinessWeek*.[35]

In February 2000, journalist Stephen Mayne launched a similar, but for-profit, guerrilla blog called Crikey to cover the underside of corporate governance in Australia.[36] Aided by a small staff of freelancers, Mayne published online and daily by e-mail from his Melbourne suburban home, and combined bulletins with shareowner activism. Again, thousands of investors at home and abroad subscribed, tolerating Mayne's sometime blunders for his cheeky insights, inside company scoops, and independent advocacy of minority shareowners. Mayne sold the business in 2005 but stayed on as corporate governance editor.

Blogs and independent publications such as these are the antidotes to sluggish watch dogging in the establishment media. Internet channels allow neojournalists heretofore unheard-of capacity to burrow for news, gather tips, and distribute reports anywhere in the world—and at little or no cost. Barriers to entry into such media are low, and quality is consequently uneven. But such organs make it possible as never before for individual and institutional new capitalists to probe long-hidden corners of the capital market. Civil economy media are thus a powerful democratizing force. At their best, they feed ordinary people with information to distinguish dysfunction from stewardship among funds, cronyism and negligence from high performance among corporations, and conflicts from integrity among the market's many intermediaries.

License to Operate

Still, the ecosystem of civil economy groups harbors a troubling—and potentially lethal—weakness. Few organizations have anywhere near the levels of accountable and transparent governance they demand of corporations.

Critics of private enterprise contend that companies should earn a virtual "license to operate" by demonstrating responsible citizenship. But by the same token, in a civil economy, NGOs must earn an equivalent license to operate to assert legitimacy as market players. Why? Because if such groups practice autarchy and opacity in their own houses, the strong establishment forces arrayed against them can—and do—persuasively argue that such groups are secretly conflicted or hypocritical, hide ulterior motives, or are self-anointed gadflies with no title to influence. Those charges can be fatal to an NGO's new-capitalist market ambitions.

Even organizations ferociously dedicated to promoting shareowner activism are strangely silent when it comes to their own governance. Only a tiny handful openly publicizes channels members may use to effect internal change. For instance, many of the same civil society groups that advocate the option of contested board elections at corporations almost never spell out how their own members might go about challenging a slate of the organization's directors. They only rarely post their bylaws or governance procedures on Web sites. Stakeholders or dues-paying constituents often find it difficult to determine how a governing body is chosen, what its responsibilities are, and how it assures integrity of accounts and manages potential conflicts of interest, whether and how leaders are reviewed for performance, how succession is determined, policies set, or sometimes even what those policies actually are.

Worse, some civil groups champion violence or use muscle for corrupt purposes, placing themselves decisively beyond the bounds of a civil economy. Anarchist demonstrators at the Seattle World Trade Organization protests, for instance, fomented rioting. *Sokaiya* groups in Japan have posed as protectors of minority shareowners but use blackmail tactics to extract payoffs. Some anti-vivisection activists crossed the line in their campaign against Huntingdon Life Sciences, physically attacking executives and property and making bomb threats to institutional investors. These moves break the law, and they breach the civil economy's implicit constitution, which rests on the premise that players from top to bottom are accountable.

A Constitution of Activism

Work is under way on an architecture of accountability for civil groups in and outside the marketplace. For a start, the United Nations' Economic and Social Council established a protocol, last revised in 1996, for deciding whether an NGO is even worth talking to. These are baseline criteria—but they can serve as a proxy for defining if a group is legitimate.[37] The United Nations says an NGO, to earn its seal of approval, must accept the framework of a "participatory democratic state" and should be nonprofit, nonviolent, and noncriminal.

Governments, worried about potential abuses of growing NGO power, have gotten into the act, generating new guidelines and rules.[38]

The more profound momentum, though, is among civil society organizations themselves. SustainAbility kicked off the most recent round of debate with its provocative 2003 report *The 21st Century NGO*. "Despite being key advocates of corporate accountability, few NGOs have adopted the same rules as their business counterparts," the study contended. "Additional transparency and accountability will become prerequisites for NGO success in entering the mainstream and crucial for retaining their position of trust."[39] The London-based consultancy recommended that groups take steps such as embracing the AA1000 assurance standard, or signing the Global Reporting Initiative. AccountAbility, in fact, has promoted efforts to adapt GRI reporting standards specifically for civil society organizations.[40]

Where is all this leading? The more accountable civil society groups become, the more potent a new capitalist force they can represent in the civil economy ecosystem. Religious bodies, trade unions, and social responsibility advocates have invented ever-more polished templates for how to mobilize the dormant ownership tools of capitalism. When they add the turbocharger of their own transparency and accountability, they are likely to gain greater access to capital, corporate, and government partners.

Of course, not all are ready to make that transition. Many civil society groups remain locked in internal debate, unwilling to adapt their mission to a new capitalist agenda or embrace transparency. Their motives for shareowner activism will remain suspect. Corporate executives have experience stretching back to the Dutch East India Company of grappling with that type of challenge. What is different, though, is the new breed of grassroots lobby that persuasively merges the social and financial interests of citizen investors to form a consensus adequate to wield effective ownership clout. To integrate these pressures, parties across the spectrum need fresh templates for action. We offer them in our concluding chapter.

TAKEAWAYS

- Civil society groups are potent in the new capitalist ecosystem when they align shareowner value with corporate social responsibility.

- Investors tried to press corporate social responsibility as long ago as 1602. But Campaign General Motors, in 1970, opened a new front by harnessing the values of social justice campaigners to the financial power of rising pension fund owners.

- Faith-based citizen groups developed the first working prototype of a civil economy organization pursuing social missions through capital. Ten basic principles underpin their efforts.

- Trade union pension funds pioneered trustee training and Internet mobilization of citizen investors.

- Street protests against globalization pushed more civil society groups such as environmental lobbies to translate their objectives into a business context. They found allies in new capitalist funds.

- Civil society groups can be of any political or social persuasion. They gain power in the market only when they can form consensus with new capitalist funds, and they risk their legitimacy if they are seen abusing ownership interests in favor of other agendas.

- Scholars have begun focusing on the impact of citizen investors, generating findings that will influence the civil economy going forward.

- While mainstream media can be sluggish watchdogs over the capital market, corporate boards have come under unprecedented scrutiny thanks to blogs and Internet publications.

- NGOs often fail to earn a "license to operate" in the investment world because many do not meet the transparency and accountability standards they demand of corporations.

PART FOUR

The New Capitalist Agenda

Action Memos

The New Capitalist Agenda

ere are two stories of modern business life.

On January 3, 2004, the NBC television network began broadcasting *The Apprentice,* a "reality" business game show presided over by Donald Trump, the real estate developer and 1980's business icon. Contestants show off their business acumen, and at the end of each episode, Trump gleefully fires one of them. The contestants learn the path to winning, that is, not being fired: overtake your colleagues either by outperforming them or by destroying them. The show is presumably meant to be a metaphor of the business world: it's a place with many losers and few winners, a place where managers commonly get ahead by using cooperation as a mask for deception, disloyalty, and betrayal. *The Apprentice* paints business as a kind of "circular firing squad," as Yale University's Jeff Sonnenfeld has written.[1] According to NBC's Web site, *The Apprentice* soon became a "cultural phenomenon" among viewers in the key 18–49 age category. "You're fired!" became such a catch phrase that Trump even tried to trademark it.[2]

Eighteen months later, U.K. Prime Minister Tony Blair received a letter from the CEOs of companies responsible for mining more than 10 percent of the world's fossil fuels: powerful people indeed. They had written because Blair was about to chair a conference of the leaders of the world's eight largest industrial nations about how to address climate change. But the corporate leaders' message was not what many environmental campaigners feared. It asked the government to promote a *tougher* regime of emissions controls without which, they argued, their businesses might end up being environmentally unsustainable. This merits repetition: executives of the world's biggest companies were working together to lobby for a more socially responsible regime of environmental regulation.

The Trump story represents a caricature of business with which we are all familiar. The second story represents a new and, to some, puzzling development. But at root, the Downing Street initiative is the civil economy in action. The CEOs who signed the letter, and their boards, had already been urged to behave in this way by many of their civil investors. Remember the eighth rule of the capitalist manifesto? Seek regulations that ensure your operations do not cause collateral damage. Joining the initiative did not require altruism on the part of the CEOs any more than it requires altruism to persuade them to make a profit. It was a rational action to create an even playing field for all energy companies, so that their operations could be sustainable and so benefit their owners, the new capitalists.

This is not to say that Trump is persona non grata in the civil economy. An open marketplace accommodates the activities of a boss such as that depicted in *The Apprentice* as much as it does the actions of the CEOs who wrote to Tony Blair. But it is the chief executives behind the letter whose thinking in this instance most closely represents that of the new capitalists.

In this book, we have tried to set out the different forces shaping the civil economy. First are the new capitalists, the hundreds of millions of owners of our large public companies. Like capitalists of old, they demand that companies be profitable. But because there are so many of them, and because they are so diversified, they also make different demands on companies.

Surrounding these new owners, a new business ecosystem is growing. Shareowners are flexing power as never before. Constitutional reforms are transforming boards of directors. New institutions are being created to monitor company performance, and to do so according to new metrics reflecting the new capitalists' broader concerns. In addition, citizens' groups are finding the capital markets a new avenue through which to influence corporate behavior.

You, the readers of this book, are not just observers of change. You're participants in it. In this concluding chapter, we address what the civil economy means for all of us—for those who work for and manage our giant corporations; for those who invest our own and other's money; for those who monitor company performance or advise on company policy; and for all of us as citizens, workers, savers, and consumers. What specific steps can we take to raise our own game to safeguard our interests and ensure success in this emerging world?

Memo to Corporate Directors and Executives

Our recommendations on how you can secure competitive advantage cover two fields: *management practice* and *management accountability*. At the end of the day, most of our large corporations are owned by millions of people. The time has come to reengineer management thinking to take this bedrock fact into account.

Management Practice

Our first suggestion is to talk the talk. After all, one of the first tasks of a manager is to motivate. In the past, management scholars have agonized about why we devote so much of our lives to the companies that employ us. Is it possible that we dedicate so much human energy and creativity simply to raise quarterly earnings? That seems a hollow explanation. Is it possible that we come to work only to collect the maximum salary? That seems at odds with the selfless behavior and teamwork that researchers, again and again, have found underpins activity in so many good companies. And while organizational psychologists can doubtless tell us why we get satisfaction from teamwork, they tell us little about the goals to which that teamwork is directed.

The civil economy does precisely that. It explains a new and broader motivation for company activity, combining the profit motive with respect for wider social goals. Indeed, the profit motive itself becomes a social goal. As in the past, the prime purpose of a business is to improve the value of the capital invested in it. But today, that capital is the people's capital. Therefore, the effective manager in a civil economy aims to create wealth for all—or at least not to destroy it. Think of the person who sat next to you on the train, or passed you on the sidewalk. Think of the teacher in West Virginia, the car worker in Durban, the retired miner in Wales. Think of the nurse in Sweden, the insurance salesman in Nagoya. These are the ultimate beneficiaries of company profits.

We can predict what new capitalists demand of companies. The blueprint is described in the capitalist manifesto outlined in chapter 3. The ten "rules" tell how to generate the greatest benefit for large numbers of diversified shareowners. But what are the manifesto's implications for the way executives go about the day-to-day task of management? Do you need new practices or new attitudes to meet these new demands?

Yes and no. The first rule of the manifesto is familiar to most managers: *be profitable and create value.* The problem is that it's so familiar that many managers in the conventional economy ignore it, instead spending money on ventures that have little prospect of creating value. Maybe you recognize the phenomenon: dedication and enthusiasm to a business are reflected in excessive optimism about prospects. Then, through the magic of the spreadsheet, that optimism is turned into a complex financial schedule, where scores of untested assumptions create a plan built on sand.

In other words, too many corporate executives believe that they are meeting shareowners' wishes by promoting schemes that look good on paper but don't actually deliver real value. In many cases of corporate scandal, executives will recount that they felt under pressure to "make the numbers." Yet those numbers were their own inventions; they crafted figures to persuade Wall Street that somehow the organization had developed a Midas touch.

Usually the critical numbers presented by failed companies were not just about profitability but also about growth. Enron and WorldCom were, and could have stayed, profitable but slow-growth utilities. It was only executives' grab for chimerical growth that brought them crashing down.

That's why the second rule of the capitalist manifesto is so important. Companies should *grow only where they can create value.* This may seem obvious. But too many managers systematically seek to grow, even though only a few of them will prove successful. Pull out your last business plan, for example. Our guess is that it aims to hold or to gain market share. But not every company can gain market share. Yet as a Bain & Company survey revealed, around 90 percent of companies aim for growth rates that are more than twice that of the economy.[3]

Of course growth is important, and of course the universal owner will want to encourage entrepreneurship. But companies that grow without meeting their cost of capital actually destroy value. And the faster they grow, the faster they destroy that value.

Figure 9-1 describes four options facing a manager: either grow the business or don't grow the business; either earn a return above the cost of capital or earn a return below the cost of capital. Clearly every business would like to be in the upper right quadrant, where it beats its cost of capital *and* grows. But what if it isn't possible to earn your cost of capital? If you can't beat cost of capital, what should you do: grow or decline? In a civil economy, the answer of course is to decline. If you grow when you have no chance of making a true economic profit, you're akin to the apocryphal merchant who loses money on every sale but tries to make up for it in volume. Nevertheless, we see company after company chasing "growth" rather than profitability.

Growth and Return: The Manager's Choice

When plans go wrong, company executives often blame investors for goading them into going for fast returns. When they talk about investors, though, they really are talking about the traders of Wall Street,

FIGURE 9-1

Growth and return: the manager's choice

	Earn below the cost of capital	Earn above the cost of capital
Grow	Maximum value destroyed	Maximum value created
Don't grow	Storm weathered	Opportunities missed

for whom it often makes sense to encourage growth. If companies are growing, then the "volatility" in the value of their shares is likely to be high—which means an opportunity to buy and sell, generating lucrative brokerage fees and trading profits. This all makes a great story for the broker who is trying to persuade a client to buy or sell. No wonder almost every corporate scandal broke out at a company that was growing rapidly, pretending that its profits put it in the upper right quadrant when in fact it was in the upper left.

New capitalists require a different strategy. First, be careful when you talk about "what your shareowners want." Remember that your ultimate shareowners are not hot-money traders; they are everyone. Traders are just traders. They have only a tangential interest in the long-term success of your company. They are mainly interested in events that will create opportunities to buy and sell. Traders are certainly important for price discovery, but they are only the thin veneer atop the ownership base. The real owners are not day traders; they are citizen investors who have a stake in your company's core profit-making ability over time, and they demand proper financial discipline.

It's not that the civil economy is inhospitable to risk. Discipline demands only that managers avoid paying for *indiscriminate* growth. Indeed, if there really are opportunities to grow profitably, new capitalists want those opportunities exploited to the maximum. They are willing to accept significant risks associated with a project, provided they are proportionate to the expected return. Why? Because citizen investors are highly diversified. If one project—indeed, even one company—goes down, it will have had only a small effect on their portfolio. The civil economy supports risk taking but not empire building.

Civil owners are eager to make capital available for good business opportunities. At the same time, they will want to be sure that companies follow the fourth rule: *Don't waste capital*. Companies that have driven excess capital out of their business, often by using new business software, have generated extraordinary benefit. Managers must focus equally on capital minimization as one element of economic profit maximization.

The civil economy also requires new strategies for executive pay. Shareowners want real returns and profitable growth, so you would expect that they would want company employees to be rewarded on those grounds. But the way we calculate remuneration, particularly CEO remuneration, leaves much to be desired.

Employees should be rewarded for performance. That should include incentives related to returns achieved by the company's share-owners. But most employees have only limited control over the share price, so being excessively rewarded in this way is unlikely to be productive. Remember, share price is ultimately the financial scorecard, not the game itself. So incentivize workers, up to and including the CEO, to play their part in the game better, rather than to find ways to bet on the final score.

Also, most of us work for many motives; including, but not limited to, maximizing earnings. Management literature says we prefer a positive working environment, challenges, friendship, teamwork, professionalism, status, the feeling of having made a contribution to something worthwhile. In other words, absolute financial reward is not an omnipotent motivator. So when the third rule of the capitalist manifesto tells you to *pay people fairly to do the right things,* it's not referring just to how you calculate pay. It is about *all* the ways that you manage and reward those who work for you. It is about the culture of a workplace.

According to the fifth rule, citizen owners want companies to *focus where their skills are strongest.* We have already noted that clever spreadsheet analysts can justify almost any business decision: "If you torture the figures for long enough you can get them to confess to anything," journalist Gregg Easterbrook famously wrote. Moreover, the longer the period over which your projections are made, the greater the uncertainty of the result. Yet new capitalists seek sustainability over time. How can you test that business plans make sense, or that the company really is working to its strengths?

Competitive logic can come to your rescue. Companies that meet customer needs better, and at a lower cost than their competitors, are likely to be profitable. Of course, there are millions of customers, and millions of ways to meet their needs. Thus there are many different ways to be successful in business. However, you are unlikely to be successful if someone else can do the job better. Thus you should treat with skepticism any business plan that purports to show a profitable business without giving a credible reason why that business will be the best.

In other words, pay attention to the assumptions behind the figures, as well as to the figures themselves.

Under a civil economy style of management, then, it's better to start the planning process by looking at the skills of the organization and linking them to market opportunity, rather than the other way round. And leave financial modeling to the end of the process, after you have established the competitive strengths of the business. With this approach, you as a manager will rarely have to find an entirely different field of business where the grass is supposedly greener. You'll be able to focus on how to develop and hone your organization's skills to meet customer needs better.

It is that need for improvement that means that you should constantly be seeking to *renew the organization* and boost its performance (rule 6). This is hardly news. It is difficult to think of any company that would still be in business if it were using the same systems, with the same products and the same levels of efficiency, that it had even ten years ago. What is new, however, is that today corporate regeneration must respond to the external forces of accountability that the civil economy has wrought.

Simon Zadek, chief of AccountAbility, describes some of them. The "global goldfish bowl" makes it impossible for you as a manager to do in one place what you don't want to be known for globally. Suppliers and customers are waking up to the fact that there are dangers in trading with companies that do not understand whether or not their behavior might be deemed irresponsible. Branded goods producers have come to that realization after sourcing scandals sullied their reputations. Moreover, it's not just *your* actions that affect your license to operate, it's the actions of your *entire industry*. For example, Zadek notes that "Diageo's very survival as the world's largest and most profitable drinks company depends on its ability to encourage the whole sector to be responsible, since it is the sector's behaviour which will shape the regulatory future."[4]

Taking these observations to their logical conclusion, you need to be aware of the need either to undertake self-policing or, as the eighth rule says, *to seek regulations that ensure operations do not cause collateral damage*. With universal ownership, regulation can be a legitimate way to allow all involved in any industry to cast out those who would try to "win" by racing to the bottom. Eliminating such "short-termism" enables entire industries to thrive over the long term, rather than allowing a single participant to reap outsize but unsustainable short-term profits at the cost of damaging the sector for generations. But you should never abuse regulation. If companies don't *stay clear of partisan politics* (rule 9), they will subvert the citizen owner's authority.

Ultimately, managers need to think about their company's social performance not just because their license to operate might in some way be restricted if they fail to respond to social pressures. In the civil economy, the issue is much bigger than compliance. New capitalists want companies to *treat customers, suppliers, workers, and communities fairly,* as stated in the manifesto's seventh rule, because those customers, suppliers, workers, and communities are also the company's shareowners.

But what does it mean to treat people fairly? It may seem like a nice idea, but is it practical in the real world? The capitalist manifesto may look good on paper, but surely it will work only if everyone lives by the rules. It takes boldness to treat customers well, to eschew destructive growth, to resist kowtowing before the traders on Wall Street, unless everyone else does so. Of course, evidence in this book suggests that if a corporation's survival hinges on chronic rule breaking, market forces will eventually punish it: that is, its financial performance will be undermined and its stock price will fall. "Oh sure," you reply, "but that might be a long way off. If meanwhile I'm the only one obeying the capitalist manifesto, everyone else will benefit at my expense."

Good point. You are in a classic prisoner's dilemma. It goes like this. Imagine you have been unjustly arrested in an unstable country and flung into jail. An interrogator comes to your cell.

"I've got a deal for you," he says. "If you will sign this statement saying Joe, whom we have in the cell next door, is guilty of murder, we will throw him in jail for ten years and let you go, with only one proviso."

You weigh this all up and ask, "What's the one proviso?"

"Well," replies the interrogator, "you go free only if Joe doesn't also sign a statement, saying that you have committed the murder. Otherwise you both stay in jail for eight years."

"OK," you reply pensively. "And what if neither of us signs?"

The investigator pauses and sighs. "Well, since we won't have any statements, we'll have to let you both go after a couple of months. But look, if you just sign the form, there's a real chance I can let you go tomorrow—it all depends on what Joe does."

"But I don't even know Joe," you respond in exasperation. "He could be anyone and everyone."

"Exactly," responds the interrogator.

That is the prisoner's dilemma. In real life, businesspeople often face the dilemma: for example when they decide whether to shortchange a customer, or put pressure on an employee, or tip toxic waste into a canal. Of course, the best solution from a selfish point of view would be to be able to behave badly while everybody else sticks by the rules. But if everyone breaks the rules, there will be trouble. What should any individual do in these circumstances?

Experts in "game theory" have put a lot of work into discovering the "right" solution to the prisoner's dilemma. You might think that there is a clever answer—for example, to play collegially for a few turns and then switch tactics. But the best strategy is a simple one: tit-for-tat. That is, begin the game by assuming the other party will be collegial. If they are, respond by being collegial. Give a negative response only to a negative response. As soon as the other side switches to a collegial response, you switch too. If you play prisoner's dilemma over and over again, research shows, those tactics will bring about the best result, for you and for others.

Now think about the world of the civil economy. How should you treat the billions of owners, customers, suppliers, workers, and citizens? Of course you can benefit at others' expense if you are the only one who breaks the rules while everyone else sticks to them. But it is simply unrealistic to believe that you can get away with that strategy. We'd all be better off if everyone played by the rules. But how do you enforce them? Start by assuming that everyone is well intentioned, and then play tit-for-tat. If we all play by those rules, we optimize the outcome for everyone.

In other words, the science of games theory has reached the same conclusion as the philosophers and teachers of old.[5] Only they called it the Golden Rule: do unto others as you would have them do unto you. There should be consideration of all interests. And this is made possible because in the civil economy, unlike earlier times, we all represent all interests: citizens, owners, consumers, employees. In reaching this conclusion, we are not trying to make a moral judgment. We are simply saying, from a hard-nosed, bottom-line perspective, that new capitalists are better off if corporations conduct business according to the Golden Rule.

Games theorists, however, make one simplifying assumption. They assume we all know whether the other player acted in our best interest or not. In business, though, it's not so easy. You don't really know until it's too late whether the supplier made every effort to ensure the goods were up to scratch, whether the fund manager really undertook his or her duty of ownership. Even worse, the other party might have thought that he or she had behaved fairly when *you* did not. In that case, in the game of tit-for-tat, you would end up getting punished for an action that you were unaware you had taken.

That is why the last rule of the capitalist manifesto is so important. *Communicate what you are doing and be accountable for it.* Unless everyone understands the rules of the game, we cannot successfully escape the prisoner's dilemma. You as a manager need to clarify to your employees, your customers, your suppliers, and your owners just how you are interpreting the rules. What is the security of staff employment, and why? What are the services that you will deliver according to what standards? How do you plan to build shareowner value? This clarity becomes ever more important as the services that we offer become more and more complex, where it is costly, if not impossible, for us to know how well a job has been done, and have to trust that suppliers will behave toward us as they would have us behave toward them.

This is not a new problem. Hippocrates, the Greek father of medicine, knew that the patient could never properly understand or evaluate the specialized skills that he taught his students, and he also knew that if the students abused their training, they could cause enormous damage. Therefore he made his students swear the Hippocratic oath, that they would not abuse their knowledge.

Today's managers in the emerging civil economy also have skills and powers over money, products, and people. They too might reflect on the appropriate code by which they should conduct themselves. It would be based on the need to maximize value for the shareowners of their enterprise, to be open about their activities, to avoid harm to society, and to treat all stakeholders fairly.

Management Accountability

Good management practice is likely to be sustained only if it is accompanied by structures that ensure that management is accountable to its owners. Here are a few practical ways you can ensure that such structures are in place. Not all will be appropriate for your company—that will depend on its size and circumstances. But hopefully these ideas can be useful pointers.

Make board elections meaningful. Every public company should have rules allowing shareowners to both elect and remove directors by majority rule, and to influence the nomination of candidates for the board. This is a fundamental requirement. Boards must be accountable to shareowners, and must be *seen* to be accountable to shareowners.

Put critical shareowner issues to the vote. In a few countries, boards have exclusive power to make vital decisions affecting value—such as whether to impose takeover defenses—without consulting shareowners. This arrogation of authority has no place in a civil economy. Big decisions with the potential to affect investor rights dramatically should be subject to a vote, giving the outcome legitimacy and signaling the extent of shareowner confidence in management and the board. If you are uncertain about what is "vital" and what is not, remember that the owners are entitled to the residual value in your business; if the matter under consideration fundamentally affects either residual value or the nature of the business going forward, err on the side of shareowner input through the ballot box.

One issue on which companies might want to seek shareowner approval is CEO pay, which has too regularly escaped shareowner oversight. To ensure that the board's remuneration committee is truly serving universal owners, its report could go to an annual nonbinding vote of confidence. British, Dutch, Swedish and Australian companies already use such ballots, injecting a healthy scrutiny that helps legitimize CEO pay and keep it in line with performance.

Split the chairman's and chief executive's jobs. Everyone in a public company should be accountable. But when the positions of board leader and management chief are fused, the CEO can essentially become his or her own boss. This isn't about building rival power centers in a single company. The jobs are very different. The board chairman should be an independent nonexecutive who can ensure that directors are on duty for all shareowners, including helping, assessing, and, if necessary, replacing the CEO.

Professionalize the corporate governance office. Many companies have named a corporate governance officer, usually the company secretary. But the title is only a start. The time has come to professionalize the job with recognized ethical and training standards and authority. Today most serve as compliance officers, responsible for ensuring that the company meets all governance regulations; or they behave as investor relations officers, promoting the company's stances to the market. Both are noble jobs. But governance involves other tasks, too. Governance executives need to have a native understanding of new capitalist interests if they are to advise directors on strategy. They need exposure to shareowners through regular dialogue, workshops, and one-on-one meetings. Only in that way will they avoid getting infected by the "groupthink" that sometimes develops at all organizations, including corporate offices, and understand the owners' viewpoint. Finally, consider making the governance officer report to the board and the independent chairman, rather than to management.

Modernize reporting. The board audit committee should press to make sure that an outside audit—by accounting or other bodies—includes an assessment of a company's extra-financial assets through reliance on civil economy-style standards such as the Global Reporting Initiative or value-analysis methods developed by an accounting firm. Every company should be reporting to shareowners on the full range of things they need to know to carry out their role as owners. Conventional accounting alone doesn't do that, so when the annual report is prepared, ensure that it contains all the information the company's new capitalist owners might want to know. Remember, the Coloplast experiment and Rivel research suggest you'll be rewarded if you provide such information.

Empower a stakeholder relations effort. No company lives in a self-contained environment. Stakeholders—employees, customers, suppliers, regulators, and others—clearly affect a company's culture and profitability. Directors need a regular channel to monitor that the company is nurturing productive relationships with key stakeholders, to ensure that such constituents are assets contributing fully to long-term value, rather than hidden liabilities set to explode sometime in the future.

Memo to the Institutional Investor

Institutional investors are the motor of the civil economy. As we saw in chapter 4, there are hurdles to overcome if these motors are to run at maximum efficiency. The investment industry has largely been structured around the buying and selling of securities and the gathering of assets, not around prudent ownership of companies.

Nevertheless, investors have greatly increased their clout in the marketplace in the past twenty years. Today, pension funds and their fund managers are engaged in taking the next steps to fulfill their fiduciary duty to conduct successful stewardship of companies. While the fund management industry obsesses about its ability to create "alpha" (that is, to outperform the market), in reality what's known as "beta" (that is, the general market return) still largely determines whether funds can actually pay the pensions they promise.

Let's start our discussion of institutional investors by looking at management practice.

Management Practice

There are four key things that institutional investors, as agents of new capitalists, can do to best fulfill their roles.

Cooperate with each other as co-owners of companies. In buying and selling shares, fund managers can compete fiercely. But in improving company performance, they have common cause. The most effective institutions will be those who can find a mechanism for working together. These might be informal networks. Hermes, for example, has people employed full time to establish relationships with other fund managers, so that they can share perspectives on problem companies and issues. They can do so through industry bodies, such as the International Corporate Governance Network or the Global Institutional Governance Network, or through the good offices of commercial services.[6] Opportunities for pension funds and fund managers to join such initiatives are multiplying, not just in pressing for better performance from the companies in which they invest, but in a broader promotion of shareowner rights.[7]

Professionalize ownership skills as distinct from stock trading. For some funds, this may seem paradoxical—surely the aim should be to bring together the ownership and trading of shares. But in fact, the skills and disciplines of share traders are very different from those of owners. By analogy, the person who gambles on the horse race may well know a lot about the sport, but may not necessarily be the best individual to train the horses. Ownership is likely to require new people with new skills, which can then be integrated as a core part of investment management, rather than as an afterthought or as a checklist in a compliance exercise.

Develop a program for shareowner engagement, even activism. Investors used to consider activism a last resort. Funds far preferred to sell out of troubled companies rather than take them on. Today, many managers are building "high-conviction" portfolios with very large holdings in a smaller number of companies. This means you can't sell out of problem companies; you have to act as an owner. Handled skillfully, returns can be superior.

Encourage long-term risk research. Be vigorous in developing innovative means to pinpoint extra-financial risks that portfolio companies face. One pilot project—the Enhanced Analytics Initiative—is an example. Members steer a percentage of brokerage commission money only to investment analysts that incorporate recognized but hard-to-measure risks, such as governance, workforce management, and environmental liability. New capitalists have a direct interest in research that routinely addresses these risks.

Match Tactics with Structures and Incentives

The four new strategies just mentioned can improve portfolio performance. But just like companies, investment institutions can sustain gains only if they match tactics with the right structures and incentives. Therefore you might also want to heed the following tips.

Practice what you preach. Funds cannot credibly demand governance standards of corporations that they will not meet themselves. Catering to citizen investors, fund managers should be transparent about how the fund operates, pays staff, acts as a steward of savers' capital, and manages conflicts of interest. A good early model exists in the International Corporate Governance Network's Statement on Institutional Shareholder Responsibilities.[8] Equally, a civil owner fund should be accountable to its members or client investors, as well as its sponsor or management. It should have an active and skilled governing body whose representatives can legitimately speak for member interests—thanks, for example, to meaningful trustee elections, in the case of pension plans.

Align fund manager actions with investor interests. Eradicating conflicts of interest is only half the job. Funds should ensure that agents are acting positively in alignment with new capitalists' interests. That means overhauling money manager incentives that today routinely reward short-term performance and narrow financial analysis. For example, the International Finance Corporation, the investing arm of the World Bank, has linked remuneration for portfolio managers to their weighing of long-term perspectives and extra-financial risks. Mutual funds and money managers could make similar pay ideas standard across the industry. At a minimum, funds should orient compensation bonus calculations to longer-term performance.

When all is said and done, will your institution reap the benefit of these actions? Evidence suggests it will. Well-managed companies are worth more, as studies show. If you actively promote optimal corporate management, you are more likely to gain over those who follow old-school habits of ignoring or skirting risks at companies in their portfolios.

Furthermore, money managers will find that, like all civil economy developments, the demand for them to take on ownership responsibilities is likely to become more intense. It is spurred by the media, by retirees and savers, by government regulations, and even by companies themselves demanding more responsible owners. Even the most traditional funds feel the brunt of rising demands from citizen investors. To be successful, more fund managers are having to demonstrate not only that they boast good relative and absolute performance, but that they are doing their part to ensure proper stewardship of the economy.

Memo to Individual Investors and Beneficiaries

In the old economy, companies were the focal point. But at the center of the civil economy universe is the individual citizen, the new capitalist, with stakes in a pension plan, retirement savings account, or insurance annuity. As the civil economy matures, they—you—have the means to make key decisions over how assets are managed. If you do nothing with those tools, financial agents are more likely to drive like that proverbial rental car. If, on the other hand, you wield those tools, you can claim influence over the financial future.

We are not talking about slitting open scads of thick envelopes from portfolio companies, poring through volumes of annual reports, and dutifully voting each proxy ballot. We acknowledge that few individual investors have the time, expertise, or desire to do that. Indeed, few choose their own stocks, preferring instead to invest through collective vehicles such as mutual funds and unit trusts. Therefore, the route to securing the investors' interests boils down to one main decision: which agent(s) will you pick to manage your savings?

Choosing an Agent

The choice used to be easy, and for some it still is. Some distant authority—pension officials at the company you work for, or the state, or the insurance plan—made the selections for you. But those days are coming to an end as sponsors shift risks to employees and savers—from defined-benefit to defined-contribution retirement plans, for instance.

Where some central authority still does hold decisive sway in overarching investment decisions without anyone representing the ultimate beneficiary, the system fails the most elemental test of accountability. Such a lack of accountability is likely to corrode the value-generating power of ownership. To protect your assets, lobby for meaningful investor representation, and ask for information from the pension or savings fund. Or, if you can, find another agent to manage your money.

Let's address the job of shopping for agents, by which we mean financial planners, investment advisers, money managers, mutual funds, insurance companies, and the like. You might well be tempted to throw up your hands in despair. Who but an expert could really tell which competitor is aligned with my interests?

But wait: there is precedent for this sort of shift in consumer decision making. Remember when there was only one telephone company in each market? People had virtually no choice in service, price, or quality. It seemed an immutable fact of life. With little notion that things could be different, we accommodated ourselves to having telecommunications parameters set for us by the monopoly. When competition appeared, many of us felt wholly unprepared to make choices. Even the very idea of tailoring telephone service to individual preferences seemed alien. But we soon learned what questions to ask, what features to look for, what prices to check. Moreover, by choosing a phone service to meet our specific needs, we found we could get far more value for our money than we ever did in the old days.

Nest eggs that help define our lives in old age, our health care choices, and our ability to nurture families are far more critical than the cost of telephone calls. Yet today too many of us cede to others the power to control decisions about our savings. These agents may and—as we have discussed—often do face business pressures that make them act in ways independent of our interests. When that happens, it costs each of us real money. But we now often have choices. We can identify which funds and agents are structured to work for us.

The Key Criterion

Here, then, is our single most important recommendation to individuals in the civil economy: *select funds based on their readiness to pledge real allegiance to you.* Start with the fees they charge; both the absolute amount and the structure. Fund companies are entitled to earn a profit, but fees should be both reasonable and transparent to you; after all, it's your capital at risk. Then consult the increasing number of both free and paid services that grade funds on the basis of their own governance and stewardship records, as well as their performance abilities. Or you can ask key questions yourself after comparing financial performances. Are portfolio managers paid in ways that value long-term performance and consideration of extra-financial drivers of value? Are fund directors independent? Is there a potential for conflicts of interest? How does the fund vote its shares? What resources does it have to act as an engaged owner of portfolio companies? Rule out any agent that cannot or will not respond. Then make your pick from among those with the best profile as value generators and new capitalist-style owners.

Memo to Analysts, Advisers, and Auditors

It's not news that information is power. And the fact that information that should have helped investors has been misdirected and misused is old news. What we have tried to illustrate in this book is the systemic nature of the abuse of information and a blueprint for avoiding it in the future.

Use Information Wisely and Accountably

That blueprint starts with two imperatives to analysts, advisers, and auditors. First, do not confuse agents for principals, the ultimate owners of capital. Second, understand what drives economic value creation in the twenty-first century. Neither of those objectives is easy, but both are attainable. Following those rules will, in the first instance, provide commercial advantages to early adopters and, more broadly, harness information to fuel sustainable economic growth.

Legitimacy comes from accountability. That is the bedrock on which the civil economy rests. To whom should all players be ultimately accountable? The citizen investor.

In the real world, it's not always so easy. As we know, accountability typically flows through a cascade of agents. Let's assume that the person who has put his capital at risk is a citizen saver, in this case, a worker named Jim. Call him the principal. Jim belongs to a defined-contribution pension plan that has trustees. They are Jim's Agent Number 1. The trustees of the plan, who have good intentions but provide no means for Jim to elect someone to represent him, rely on outside advisers (Agent Number 2). Those advisers, though generally responsible, are hired by the plan. They are steps removed from Jim, and so they may readily overlook that they are ultimately responsible to him. The advisers recommend putting Jim's capital, along with that of thousands of others, into a particular mutual fund (Agent Number 3) that the same advisers have recommended time and again to a number of similar pension plans. So Jim's plan is just one among many to the mutual fund portfolio manager (Agent Number 4). The portfolio manager may, in turn, rely on an analyst (Agent Number 5) to suggest a particular investment. That analyst, of course, is compensated either by the mutual fund or a third-party service, and almost certainly has no clue that his or her recommendations will affect Jim's monthly check.

That chain of accountability can and does work, as long as each link is loyal and accountable to the one immediately before it. Any break—the analyst being swayed by an investment bank, which is influenced by the company the analyst is following; the pension adviser being paid by a mutual fund for access; the trustees acting as agents of the company rather than the retirees—can undermine the whole chain. That's why infamous public relations shills Jack Grubman and Henry Blodgett earned such public scorn. They weren't loyal to the party ahead of them in the chain: the portfolio managers to whom they provided advice. And they certainly were not loyal to the ultimate principals, the Jims and Janes whose pensions were at risk. Rather, they danced to the tune of whoever paid the highest check.

Imperatives for Analysts, Advisers, and Auditors

How do you avoid Grubman and Blodgett's fate? Think of accountability as something that flows to you from the principal.

Never confuse the agent for the principal. If you see a weak link in the accountability chain, point it out, avoid it, and try to get to the link above it.

Be free of conflicts. Don't sell products, services, or even "access" that, at best, allows your competitors to claim you have a conflict and, at worst, encourages law enforcement officials to show up at your door with a subpoena to prove you have conflicts. Even if you are convinced that any conflicts you have are potential or theoretical, make sure you disclose and mitigate them with the goal of ending them over time.

If you don't have conflicts, make it a selling point. CreditSights is a bond-rating agency. Ennis Knupp is a pension adviser. Glass Lewis is a proxy-voting agency. All are stealing market share from better-established, larger rivals by emphasizing their undivided loyalty to their clients. Being accountable is good business.

Developing New Standards of Performance Assessment

You are the information experts; you measure what works and what doesn't in this evolving free market. As we saw in chapter 7, both the drivers of the economy, and the ways to measure who benefits from them, are evolving. The old metrics are still valid and necessary but are hardly sufficient. That opens a huge opportunity for creative, nimble information agents. There is a world of business to be won by those who can best inform new capitalist investors. The emerging information moguls can be new, smaller entrants looking for a niche or large, long-established entities seeking to evolve along with the economy.

Move beyond the traditional. The Coloplast experiment and Rivel Research (chapter 7) demonstrate just how much power there is in providing context to the numbers. Develop metrics to help your clients harness that power.

Be approximately right rather than exactly wrong. Contingent liabilities and uncertain future revenue streams are inherently hard to value. They may or may not happen; if they do happen, the size of the impact is uncertain, and the time frame over which they may occur is unknown. That is a trifecta of uncertainty sure to challenge the smartest brains in the world. And it has. Wall Street's financial engineers deal with hard-to-value assets and liabilities regularly. Rather than try to nail down an exact number in advance, those financial experts accept a range of probabilities and try to explain the validity of various calculation methodologies.[9] By contrast, corporate accounting seeks exact numbers. Even worse, the exact number chosen too often is zero, since measurers consider low-probability but high-impact events—such as the *Exxon Valdez* oil spill or Merck's recall of the drug Vioxx—so remote as to not be worth noting—until they explode into major threats to corporate profitability and even survival. Remember, just because something is hard to value doesn't mean it shouldn't be reported.

Be clear on objectives; communicate the message. You need to be clear about the message you are communicating. For example, does the information aim to help traders decide how to buy and sell, or does it aim to create the best economic outcome for the company and its shareowners? And users need to know it is the truth, the whole truth, and nothing but the truth. Of course, sometimes these questions are complex and multidimensional. Sometimes there are huge payoffs in unlikely situations and no payoff in others. Yet even here, you can find ways to present information that people can understand, such as by using qualitative measures or visual displays. Indeed, some financial engineers use 3-D mapping technologies to clearly display multidimensional probabilistic outcomes.

Memo to Civil Economy Groups

The civil economy is erasing the line that once divided investors from community-based advocates. You may be, all at the same time, a pensioner, shareowner, trade union member, taxpayer, and member of a hunting club. No matter what hat you wear, you have an interest now in mobilizing capital to accomplish your financial and social objectives. If you participate in a social advocacy group, this new situation opens doors for action.

Expanding Clout

As described in chapter 8, leading-edge civil society organizations have pioneered a working prototype of "sustainable engagement." The ten principles we identified in that chapter will help a civil economy organization operate effectively and credibly in the once-alien terrain of capital markets. If they wish to expand their clout further, such bodies need to lead themselves to the next stage of development. Here are sample directions for that journey.

Build a grassroots network. Civil economy groups, though they purport to speak for great numbers of citizens in the emerging investor class, consistently punch well below their weight in shaping policy at the political level. That's because most are narrow in focus. Either they represent a discrete group—say, pension fund executives—or address a distinct policy—say, climate change. Yet the most powerful currency in politics, as any lobbyist knows, is the ability to influence votes or campaign contributions. The shareowner community has vast potential to rally votes or even generate mass targeted contributions, since funds represent the interests of tens of millions of citizen savers.

So far, though, no group in any country has surfaced with the mandate, capacity, and ambition to serve as a populist tribune of the investor class. The potential is immense. Think of the U.S. Council of Institutional Investors, which directly brings together top professionals from 140 pension funds. Then think of AARP, the advocacy group for older Americans, which boasts a whopping 36 million direct grassroots members. AARP has uninterrupted networking lines to its supporters, giving it muscle in political contests. Civil economy groups have the potential to recruit similar numbers and marshal equivalent clout to push shareowner-friendly legislation and regulation. But they can only do so if they develop an AARP for the investor class.

Heal thyself. Civil society organizations are notorious for their own inadequate governance. To earn a proverbial "license" to operate in the civil economy, they must address this challenge head-on. Groups cannot credibly demand accountability, transparency, and fresh thinking in the corporate boardroom if they themselves fall short of meeting the same challenges. Every civil economy group should undertake, in the first instance, a self-assessment to test its own governance. Does the Web site provide full information about board members and duties, staff, funding, election procedures, financial controls, and internal channels for dissent? Can members participate meaningfully at the highest levels of policy making? If not, make the appropriate changes. If best-practice governance standards do not as yet exist in a market for civil economy groups, bring peers together to create them.

Lobby mutual fund boards. U.S. regulators have opened up a new avenue for civil economy groups and other investors who are ruffled by mutual funds' investment practices. Boards are now supposed to be 75 percent independent of the parent company and, if the rule survives challenge, the chair is also meant to be independent. Since mutuals pool so much capital, these boards have enormous potential power, but few have paid them more than the slightest attention. The next step civil groups can take is to watch and lobby those boards much as they would any corporate board. Directors should be working to abolish conflicts of interest, cut unnecessary costs to clients, and ensure that each fund deploys meaningful stewardship resources when investing in equity. If directors are not accomplishing those tasks, civil economy groups now have some means to bring them to account.

Supply resources to trustees. Pension fund trustee boards suffer from a shortage of skills and research. But that is an opening civil economy groups can fill. Training courses, briefings, and toolkits such as those pioneered by Just Pensions can have an important impact. So could a think tank that generates regular policy guidance to trustees.

Memo to Politicians and Policy Makers

How can a free market work to social purpose? That is an old challenge for policy makers, but the civil economy opens a route to entirely new solutions. Laws and legislation no longer serve only as instruments to constrain corporations. Rather, they can be channels giving new capitalists the means to ensure that enterprises to which they have entrusted their savings operate in citizens' interests. Of course, that means there must be citizen investors to whom voice can be given. The rise of the civil economy therefore depends on two hugely important developments, which politicians and policy makers can foster.

Supporting the Civil Economy

First, ownership of companies must have spread broadly enough that corporate boards must take the presence of new capitalists into account when defining goals.[10] We have shown in chapter 1 that this condition is already in place in much of the developed world. Civil ownership is not yet embedded enough in emerging and transitional markets, but it is likely to become so as growth continues and income becomes more widely spread.

Second, citizen investors must be able to translate their savings into economic influence. Here is where politicians and policy makers have enormous opportunities. They can help citizens find efficient ways to channel their savings into financial instruments that offer economic influence as a driver of returns. And they can introduce rights and powers that enable citizen savers to bring their interests to the fore.

Think about assembling a civil economy in ways that mirror the astonishing success we have experienced in building civil societies around the world. Today's politicians and policy makers have the ability to draft a new constitution for capitalism, just as their forebears wrote a constitution for the nation. This mission can be a political goldmine for parties who grasp its potential.

You can build civil economies with catalytic innovations on minimal budgets. The most effective results come from intervention with a light touch, surgical adjustment of regulation and law, allowing market forces to do the heavy lifting. In fact, governments should see their role less as "players" in the civil economy and more as "rule makers and referees." Public policy should promote civil ownership institutions such as pension funds, and ensure that they are configured to act fully on behalf of new capitalist savers. At the same time, government should empower citizen investors with information they can use to hold their organizations accountable.

The goal is not to assume economic power on behalf of the people, or to microregulate corporate behavior. Instead, public policy in a civil economy endeavors to reunite ownership with authority, thus giving power back to citizen savers. Empowered owners can be an antidote to public alienation from globalization as a distant and unaccountable force controlling nations and manipulating communities. Engaged new capitalists can bolster the public legitimacy of private enterprise, and they can compel corporations to address as bottom-line risk factors the sustainability and social responsibility of their operations. In addition, empowered citizen investors are likely to foster a culture of competitiveness and performance, producing more wealth and employment.

The beauty of the equation—small public expenditure yielding big results—is that it could be a winning platform if you are a political leader under pressure to spur growth, employment, and social justice when there is little money in the public till. It is also a roadmap for international organizations such as the World Bank, the United Nations, and the OECD.

Growing a Civil Economy

The following ideas for a public policy agenda could accelerate the spread of a civil economy.

Ensure economic democracy. Many governments encourage citizen savers to invest in companies but then abet practices that deny shareowners votes and influence. Companies can issue nonvoting shares, for instance, or create pyramid structures. Both concentrate power in the hands of a minority. Advocates contend that such measures ensure that someone is responsible for undertaking ownership oversight. There is a greater danger, though, that such structures simply disenfranchise citizen investors. In general, governments should encourage economic democracy based on the principle of one share, one vote.

Encourage collective investment vehicles such as pension funds, which create broad ownership. Big pools of capital allow ownership of corporations to be widely spread. They can give citizen investors collective voice. They are the liquidity that lubricates the capital markets, provides growth capital, and allows greater risk taking. Moreover, they ensure that workers have access to retirement savings that complement traditional state social security systems. Policy makers should ensure that such institutions are encouraged and safeguarded.

This issue is of urgent importance. Around the world, where corporate pensions do already exist, arrangements are in a considerable state of flux. Historically, companies mainly offered employees a defined-benefit plan. Joining them was simple; usually it came automatically when you got your job or shortly thereafter. Firms found them cheap to administer. Actuaries set terms so that those who died young "subsidized" those who lived longer, thus sharing the overall cost. The corporate sponsor underwrote the plans.

These schemes worked well when there were large employers offering stable employment. But in an economy increasingly characterized by labor mobility, rapid change, and self-employment, too many people can now fall through the pension safety net.

Further, in an effort to reduce costs, corporations have closed many defined-benefit schemes, replacing them with long-term savings plans based on individual worker contributions. Often these plans are tailored, highly regulated, and relatively expensive. In Britain, for example, a private "stakeholder pension" will cost around 1.5 percent *per year,* largely because of regulatory costs. This annual rate will translate into fees of around 40 percent of all the money saved over the life of the pension. Clearly there needs to be a more efficient way to channel citizens' money into long-term savings.

Foster responsibility. As money is pooled into collective funds, it can drive companies toward economic growth and social responsibility. Two policy strategies can unlock such benefits. First, you can shape trust laws to make each fund accountable to the employees and pensioners who are members of the plan. Many jurisdictions do this already. Second, you can require funds to disclose whether or not they undertake ownership duties.

Revolutionize audits of pension funds. New capitalists might reasonably assume that even if the agents managing their pension money snooze while value leaks away, auditors and actuaries are there to blow the whistle on poor fiduciary practices. If so, they would be wrong. Typically, the auditor and the actuary have neither an obligation nor a motivation to evaluate the risks of a fund's stewardship practices.[11] Independent audits of pension funds do take place, just as outside auditors inspect the financial statements of corporations. But they merely check whether officials have obeyed accounting and actuarial conventions when compiling the numbers. Audits of pension funds do not assess equally vital matters that bear directly on the integrity of a fund's stewardship. They fail to judge—or even to mention—whether those running a pension fund control adequately for conflicts of interest, say, between the corporation sponsoring the plan and the members. Audits fail to assess whether agents are marshaling and measuring all available tools in a cost-effective manner to enhance and protect member savings. And they make no comment on the quality of a trustee board's or management's capacity to serve fund members. Moreover, the auditor is responsible to the managers, not the current and former employees who rely on the fund. Firms are hired exclusively by the trustee board or the plan sponsor.

You can propel the civil economy by redesigning statutory obligations of the pension fund audit. First, the audit's purpose should be recast to ensure that the exercise is accountable to plan members as well as the sponsor. Second, the outside inspection should in fact test for the integrity of stewardship in addition to compliance with accounting rules. A simple step would be to require the pension fund to supply detailed information about if and how it acts as an owner.

Modernize fund trustee governance. Fund oversight is a critical objective in any civil economy public policy. You can spur funds to act like owners by ensuring that a certain percentage of pension and insurance fund trustees are elected by the employees/savers themselves. You can mandate architecture that empowers trustee boards. Government policy could aim to ensure that trustee boards meet high disclosure standards so that members can readily monitor whether their funds truly are exercising ownership responsibilities. Share voting records, for instance, could be made available. Funds could disclose trustee attendance records, plus details of the trustees' professional backgrounds and potential conflicts. Policies on management of conflicts could be clear and public. Members should be able to tell if and how their collective savings are helping press companies to improve records on financial, social, environmental, and ethical practices. Further, policies could encourage new levels of trustee training, conflict management, disclosure, and ethics.

Recruit public-sector financial bodies to push accountability. Today we see anomalies in the way public bodies treat the financial levers at their disposal. For example, the United Nations strongly advocates corporate social responsibility—but is only now getting around to addressing whether its own pension system uses its influence to achieve these goals. On the other hand, certain governments have been innovative in enlisting financial tools to bolster civil economy public policies—pointing the way for other markets. For instance, the U.K. government had the Bank of England found ProNed, which jump-started corporate board recruitment of high-quality nonexecutive directors. The Brazilian Development Bank, a state-controlled lending institution, now sets minimum corporate governance standards before investing in a company. So does the World Bank Group's International Finance Corporation. The national Canada Pension Plan takes long-term corporate issues into account when it invests. And some countries are mulling rules that would encourage civil service pension fund investments to consider governance, including a demand for governance ratings at companies in which they invest. Bovespa, Brazil's leading stock exchange, created a premium trading channel—the Novo Mercado—for companies meeting higher accountability and transparency standards. So have the Bangkok and Milan exchanges. Using these types of capital levers, you can spur better corporate performance without direct intervention in the market.

Drive funds to address long-term extra-financial risks. A multitude of options can wean private-sector funds away from short-term, uncivil investing. The United Kingdom, for instance, helped sponsor the Carbon Trust, which bankrolls investor-oriented research on greenhouse gas emissions and climate change. More important, London adopted a simple disclosure rule in 2000 that must be considered the archetype of new capitalist public policy. Under the regulation, each private-sector fund had to state annually whether it addressed social responsibility in its investment strategies. A fund could fully comply by declaring that it wanted nothing to do with the topic. It turned out, however, that funds feared losing market share if they admitted utter disinterest. So at almost no cost to the Treasury, the rule triggered a cascade of fresh institutional investor focus on civil economy factors affecting corporations.

You can go farther. Laws in most capital markets require listed companies to commission an outside audit of financial statements. In a civil economy, companies can be asked to demonstrate either that they meet acceptable governance standards when they go into the stock market for equity capital, or explain why they don't. States can spur use of governance and social responsibility ratings or assessments by requiring such evaluations as part of the annual audit. Or they can rely on incentives instead of directives. Public policy can grant favorable tax, red tape, or other treatment to corporations that have such ratings done. Alternatively, they can take the disclosure route and obligate companies to declare regularly whether they have commissioned such independent assessments and, if not, why not. Our preference, consistent with light-touch, governmental regulation, is disclosure.

Overhaul reporting standards. You can spur market players to accelerate reform of accounting and reporting standards to include under-measured drivers of value such as human capital, intangibles, and social, environmental, governance, and ethical risks and assets. Policy should nurture experimentation but avoid proliferation of conflicting standards. The process of developing standards should be transparent and inclusive of market participants with a stake in the outcome.

Strengthen corporate audits. In some markets, rules fail to charge the outside independent auditors with attesting to the integrity of a board's stewardship. They can even ignore "puffery" as long as the company obeys the letter of accounting rules. Worse, markets are unclear whether the auditor works for the corporate management, the board, or the shareowners. To advance the civil economy, we need to end the confusion. The outside audit should be conducted for the shareowners. And it should issue a judgment not only on whether the audit complies with rules, but whether the accounts represent a "true and fair" picture of the company, and how the board is following practices designed to align managerial performance with shareowner interest.

Reengineer foreign aid. Nations with robust corporate governance traditions can reinvent overseas development aid programs to nurture indigenous civil economy institutions in struggling countries. One model is the United States' Center for International Private Enterprise, which helps build civil economy organizations such as director-training institutes in emerging markets. Another model is the Global Corporate Governance Forum. Backed by the OECD, housed at the World Bank, and financed by donor countries, the forum encourages local market corporate governance improvements.

Encourage best practice. As a policy maker, you can set minimum standards for various market participants, such as credit-rating agencies. But you can also publicly state what criteria are necessary to gain governmental imprimatur so as to open the field to more competitors. Moreover, you can reevaluate those standards periodically, lest they become tools of entrenchment for insiders rather than supports for capital markets.

Memo to Economists and Researchers

We have seen how new capitalists are creating profound changes in the way large companies—key drivers of our economic prosperity—are owned and made accountable. This opens a whole new field of inquiry for economists and researchers.

In chapter 2, we noted that, to a degree, economics has been a victim of its own success. Over time, economists discovered that they can use elegant mathematical models to describe much market behavior. To gain that mathematical precision, however, they made many simplifying assumptions, which often divorced economics from the real world—and from many of the interesting questions it might have addressed.[12]

If you took an introductory economics course, you will have encountered these assumptions. For instance, that there is often perfect competition where no company enjoys a competitive advantage, or that there is continuous liquidity and a continuous market to provide price discovery. Or, crucially, that the firm is an institution whose aim is to "maximize profit." But few economists asked whether this was indeed the case. Fewer still asked what constitutes profit, or how or for whom that profit is made. Yet if you work in business, you know that the answer to these questions varies enormously from company to company.

Equally, you know that how an enterprise answers these questions helps determine whether that company will grow and prosper.

So the civil economy is a call to action for our economic thinkers. Economics needs another starting point. It needs to focus on the phenomena we see in the world and help us to explain them, even if that means abandoning certain elegant theoretical constructs. To most people it would seem self-evident that the constitution of a company, or its ownership, or the way it measures success, or the way in which it is monitored, or the actions of civil society, will affect what it does. If the economists' starting point is that firms are "black boxes" that can be assumed to maximize profits, this precludes at a stroke some of the most interesting questions we might want to ask about company behavior.

Happily, some economists and historians take a different, less mathematical approach. David Landes, professor emeritus at Harvard, has considered what characteristics of a society would be most likely to nurture growth and prosperity. He concluded that they would be ones that "knew how to operate, manage and build the instruments of production ... [and] ... impart this knowledge and know how to the young ... [c]hoose people for jobs by competence and relative merit ... afford opportunity for individual or collective enterprise ... [a]llow people to enjoy the fruits of their labour ... This ideal society would also be honest ... People would believe that honesty is right (also that it pays) and would live and act accordingly. [13]

Today the challenge is to help new capitalists better understand how the genius of the giant corporations we all co-own can be vehicles to achieve social purpose. What structures and cultures can help manage production, transfer knowledge, afford opportunity, and promote honesty? Here is an agenda for research by a new breed of economist: a civil economist. Answers would contribute critically to prosperity and social welfare.

- Economic theory says that companies should maximize profits for their owners. Yet most of us would observe that although many companies behave well, most fall short of this ideal. What factors stop companies from fully meeting owners' interests? What bits of the capitalist manifesto do they find most difficult to implement, and why?

- Economic theory is well aware of the principal-agency problem. In a nutshell: if you delegate a task to an agent, he or she may not carry out that task as you would wish, and hence will require the right incentives to do the job properly. How then can we best design the circle of accountability we met in part I to ensure that companies are run for their citizen investors? Is it likely to vary from company to company, within various industries or economic sectors, or from country to country?

- Economic theory understands that information is important. How does the information produced by companies, auditors, and others affect behavior? How can output be redesigned to generate the most beneficial outcome, rather than simply assisting with share-trading decisions?

To address these questions, civil economists will need to gain cross-disciplinary expertise in psychology, political science, organizational behavior, and law, as well as finance and statistics. In doing so, they will be returning to the roots of their subject. Remember, Adam Smith was a professor of moral philosophy. He knew only too well that successful business can only exist and commercial activity could only be based on rules and justice. "Society," he said, "cannot subsist amongst those who are ready to hurt one another." [14] That is why, a century and a half years later, Alfred Marshall noted that the success of companies depended on a "spirit of honesty and uprightness in commercial matters," as well as laws, institutions, customs and practice, information flows, and the rest. [15]

Today, we tend to view corporations as the instruments of capital. That is also the starting point for most economists. Intriguingly, many early observers did not see the corporation in quite this way. To them, corporations were a "democratic" form of organization because they could give expression to management talent, even when that talent did not itself own capital. Perhaps we should start to think of the corporation not as the instrument of narrowly held capital designed to exploit the labor and resources of the world, but as a vehicle through which citizens-as-*owners* can create a store of value to ensure their income in the future and, equally, a vehicle through which the same citizens-as-*workers* can receive full compensation for their efforts based on competence and relative merit. That would be a radical new perspective for civil economists to bring to our economic thinking.

The New Culture of Business

In this chapter we have laid out straightforward actions that companies, managers, intermediaries, owners, and others can take to address the emerging civil economy. Ideas take off from the issues we identified in the rest of this book.

By contrast, actions taken in the old, traditional economy often remind us of the Isaac Bashevis Singer stories of the legendary Russian village of Chelm and its famously loopy council of "Wise Men." In one episode, a gigantic pothole has opened in the dirt carriageway into town, causing major injuries to residents as they come and go. Villagers judge the problem grave enough to summon the Wise Men to devise a solution. After days of closed-door deliberations, the council issues its decision. It chooses not to fill the pothole but, instead, to construct a hospital beside it.

The Wise Men's approach fails Chelm just as the habit of avoiding straightforward solutions fails the global economy. Yet, as we have seen, there remain many examples of off-the-point policies that stem from outdated traditions of uncivil markets. Think of U.S. lawmakers crafting reams of new pension fund reporting rules instead of mandating employee trustees; the company scrambling to block investor access to proxies instead of forging a strong dialogue with shareowners; the mutual fund spending money to fight rules on independent fund directors instead of on stewardship resources. Blown astray by pressures unanchored to the demands of new capitalists, they still operate as if the world's corporations were owned as of old.

Dramatic shifts in capital have made citizen investors into the owners of the global economy. This development is bringing dramatic change. Vanguard corporations are pioneering capitalist manifesto–style methods of generating sustainable value from accountability. Civil funds are transforming their equity blocks into real expressions of priorities for citizen owners. Community groups are embracing capital to achieve social objectives. Monitors increasingly are independent and focused on investor interests. Modern measurements of performance based on long-term risk and long-term opportunity are fast supplementing conventional accounting standards. More governments are recognizing the political and economic payoffs of civil economy public policy.

As capital ownership spreads still more widely, these forces combine to strengthen the demand for a new culture for business. Properly nurtured, this culture has the ability to remake the world of commerce into a civil economy. Those individuals, companies, funds, civic groups, monitors, and politicians who correctly interpret and act on the signals of what is happening will not only work to everyone's benefit, they will enhance their own chances of coming out on top.

EPILOGUE

This book has mapped out the growth of a civil economy.

Today our corporations are owned, not by the wealthy few, but by the many. They are facing pressure to transform into institutions that are accountable not to themselves but to their citizen owners. Investors are starting to behave as responsible proprietors. Monitors are emerging to police the new economy. The old politics of worker versus capitalist is being replaced by the world of the citizen investor. Bit by bit, a new consensus is emerging, in which company managers focus on the delivery of value to shareowners, and where new capitalists are recognized as those owners.

We have given scores of examples of how citizen investors directly and indirectly are reshaping the corporate agenda. Some readers may think the notion of a civil economy utopian: that it suggests an automatic reconciliation of different social and economic interests; that it somehow resolves the real tensions between entrepreneurship and accountability; that it can dispose of temptations that arise when managers are given delegated powers.

That conclusion would be wrong. You'll remember that in chapter 1 we showed how a civil economy mirrors civil society. Civil society is not utopian; it does not pretend that by giving everyone a vote and freedom of expression somehow all social debate is automatically resolved. It simply says that in a civil society we have a mechanism for raising, engaging in, and finding a way of addressing problems. In a civil economy, widespread economic ownership means that the economic and social purposes of business both affect the same constituencies. There is therefore every chance that we can maximize overall benefits if we challenge corporations to act in the interests of their owners by carrying out the capitalist manifesto.

The reward can be great if progress continues. To begin with, we can recover that $3 trillion of lost savings that we identified in the first pages of this book. We can create millions of jobs. We can rein in unsustainable production, ensuring companies work for a fusion of profit and social purpose.

We have focused on six key players who will act out the drama of the civil economy:

- Company boards and managers, who need to be accountable

- Investment funds, which need to be responsible

- Monitors, who need to be independent

- Standards and measures, which need to be relevant

- Civil society groups, which need to be open to earn market access

- Lawmakers and regulators, who need to empower new capitalists

Perhaps you are one of these actors. If so, you have a vital role in determining the future of the civil economy.

But while all these actors are important, it is not they who will write the script of the civil economy. Ultimately, these actors are agents of a principal; and that principal is the citizen investor. We, the people, are not just the audience. We, the citizen owners, can direct this drama and decide its outcome. Otherwise the actors will simply improvise their parts.

But owners will be heard only if they give voice to their interests. Given the size of the rewards, it is worth reflecting how we can influence the civil economy: through screening the funds that manage our savings and pensions; contacts with company boards; participation in civil society groups such as churches and trade unions; and in our choice of candidates in political elections.

Perhaps one final story will illustrate the point.

On June 30, 2005, in a basement conference room at its headquarters, the United Nations has called together representatives of the largest capitalists in the world. Their combined investments dwarf those of Bill Gates or the sultan of Brunei.

The United Nations needs help. In the developing world, millions are hungry, billions need more productive work. This day, the U.N. is not looking for investors' charity. It wants to understand how to persuade big investment funds to encourage companies to invest in the developing world, where capital is scarce and hence returns should be higher. And when that capital is invested, the U.N.'s mandarins want to know that it will be used in a way that is socially responsible.

Initially, some progress is made. But after a while the capitalists' representatives point out that they themselves are limited in what they can do. "You've got to understand," they say, "that we are only representatives. We are fiduciaries for the real owners of this capital. Unless we are mandated otherwise, we can't readily change the way we behave."

Who then were the real owners of the capital in the room? They were more than 15 million people from around the world. Their representatives were investment officers from the globe's largest pension and savings institutions. They would soon sign the United Nations Principles for Responsible Investment on behalf of workers and retirees from the United States, Norway, France, the Netherlands, Australia, Britain, Thailand, Brazil, South Africa, Canada, Sweden, Germany and New Zealand. It is likely that some of those workers and retirees will be readers of this book. Today, we are the capitalists. And it is on our behalf that investment funds and companies behave the way they do.

The money that circulates in global capital markets is our money. The companies it owns are our companies. How those companies behave, how the civil economy develops, is ultimately up to us, the new capitalists. Our money, our companies, our choice.

Notes

Preface

1. GE vice president Bob Corcoran, conversations with Stephen Davis, December 2005.

Chapter 1

1. Market capitalization and ownership statistics as of February 2006, http://finance.yahoo.com.

2. *Pensions & Investments*, January 26, 2004.

3. James P. Hawley and Andrew T. Williams, *The Rise of Fiduciary Capitalism* (Philadelphia: University of Pennsylvania Press, 2000); Chris Mallin, "Shareholders and the Modern Corporation" (paper presented at the Corporate Governance in Practice conference, London, April 19, 1999); The Conference Board, *Institutional Investment Report: Turnover, Investment Strategies, and Ownership Patterns* (The Conference Board: New York, November 2000); Fabrizio Barca and Marco Becht, eds., *The Control of Corporate Europe* (Oxford: Oxford University Press, 2001).

4. John C. Bogle, *The Battle for the Soul of Capitalism* (New Haven: Yale University Press, 2005), 74.

5. The Conference Board, *Institutional Investment Report 2005: U.S. and International Trends* (The Conference Board: New York, 2005).

6. Office of National Statistics (UK), share ownership 2004, www.statistics.gov.uk/.

7. See Nell Minow and Robert A. G. Monks, *Watching the Watchers: Corporate Governance for the 21st Century* (Oxford: Blackwell Publishers, 1996).

8. Peter F. Drucker, *The Unseen Revolution: How Pension Fund Socialism Came to America* (New York: Harper & Row, 1976).

9. *Second Report of the Pensions Commission* (London: HMSO, 2005), 51.

10. *Federal Reserve Bulletin* (January 2000) and *Investor's Business Daily* (September 13, 2000).

11. The wealth gap is wide, but not perhaps as wide as some statistics suggest. Many measure affluence by what economists call "marketable wealth," meaning the investments

or cash someone can readily spend. Usually the figure does not include pension entitlements. When retirement savings are added in, wealth appears somewhat more broadly distributed. And since it is typically through pension entitlements that many of us have our interest in company shares, wealth statistics alone often mask the degree of common ownership.

12. Marco Becht and Colin Mayer, "Introduction," in *The Control of Corporate Europe*, eds. Fabrizio Barca and Marco Becht (New York: Oxford University Press Inc., 2001), 32.

13. The Conference Board, "U.S. Institutional Investors Boost Control of US Equity Market Assets," press release, October 10, 2005.

14. OECD data, quoted in RBC Financial Group, "Current Analysis," September 2003.

15. Pierre Delsaux (corporate governance head, International Market Directorate, European Commission), speech delivered at the International Corporate Governance Network, Frankfurt, February 7, 2006.

16. Tokyo Stock Exchange, "2004 Share Ownership Survey," www.tse.or.jp/english/data/research/english2004.pdf.

17. *Pensions & Investments*, September 20, 2004.

18. The Conference Board, *Institutional Investment Report 2005*, 55.

19. Michael C. Jensen, "Eclipse of the Public Corporation," *Harvard Business Review*, September–October 1989, 61–74.

20. McKinsey & Company, "Global Investor Opinion Survey on Corporate Governance" (London: 2002).

21. There is a rich literature addressing the relationship between corporate governance and performance. Conclusions are hardly uniform, but the weight of evidence points to good governance coinciding with superior stock price performance. Among the soundest cases are the following: (1) Art Durnev and E. Han Kim, "To Steal or Not to Steal: Firm Attributes, Legal Environment, and Valuation" (paper delivered at 14th Annual Conference on Financial Economics and Accounting (FEA), San Diego, CA., September 22, 2003, http://ssrn.com/abstract=391132. Durnev and Kim show a "positive relation between firm valuation and corporate governance"—especially where home regulations and laws are weak. If a company shows a 10 percent increase in corporate governance scores, it can expect a more than 13 percent jump in market value. If it makes similar improvements in transparency, market value can climb by more than 16 percent. (2) Bernard S. Black, Hasung Jang, and Woochan Kim, "Does Corporate Governance Predict Firms' Market Values? Evidence from Korea," *Journal of Law, Economics, and Organization* 22, no. 2 (Fall 2006), http://ssrn.com/abstract=311275. The authors found that a company that embraces sweeping governance reform, moving from worst to best, should see a 96 percent jump in market value. Even modest improvements in board practices and transparency yield a 13 percent boost in stock market value. The paper offers "evidence consistent with a causal relationship between an overall governance index and higher share prices in emerging markets." (3) McKinsey & Company (*Global Proxy Watch* 6, no. 30 [July 26 2002]) found in 2002 that companies featuring better governance have higher price-to-book ratios, showing that investors who say they will pay a premium for best practices actually do so. Research predicts that a firm moving from worst to best could swell in value by up to 12 percent. (4) Paul A. Gompers, Joy L. Ishii, and Andrew Metrick, "Corporate Governance and Equity Prices," *Quarterly Journal of Economics* 118, no. 1 (February 2003): 107–155, available at http://ssrn.com/abstract=278920. This analysis

demonstrates that firms with stronger governance features had "higher firm value, higher profits, higher sales growth, lower capital expenditures, and made fewer corporate acquisitions." (5) Deutsche Bank's "Beyond the Numbers: UK Corporate Governance Revisited" (London: July 2005) found that in Britain "good governance is lower equity risk which should translate into higher valuation multiples." Its March 2006 update, this time analyzing 204 companies in the Asia Pacific region, concluded that the "momentum" of corporate governance reform at a company is a key influence on equity price performance.

22. Author Pitt-Watson was CEO of Hermes Focus Asset Management until 2006.

23. Joseph Healy, "Corporate Governance and Shareholder Value," ANZ Investment Bank study (Auckland, March 24, 2000); and Joseph Healy, "The Shareholder Value Performance of Corporate New Zealand," ANZ Investment Bank study, (Aukland, February 24, 2000).

24. Figures are based on a conservative estimate of $30 trillion in global stock market value in 2004. Although most corporate governance research relates to equity ownership, recent research suggests that good corporate governance can also reduce the cost of debt financing. (See, for instance, Hollis Ashbaugh-Skaife and Ryan LaFond, "Firms' Corporate Governance and the Cost of Debt: An Analysis of U.S. Firms' GMI Ratings," April 2006, http://www.gsm.ucdavis.edu/faculty/Conferences/Hollis.pdf. We have not considered the effect of a reduction in the cost of debt in this analysis, but it could be several multiples of the equity-only estimated benefits.

25. Jacques Bughin and Thomas E. Copeland, "The Virtuous Cycle of Shareholder Value Creation," *The McKinsey Quarterly*, no. 2 (1997), 156.

26. *New York Times*, September 11, 2005.

27. Simi Kedia and Thomas Philippon, "The Economics of Fraudulent Accounting," working paper 11573, National Bureau of Economic Research, Cambridge, MA, August 2005.

28. James P. Hawley and Andrew T. Williams, *The Rise of Fiduciary Capitalism: How Institutional Investors Can Make America More Democratic* (Philadelphia: University of Pennsylvania Press, 2000).

29. In Europe alone, there is the Association of British Insurers, Deminor, European Corporate Governance Service, Pensions and Investment Research Consultants, Manifest, and RREV (and that is a partial listing). In the United States, still the world's largest capital market, the Corporate Library, GovernanceMetrics International (GMI), Institutional Shareholder Services, Egan Jones, Proxy Governance, and Glass Lewis compete. Australia has Corporate Governance International and Proxy Australia, South Korea has the Center for Good Corporate Governance and the Korea Corporate Governance Service, and Brazil has LCV.

Chapter 2

1. "Recollections of Vadim Orlov," National Security Archive, http://www2.gwu.edu/~nsarchiv/NSAEBB/NSAEBB75/asw-II-16.pdf.

2. Karl Marx and Friedrich Engels, *The Communist Manifesto* (London: Penguin Books, 1967), 235.

3. John F. Kennedy, Inaugural Address, January 20, 1961.

4. J. F. C. Harrison, *Common People: A History from the Norman Conquest to the Present* (New York: Flamingo, 1984), 211.

5. For example, see the discussion in Roger Backhouse, *Penguin History of Economics* (London: Penguin, 2002), 29–50.

6. Adam Smith, *The Wealth of Nations*, bk. I (1776; rept. New York: Alfred A. Knopf, Inc., 1991), 1:3.

7. C. A. Oakley, *The Second City* (Glasgow: Blackie & Co., 1947), 16.

8. James R. MacDonald and James Kier Hardie, *From Serfdom to Socialism*, quoted in Gordon Brown and Tony Wright, *Values, Visions and Voices* (Edinburgh: Mainstream Publishing, 1995). Even as recently as the 1990s, the U.K. Labour Party was still committed to "the common ownership of the means of production, distribution and exchange."

9. Franklin D. Roosevelt, Inaugural Address, March 4, 1933.

10. Quoted in Samuel Eliot Morison and Henry Steele Commager, *The Growth of the American Republic* (New York: Oxford University Press, 1962), 227.

11. See, for example, Backhouse, *Penguin History of Economics*, 306: "After the Second World War, economics became a much more technical subject, and mathematical techniques were systematically applied to all its branches. This was not a neutral development . . . as theories were refined in such a way that they could be treated using available mathematical tools. The meaning attached to such basic terms as 'competition,' 'markets' and 'unemployment' changed. Many theories were developed that only had tenuous links, if any, to the real world."

12. Paul Frentrop, *A History of Corporate Governance* (Brussels: Deminor, 2003), 86.

13. Ibid.; Larry Neal, "Venture Shares of the Dutch East India Company," unpublished paper (New Haven: Yale School of Management, March 2003).

14. Arianna Huffington, *Pigs at the Trough: How Corporate Greed and Political Corruption are Undermining America* (New York: Crown Publishers, 2003).

15. Günter Ogger, *Nieten in Nadelstreifen: Deutschlands Manager im Zwielicht* (Munich: Droemer Knaur-Verlag, 1992).

16. Joel Bakan, *The Corporation: The Pathological Pursuit of Profit and Power* (New York: Free Press, 2004).

17. Adam Smith, *The Wealth of Nations*, bk. V (1776; rept. Edinburgh: Brown and Nelson, 1827), 1:311.

Chapter 3

1. Milton Friedman, cited in the *New York Times*, September 13, 1970.

2. Plato, *The Republic*, quoted in Peter Singer, *How Are We to Live? Ethics in an Age of Self Interest* (Oxford: Oxford University Press, 1997), 5.

3. Paul Frentrop, *A History of Corporate Governance* (Brussels: Deminor, 2003), 42–143.

4. *Louis K. Liggett Co. et al. v. Lee, Comptroller et al.*, 288 US 519 (1933), 548, 567, quoted in Joel Bakan, *The Corporation: The Pathological Pursuit of Profit and Power* (New York: Free Press, 2004), 19.

5. Johnston Birchall, *Co-op: The People's Business* (Manchester, England: Manchester University Press, 1994), 134.

6. In talking about corporate ethics, we are not seeking to make a normative judgment. We simply note that corporations cannot exist without a common understanding of what behavior is appropriate. For example, see Gerry Johnson and Kevan Scholes, *Exploring Corporate Strategy: Texts and Cases*, 3rd ed (Upper Saddle River, NJ: Prentice Hall, 1993).

7. Thomas Peters and Robert Waterman, *In Search of Excellence* (New York: Harper and Row, 1982), 238.

8. Cited in Bakan, *The Corporation*, 34.

9. Adolph Berle and Gardiner Means, *The Modern Corporation and Private Property* (Somerset, NJ: Transaction Publishers, 1991), 312ff.

10. This list is based on the Hermes Principles, cowritten by author Pitt-Watson, and adopted by Britain's largest pension fund as its objectives for the companies in which it invests. Tony Watson and David Pitt-Watson, *The Hermes Principles: What Shareholders Expect of Public Companies–and What Companies Should Expect of Their Investors.* (London: Hermes Pensions Management Ltd., 2004)

11. While we note that most investment, on a capital-weighted basis, is from pension funds, the same arguments can be made if saving for a college education or a vacation, or even just to "get richer."

12. See also chapter 6 for a discussion of EVA, a metric for measuring corporate success at creating value.

Chapter 4

1. Quoted in Thomas Friedman, "There Is Hope," *New York Times*, October 27 2002.

2. In the United States alone, workers and retirees have saved $12.9 trillion in designated retirement savings. While most experts believe individuals, generally, keep too much of their assets in low-risk securities, the "risk" asset of choice seen in chapter 1 is clearly equity.

3. *Global Proxy Watch* 8, no. 42 (November 19, 2004).

4. Luh Luh Lan and Loizos Heracleous, "Shareholder Votes for Sale," *Harvard Business Review*, June 2005, 20–24.

5. *Pensions & Investments*, September 15, 2003, 10.

6. The S&P was capitalized at $11.4 trillion as of August 5, 2005.

7. By contrast, the vast majority of the return to the beneficiaries is the return of the general market, not the difference in return between broadly diversified mutual fund number 1 and broadly diversified mutual fund number 2. In fact, various studies show that more than 100 percent of the return to an investor is, on average, created by the overall market. How can that be? Well, on average, mutual funds are destroyers of value, not creators of value. The reason is fees, combined with the law of averages. The thousands and thousands of mutual funds in the world basically define the market, so, in aggregate, they return around the market average to investors. Subtract fees from that and you quickly understand the source of the underperformance. Indeed, truly talented mutual fund managers such as Fidelity's Peter Lynch or Legg Mason's Bill Miller, who consistently beat the market, are so unusual that they are hailed as superstars. That acclaim, in itself, is perverse proof of how the industry generally underperforms.

8. Quoted in "Tom Jones to Keep Citigroup Fund Unit on Song," *Financial Times*, June 16, 2003.

9. Most mutual funds don't want to be too different from their peers. Being different is a definite risk. Get it right, and you improve returns dramatically, which will attract new investors, and mutual funds will get paid for that. But get it wrong, and the mutual fund will be flooded with redemptions. The asymmetric risk/reward spectrum encourages mutual funds to stay within the pack and rely on all those marketing resources— rather than performance differences—to bring in assets. Indeed, the industry even calls the difference from the broad market indices "tracking error," as if it's something undesirable, rather than evidence that the mutual fund manager is actively selecting stocks, for which he or she is getting paid. The net result is that many mutual fund managers hold

overlapping portfolios, not just of the same names, but similar proportions of the same names.

10. Quoted in "Saint Jack On The Attack," *Fortune,* January 20, 2003, 112.

11. "How to Fix the Mutual Funds Mess," *BusinessWeek,* September 22, 2003, 106. Another venture, FundExpenses.com, also tracks mutual fund fees.

12. See Andrew Clearfield, "'With Friends Like These, Who Needs Enemies?' The Structure of the Investment Industry and Its Reluctance to Exercise Governance Oversight," *Corporate Governance: An International Review* 13, no. 2 (March 2005), 114; and UNEP Finance Initiative and World Business Council for Sustainable Development, "Generation Lost: Young Financial Analysts and Environmental, Social and Corporate Governance Issues," 2005, http://www.unepfi.org/fileadmin/documents/ymt_summary _2005.pdf.

13. *Global Proxy Watch* 7, no. 41 (November 14, 2003). See also *Mutual Funds, Proxy Voting and Fiduciary Responsibility* (Washington, DC: Social Investment Forum, April 2005).

14. Jim Hawley, Andrew Williams, and John Cioffi, "Why Did Institutional Investor Governance Activism Fail? Towards a New Model of Corporate Governance Monitoring" (unpublished manuscript, The Center for the Study of Fiduciary Capitalism, Saint Mary's College of California, April 2003).

15. Op cit., "How to Fix the Mutual Funds Mess."

16. S.1992, sponsored by Sen. Edward Kennedy, passed the Health, Education, Labor and Pensions Committee in March 2002.

17. These defined contribution, or DC, plans are fast replacing defined-benefit, or DB, schemes in many markets. DC plans shift risk to individuals; payouts hinge largely on members' investment decisions. In DB plans, payouts were prescribed in advance. In 2000 alone, the number of DB plans in the United States shrunk by 4.1 percent, according to the Department of Labor.

18. Mirror Group retirees eventually recovered much of the lost cash. U.K. taxpayers paid £100 million, and a group of auditors, investment banks and others settled out of court for another £276 million.

19. *Pension Plans: Additional Transparency and Other Actions Needed in Connection with Proxy Voting,* GAO-04-749 (Washington, DC: US Government Accountability Office, 2004).

20. Investor Responsibility Research Center. Of the 1,077 proposals IRRC tracked, 794 were classified as narrow "governance" resolutions, and the rest as "social."

21. See www.dwp.gov.uk/asd/. Vereniging van Bedrijfstakpensioenfondsen (VB), the Dutch industrywide pension fund association, issued a similar review of fund governance in June 2004; see www.vvb.nl.

22. Allen Sykes, *Capitalism for Tomorrow* (Oxford: Capstone, 2000), 4.

23. Quoted in "Compulsory trustee knowledge is a bridge too far, says Myners," *Pensions Week,* May 16, 2005.

24. The following derives from an interview with Peter Clapman by Stephen Davis.

25. Investor Responsibility Research Center.

26. Stephen Davis, *Shareholder Rights Abroad: A Handbook for the Global Investor* (Washington, DC: IRRC, 1989); and Lauren Talner, *The Origins of Shareholder Activism* (Washington, DC: IRRC, 1983).

27. "Governor's Plan Could Erode CalPERS Clout," *Sacramento Bee* (California), February 28, 2005.

28. Ironically, Ronald Reagan had first gained political fame as governor of California, a position he attained by defeating Jesse Unruh.

29. Rachel Ongé Lerman, Stephen Davis, and Corinna Arnold, *Global Voting: Shareholder Decisions 1991–1992* (Washington, DC: IRRC, 1993).

30. Stephen Davis and Karel Lannoo, "Shareholder Voting in Europe," *Center for European Policy Studies Review* 3, (Summer 1997), 22.

31. International Corporate Governance Network, "Cross Border Proxy Voting: Case Studies from the 2002 Proxy Voting Season," http://www.icgn.org/organisation/documents/cbv/cbv_crossborder_voting_may2003.pdf

32. *The Times* (London), June 14, 1993.

33. For instance, see *Pensions & Investments*, July, 21 1997.

34. Tim C. Opler and Jonathan S. Sokobin, "Does Coordinated Institutional Activism Work? An Analysis of the Activities of the Council of Institutional Investors," Working Papers Series 95-5, Dice Center for Research In Financial Economics, October 1995. Available at SSRN: http://ssrn.com/abstract=46880 or DOI: 10.2139/ssrn.46880.

35. Some of the most influential include the NAPF, the Association of British Insurers, the U.S. Council of Institutional Investors, the Australian Council of Superannuation Investors, the Canadian Coalition for Good Governance, the Irish Association of Investment Managers, and France's Association Française de la Gestion Financière.

36. *Financial Times*, April 19 2005.

37. See Mathew Gaved, *Institutional Investors and Corporate Governance* (London: Foundation for Business Responsibilities, 1998); Anthony Williams, *Who Will Guard the Guardians?* (London: Management Books, 2000); Minow and Monks, *Watching the Watchers*; and Sykes, *Capitalism for Tomorrow*.

38. This "comply or explain" type of code is rapidly becoming the norm for non-U.S. regulators seeking to solve problems without unintentionally creating others. "Comply or explain" first came to prominence following the Cadbury Commission's recommendations regarding the U.K. corporate sector in 1992.

39. Principle 11.4 in Paul Myners, *Institutional Investment in the United Kingdom: A Review* (London: HM Treasury, March 6, 2001), www.hm-treasury.gov.uk/media/2F9/02/31.pdf.

40. Sponsors are professional investor bodies: the Pensions Investment Association of Canada, France's AFG, and the Netherlands' VB. See also Eurosif, which includes fund managers focused on socially responsible investment.

41. See latest endorsement figures at www.enhanced-analytics.com.

42. See, for instance, the Carbon Disclosure Project, the Investor Network on Climate Risk, and the Institutional Investors Group on Climate Change.

43. See http://www.pharmafutures.org/.

44. Merrill Lynch found a similar solution, combining its asset management unit with BlackRock, while maintaining a minority interest in the combined entity. Interestingly, Merrill Lynch had explored a transaction similar to Citicorp's with Legg Mason a year earlier, for much the same reasons.

45. Much of the discussion of hedge funds was first published in Stephen Davis and Jon Lukomnik, "Who Are These Guys? Welcome to the Hedge Fund Era," *Compliance Week*, April 5, 2005, www.complianceweek.com.

46. Author Lukomnik was elected to the Board of Sears Canada on May 9, 2006.

47. Sears Holdings Corporation's Form 10Q SEC filing for the period ended October 29, 2005.

48. One policy idea would be to compel boards to seek shareowner approval before undertaking major layoffs. Such a measure would compel directors to frame a persuasive case that reducing staff is in investors' long-term interests. Otherwise, downsizing could be a knee-jerk move to boost short-term stock prices at the risk of hollowing out the company. Critics, though, might worry that such a measure could involve investors in micromanagement. See Stephen Davis, "Corporate Downsizing: Let Shareholders Vote," *Pensions & Investments*, April 29, 1996, 14.

Chapter 5

1. Louis Cabot, "From the Boardroom," *Harvard Business Review*, Autumn 1976, 41.

2. Enron, for example, had as head of its audit committee the highly regarded former dean of Stanford Business School.

3. Peter F. Drucker, *Management: Tasks, Responsibilities, Practices* (New York: Harper Business, 1993), 628–629.

4. Cabot, "From the Boardroom."

5. Bryan Burrough and John Helyar, *Barbarians at the Gate* (New York: Arrow Books, 1990), 96–97

6. *Re Brazilian Rubber Plantations and Estates Ltd [1911] Ch 425 at 437*

7. Cited in *Global Proxy Watch* 6, no. 9 (March 1, 2002).

8. "McCall To Quit Stock Exchange After Pay Furor," *New York Times*, September 26, 2003.

9. MVC Associates International, www.mvcinternational.com. Ten funds cited the research in a November 30, 2005, letter to the U.S. Securities and Exchange Commission asking for stricter disclosure rules.

10. Michael C. Jensen, Kevin J. Murphy, and Eric G. Wruck, "Remuneration: Where We've Been, How We Got to Here, What Are the Problems, and How to Fix Them," Finance Working Paper 44, ECGI, Brussels, July 12, 2004, 31.

11. Joanna Potts and Christian Humphries, eds., *Phillips Guide to the State of the World* (London: Phillips, 2004), 124. (The U.S. aid budget in 2001 was $11,429.)

12. Jensen, Murphy, and Wruck, *Remuneration*, 45.

13. "The Corporate Library Publishes CEO Employment Contracts Online: Announces Best and Worst in Contract Provisions and Responsiveness from Mom's First Class Airfare to the 'Ministry of Disinformation,'" PR Newswire, The Corporate Library, February, 24, 2000. Also see Geoffrey Colvin, "Where's the Beff: It's in the Contract," *Fortune*, April 3, 2000, 70.

14. Quoted in "Warm Words," *Financial Times*, September 30, 2002.

15. Jon Lukomnik, "Shareholder Activism: Two Alpha-Generating Strategies in One," in Marvin L. Damsma, Jon Lukomnik, Maarten L. Nederlof, and Thomas K. Philips, *Alpha, The Positive Side of Risk* (Washington Depot, CT:. Investors Press, 1996).

16. Lucian Bebchuk and Jesse M. Fried, *Pay Without Performance: The Unfulfilled Promise of Executive Compensation* (Cambridge: Harvard University Press, 2004), 206.

17. Delaware General Corporation Law, quoted in Minow and Monks, *Watching the Watchers*, 182.

18. Gavin Grant, "Beyond the Numbers: Corporate Governance in Europe," Deutsche Bank, London, 2005, 60 and 68.

19. Leslie Crawford, "Spain Sets First with 'Lover's Guide' to Boardrooms, *Financial Times*, May 10, 2005, 10.

20. Barry Metzger, *Global Corporate Governance Guide 2004: Best Practice in the Boardroom* (London: Globe White Page, 2004).

21. Robert Monks and Nell Minow, *Corporate Governance* (Cambridge, MA: Blackwell Business, 1995) 206.

22. William B. Chandler III and Leo E. Strine Jr., "The New Federalism of the American Corporate Governance System," NYU Center for Law and Business Research Paper No. 03-01; University of Pennsylvania Institute for Law & Economic Research Paper 03-03, available at SSRN: http://papers.ssrn.com/sol3/papers.cfm?abstract_id=367720 or DOI: 10.2139/ssrn.367720. Accessed March 13, 2003.

23. Metzger, *Global Corporate Governance Guide 2004*, 29.

24. Chuck Lucier, Rob Schuyt, and Edward Tse, "CEO Succession 2004: The World's Most Prominent Temp Workers," *Strategy + Business* Special Report, Summer 2005.

25. Grant, "Beyond the Numbers: Corporate Governance in Europe."

Chapter 6

1. Quoted in *Class Action Reporter*, May 2, 2002.

2. *U.S. Securities and Exchange Commission* v. *Citigroup Global Markets Inc.*, U.S. District Court, Southern District of New York, April 28 2003. See the complaint at www.sec.gov/litigation/complaints/comp18111.htm.

3. This chapter focuses on information intermediaries, but we note that other intermediaries also play a role in defining the relationship of owners and corporations. Compensation consultants and executive recruiters, for example, have been accused of being quiescent in the face of explosive growth in executive compensation.

4. "Amy Feldman and Joan Caplin, "Is Jack Grubman the Worst Analyst Ever?" CNNMoney.com, April 25, 2002, money.cnn.com/2002/04/25/pf/investing/grubman/.

5. "Ex-Qwest Officials Charged," *Washington Post*, March 15, 2005.

6. 2002 GDP figures.

7. Global Research Analyst Settlement Distribution Funds, www.globalresearchanalystsettlement.com.

8. You can read the text of the principles at the National Association of State Retirement Adminstrators' Web site, www.nasra.org/resources/investorprotectionprinciples.pdf.

9. The group was founded by Independent Minds, IRIS, and Delta Lloyd Securities. The chairman is George Möller, CEO of Robeco.

10. Carol Graham, Robert Litan, and Sandip Sukhtankar, "The Bigger They Are the Harder They Fall: An Estimate of the Costs of the Crisis in Corporate Governance," Policy Brief 102, the Brookings Institution, Washington, DC, August 30, 2002. The $35 million figure is the base case. The authors estimated the range at $21 billion to $50 billion. Carol Graham, additional conversation with Jon Lukomnik, April 2005.

11. Alan G. Hevesi, "Impact of the Corporate Scandals on New York State," Office of the State Comptroller, Albany, NY, August 2003.

12. The authors are indebted to Tim Bush for his analysis of the U.S. accounting system. Many of the observations in this section are drawn from, or influenced by, his paper "Divided by Common Language: Where Economics Meets the Law: US versus non-US reporting systems," Institute of Chartered Accountants in England and Wales, London, 2005.

13. Quoted in ibid.

14. Ibid.

15. "Many Big Firms Buy Tax Shelters from Auditors," *Wall Street Journal*, February 25, 2005.

16. Pat McGurn, "Tax Debt Piled Up for Sprint Execs," *USA Today*, February 7, 2003.

17. Ibid.

18. *Caparo Industries plc* v. *Dickman and others [1990] 1 All ER568[1990] 2 WLR 358* www.icaew.co.uk.

19. PCAOB 2005 budget, www.pcaobus.org.

20. ISS 2005 Proxy Season Preview and Policy Update, December 13, 2004, www .issproxy.com.

21. "Arthur Andersen, Final WorldCom Defendant, Settles," press release, Office of New York State Comptroller Alan Hevesi, Albany, April 26, 2005.

22. See www.cfraonline.com.

23. "The Boss on the Sidelines; How Auditors, Directors, and Lawyers are Asserting their Power," *BusinessWeek*, April 25, 2005. 86.

24. *Global Proxy Watch*, October 28, 2005. See also www.hermes.co.uk/pdf/corporate _governance/commentary/Hermes_APB_consultants_paper160304.pdf.

25. Morley Fund Management, "Audit Reform: A Focus on Purpose and Transparency," London, December 2004.

26. Quoted in Hilary Rosenberg, *A Traitor to His Class* (New York: John Wiley, 1999), 193–194.

27. John Connolly, CEO of Institutional Shareholder Services, interview with Stephen Davis, May 20 2005.

28. ISS letter to the U.S. Securities and Exchange Commission, September 15, 2004. http://www.sec.gov/divisions/investment/noaction/iss091504.htm.

29. For example, see Gretchen Morgenson, "And They Call This Advice," *New York Times*, August 21, 2005.

30. SEC letters to Kent S. Hughes, Managing Director, Egan-Jones, May 27, 2004, and to Mari Ann Pisarri, Esq., Pickark and Djinis LLP, Counsel for ISS, September 15, 2004. See http://www.sec.gov/divisions/investment/noaction/egan052704.htm and http://www .sec.gov/divisions/investment/noaction/iss091504.htm.

31. Egan-Jones Rating Company, www.egan-jones.com.

32. Quoted in "Corporate Watchdogs Fight Scandal—and Each Other," Associated Press, May 10, 2005.

33. U.S. Securities and Exchange Commission Office of Compliance Inspections and Examinations, "Staff Report Concerning Examinations of Select Pension Consultants." May 16, 2005.

34. Ibid.

35. Ibid.

36. "SEC Looking at Pension Consultants," *New York Times*, May 17, 2005.

37. Ibid.

38. See www.ennisknupp.com.

39. Nelson/Thomson Financial 2003 Pension Fund Consultant Survey, www.nelson information.com/industry_insight/pfc2003.pdf.

40. In 2005, Standard & Poor's announced it was closing its separate governance service unit covering North American companies.

41. https://www.creditsights.com/about/.

42. See Egan-Jones, www.egan-jones.com.

Chapter 7

1. Data from the American Institute of Certified Public Accountants, www.aicpa.org.

2. "In the Dark: What Boards and Executives Don't Know about the Health of Their Businesses," white paper (New York: Deloitte, Touche Tohmatsu, 2004).

3. "Why the Economy Is a Lot Stronger Than You Think," *BusinessWeek*, February 13, 2006, 62.

4. Quoted in "Measuring the Value of Intellectual Capital," *Ivey Business Journal*, March 1, 2001, 16.

5. H. Thomas Johnson and Robert S. Kaplan, *Relevance Lost: The Rise and Fall of Management Accounting* (Boston: Harvard Business School Press, 1987), 5.

6. H. Thomas Johnson, *Relevance Regained: From Top-down Control to Bottom-up Empowerment* (New York: The Free Press, 1992), 116.

7. Cited in Deloitte Touche Tohmatsu, "In the Dark," 29.

8. AQ Research–EAI Roundtable Report, 2005, www.aqresearch.com/downloads/EAI_revised_2.pdf.

9. GE 2005 proxy statement. http://www.gc.com/ar2004/proxy/statement.jsp.

10. EVA® is a trademark of Stern Stewart & Co.

11. The standards and metrics in this section address value creation by management overall. Individual drivers of value creation are addressed in the "sustainability" and "enhanced disclosure" discussions, which follow.

12. See www.sternstewart.com/evaabout/whatis.php.

13. Ibid. Some practitioners prefer to use net operating profits after taxes.

14. "AIG Provides Details of Executive Compensation," *New York Times*, June 28, 2005.

15. "Jurors See Tyco CEO's $2M Party," CNNMoney.com, October 29, 2003.

16. Authors Davis and Lukomnik were cofounders of GMI but have no roles or responsibility at the company. They do hold small subordinated equity positions in the company, now controlled by a joint venture of State Street Bank and ABP, the Dutch civil service pension fund.

17. GovernanceMetrics International, see http://www.gmiratings.com/(nxl0x455izt2kvqs22b0svbq)/Performance.aspx.

18. Lawrence D. Brown and Marcus L. Caylor, "Corporate Governance and Firm Performance," December 7, 2004, available at SSRN: http://ssrn.com/abstract=586423 or DOI: 10.2139/ssrn.586423.

19. GovernanceMetrics International, www.gmiratings.com.

20. Gavin Grant, "Beyond the Numbers: UK Corporate Governance Revisited," (New York: Deutsche Bank, July 2005).

21. Calculated by First Boston Corporation. See "Oil Spill Gave Big Push to Valdez Principles," *Anchorage Daily News*, November 5, 1989.

22. "Comments by Joan Bavaria on the Occasion of CERES' Fifteenth Anniversary Conference," April 14, 2004, cited in Trillium quarterly newsletter, http://207.21.200.202/pages/news/news_detail.asp?ArticleID=348&status=CurrentIssue&Page=HotNews.

23. Ibid.

24. See www.unglobalcompact.org.

25. See www.accountability.org.uk.

26. See www.fairtrade.net.

27. See www.ilo.org.

28. See www.iso.org.

29. See www.sa-intl.org.

30. See www.transparency.org.

31. See http://globalreporting.org.

32. Allan Fels, *The Australian Financial Review*, October 2003, http://www.anzsog. edu.au/news/article2_oct2003.htm

33. Sir David Clementi, speech given to ICGN, London, July 8, 2005.

34. Alison Thomas, "A Tale of Two Reports," *EBF* 16, Winter 2003/2004, www.ebr360. org/downloads/ebf_issue16.pdf.

35. Ibid.

36. Ibid.

37. Brian Rivel, "Perspectives on the Buy-Side: How Are Decisions Made?" Rivel Research Group, paper presented at the Grant & Eisenhofer Conference, New York, June 9, 2005.

38. David Phillips, "Rethinking Governance, Reporting and Assurance for the Benefit of Wealth Creation and Social Development in the 21st Century," comment draft, 2005.

39. Deloitte Touche Tomatsu, "In the Dark."

Chapter 8

1. Quoted in David Bollier, *Citizen Action and Other Big Ideas: A History of Ralph Nader and the Modern Consumer Movement* (Washington, DC: Center for the Study of Responsive Law, 1991), available at www.nader.org/history/.

2. Frentrop, *History of Corporate Governance*.

3. Quoted in Talner, *Origins of Shareholder Activism*.<<p. no.?5>>

4. *Investor Responsibility in the Global Era* (Washington, DC: IRRC, 1998), 25.

5. Jan Hofmeyr, Stephen Davis, and Merle Lipton, *The Impact of Sanctions on South Africa: Whites' Political Attitudes* (Washington, DC: IRRC, March 1990).

6. Interfaith Center on Corporate Responsibility, *The Proxy Resolutions Book 2000* (New York: ICCR, January 2000).

7. Talner, *Origins of Shareholder Activism*, 29.

8. Craig Mackenzie, "Ethical Investment and the Challenge of Corporate Reform" (PhD diss., University of Bath, 1997). Chapter 3 available at http://staff.bath.ac.uk/hssal/crm/phd/2hist0.doc.

9. Carolyn Mathiasen, *The SEC and Social Policy Shareholder Resolutions in the 1990s* (Washington, DC: IRRC, November 1994).

10. Ibid.

11. Brad M. Barber, "Monitoring the Monitor: Evaluating the CalPERS' Shareholder Activism," unpublished paper, Graduate School of Management at University of California Davis, March 2006, 19. Also see "Gadfly Activism at CalPERS Leads to Possible Ouster of President," Wall Street Journal, December 1, 2004, A-1.

12. CNN Money Morning, August 14, 2002.

13. Edelman Public Relations, *Edelman Annual Trust Barometer, 2005*, www.edelman.com/image/insights/content/Edelman_Trust_Barometer-2005_final_final.pdf.

14. Marlies Glasius, Mary Kaldor, and Helmut Anheier, eds., *Global Civil Society 2005/6* (London: Sage Publications, 2005); see http://www.lse.ac.uk/Depts/global/yearbook.htm.

15. Alister Scott, one of the campaign's founders; interview with Stephen Davis, April 26, 2005. The E-USS campaign is also the subject of a case study in Steve Waygood, "NGO and Equity Investment: A Critical Assessment of the Practices of UK NGOs in Using the Capital Market as Campaign Device," unpublished PhD thesis, University of Surrey, February 2004. The authors are grateful for permission to source this material.

16. Sir Robert Megarry's judgment came in the case known as *Cowan* v. *Scargill* See http://oxcheps.new.ox.ac.uk/casebook/Resources/COWANA_1%20DOC.pdf.

17. See www.fairpensions.org.uk for background on the campaign.

18. Ibid.

19. For instance, the Make TIAA-CREF Ethical coalition targets the New York–based educators' fund company. The Council for Responsible Public Investment presses all California civil service pension plans to adopt socially responsible portfolio practices. AsrIA, founded in 2001, rallies NGOs to promote socially responsible investment in Asia. Still others are trying to galvanize grassroots investors of mutual funds and unit trusts so that fund families face pressure to become more engaged owners. The Boston-based Ceres coalition is one. Other groups, such as the San Francisco–based As You Sow Foundation, are contacting donors to charities and endowments, trying to recruit those channels of capital to exert pressure on companies. The Responsible Endowments Coalition marshals student pressure on university funds.

20. See "EIRIS Study of the Top 250 UK Occupational Pension Funds," www.eiris .org/Pages/Pensions/Penson.htm.

21. Nicholas Hildyard and Mark Mansley, *Campaigners Guide to Financial Markets: Effective Lobbying of Companies and Financial Institutions* (Sturminster Newton, England: The Corner House, 2001); and "Confronting Companies Using Shareholder Power: A Handbook on Socially-Oriented Shareholder Activism," www.foe.org/international/shareholder.

22. Robert Kinloch Massie, "The Rise of Sustainable Governance," *Global Agenda* (World Economic Forum), January 2003, available at www.globalagendamagazine.com/2003/robertkinlochmassie.asp.

23. See www.incr.com.

24. Each is called the Institutional Investors Group on Climate Change; see www.iigcc.org.

25. See www.cdproject.net.

26. It had support from the antipoverty groups War on Want and Traidcraft. In addition, in August 2002 the Rose Foundation for Communities and the Environment issued "Environmental Fiduciary: The Case for Incorporating Environmental Factors into Investment Management Policies" (see www.rosefdn.org/images/EFreport.pdf). In a similar vein, Ceres, with Innovest, put out "Value at Risk: Climate Change and the Future of Governance" in April 2002 (www.innovestgroup.com/pdfs/climate.pdf). Britain's Chartered Institute of Management Accountants, with Forum for the Future, published a similar *Environmental Cost Accounting: An Introduction and Practical Guide* (London: CIMA Publishing, 2002). Even the World Bank joined in, when its subsidiary, the International Finance Corporation, in conjunction with SustainAbility and the Ethos Institute, released "Developing Value: The Business Case for Sustainability in Emerging Markets," www.ifc .org/ifcext/sustainability.nsf/AttachmentsByTitle/Developing_Value_full_report/$FILE/Developing+Value_full+text.pdf.

27. Jonathan Charkham, "Corporate Governance and the Institutional Investor," paper delivered at Columbia University Center for Law and Economic Studies (New York: May 23 1988).

28. Michael Useem, *Investor Capitalism: How Money Managers Are Changing the Face of Corporate America* (New York: Basic Books, 1996.)

29. The European Corporate Governance Institute, founded in Brussels by Marco Becht, commissioned papers and built a vital online archive of studies and codes—and an Internet chat room for scholars migrating into the new field studying the impact of shareowner

power. Chris Mallin started centers for corporate governance research at the Universities of Nottingham and Birmingham. France's huge Caisse des Dépôts et Consignations funded the Observatoire sur la Responsabilité Sociétale des Entreprises (ORSE), while Theodor Baums led related research at the University of Frankfurt. James Hawley and Andrew Williams opened the Center for the Study of Fiduciary Capitalism at St. Mary's College in California. Yale founded its Center for Corporate Governance, with Ira Millstein as an associate dean. Starting in 1995, similar programs began to sprout up at Cambridge University, the Center for European Policy Studies, Dartmouth College, Harvard University, Henley Management College, INSEAD, New York University, Stanford University, Stockholm Business School, and Yonsei University; at the Universities of Alberta, Amsterdam, Anahuac (Mexico City), Athens, Canberra, Copenhagen, Cranfield, Hagen, Hong Kong, Mauritius, Melbourne, Oxford, Tokyo, Toronto; and at the University of Asia and the Pacific in Manila. Y. R. K. Reddy's Academy of Corporate Governance sought to knit study centers together in India. The Asian Institute of Corporate Governance, led by Hasung Jang, opened at Korea University Business School. M. K. Chouhan chaired the Asian Center for Corporate Governance in Mumbai. The Conference Boards of the United States, Canada, and Europe added reports and conferences. And so on.

30. CNNfm, June 9 2003.

31. James Madison, "Report on the Virginia Resolutions," 1798, www.jmu.edu/madison/center/home.htm.

32. "Corporate Scandals, Corporate Responsibility and the Media: Who Should We Believe?" conference sponsored by *Business Ethics* magazine, New York City, April 21, 2005.

33. *The State of the News Media 2005: An Annual Report on American Journalism*, Project for Excellence in Journalism, March 15, 2005; available at www.stateofthenewsmedia.org/2005/.

34. James McRitchie, "Making Corporate Governance Decisions that Work for Whom?" paper presented to the World Council for Corporate Governance conference, London, May 12–13, 2005, http://corpgov.net/forums/commentary/ICCG2005.html

35. "A Crusader in Hong Kong," *BusinessWeek* (international edition cover story), May 19, 2003, 46.

36. See www.crikey.com.au.

37. Waygood, "NGO and Equity Investment."

38. The U.S. Congress, for instance, is contemplating legislation that would compel NGOs such as big-money charitable foundations to apply Sarbanes-Oxley–style reporting and governance requirements. The European Commission is mulling disclosure standards for civic groups that have lobbying arms in Brussels. The Philippines' Department of Finance has pressed community organizations to self-police through a "Council for NGO Certification" (www.pcnc.com.ph).

39. Sustainability, *The 21st Century NGO*. (London: Sustainability, 2003).

40. Other civic groups are tackling the challenge head-on, too. One World Trust, in its 2003 report "Power Without Accountability?" (http://www.oneworldtrust.org/documents/GAP20031.pdf), rated the biggest global NGOs on governance and recommended a menu of best practices. The Credibility Alliance has crafted governance and disclosure standards for the thousands of civil society organizations in India. The Charities Aid Foundation has led efforts to write a governance code for NGOs in southern Africa. The London School of Economics Centre for Civil Society has launched projects studying governance among NGOs. And vanguard individual nonprofits—notably AccountAbility, Ceres, and WWF—have taken pains to make their own governance practices best in class.

Chapter 9

1. Jeffrey Sonnenfeld, "The Last Emperor," *Wall Street Journal*, March 2, 2004.

2. See www.thesmokinggun.com/archive/0318041trump1.

3. Cited in Andrew Campbell and Robert Park, *The Growth Gamble: When Leaders Should Bet Big on New Business and How They Can Avoid Expensive Failures* (London: Nicholas Brealey, 2005), 19.

4. Simon Zadek, "Being Global Means Being Responsible," AccountAbility, London, October 2004, www.accountability.org.uk.

5. Peter Singer, *How Are We to Live? Ethics in an Age of Self Interest* (Oxford: Oxford University Press, 1997), 273.

6. For example, ISS, Glass Lewis, Egan-Jones, Proxy Governance, the European Corporate Governance Service, Corporate Governance International and the Korea Corporate Governance Service provide share-voting advice to hundreds of shareowners around the world. Equity Ownership Service (EOS), owned by Hermes, has gone even further in providing a full "stewardship service," including collective intervention in companies, to some of Europe's largest pension funds. Indeed, EOS has even sparked a spin-off competitor: Governance for Owners (GO), founded by the former head of Hermes Focus Funds. The Local Authority Pension Fund Forum (LAPFF) and Pensions Investment Research Consultants (PIRC) offer similar services for their members and clients. So do fund managers ISIS and Insight.

7. Clearly, there are hurdles to cooperation, such as regulatory filings and publicity. Experience suggests, however, that such hurdles are more fearsome in anticipation than in reality.

8. See www.icgn.org/documents/InstShareholderResponsibilities.pdf.

9. See, for example, E. Weinstein and A. Abdulali, "Hedge Fund Transparency: Quantifying Valuation Bias for Illiquid Assets," *Risk*, June 2002, S25–S28.

10. We do not argue for or against redistributive wealth policies; that is beyond the scope of this book. As we discussed in chapter 1, however, we maintain that the development of collective savings, pension, and insurance vehicles has already created conditions that are giving rise to a civil economy in much of the developed world.

11. Insights on pension fund audit practices were developed in part via Stephen Davis's e-mail exchanges with Frank Curtiss of Railpen Investments, who chairs the International Corporate Governance Network's audit and accounting committee, July 2005.

12. The lack of reality in economists' assumptions is illustrated by the famous joke about the engineer, the physicist, and the economist, shipwrecked on a desert island with many cans of food, but no can opener. "Well," says the engineer, "If we find a stone, we can cut an axe blade and open the cans." "I've got another idea." says the physicist. "Light a fire, put the cans on it, and the pressure will burst them open." "Those seem like very complicated solutions to me," says the economist. "Why don't we just assume we have a can opener?"

13. David Landes, *The Wealth and Poverty of Nations: Why Some Are So Rich and Some So Poor* (London: Abacus, 1999), 217–218.

14. Adam Smith, *The Theory of Moral Sentiments*, part 2, section 2, chapter 3, www.adamsmith.org.

15. Alfred Marshall, *Principles of Economics* (New York: Macmillan, 1946), 303.

Selected Bibliography

Ashbaugh-Skaife, Hollis, and Ryan LaFond. "Firms' Corporate Governance and the Cost of Debt: An Analysis of U.S. Firms' GMI Ratings," January 2006. http://www.gsm.ucdavis.edu/faculty/Conferences/Hollis.pdf

Association of British Insurers. *Investing in Social Responsibility: Risks and Opportunities.* London: Association of British Insurers. 2001.

Backhouse, Roger E. *The Penguin History of Economics.* London: Penguin. 2002.

Bain, Neville, and David Band. *Winning Ways: Through Corporate Governance.* London: Macmillan Press Ltd., 1996.

Bakan, Joel. *The Corporation: The Pathological Pursuit of Profit and Power.* New York: Free Press, 2004.

Barca, Fabrizio, and Marco Becht, eds. *The Control of Corporate Europe.* New York: Oxford University Press Inc., 2001.

Baums, T., and E. Wymeersch, eds. *Shareholder Voting Rights and Practices in Europe and the United States.* London: Kluwer Law International Ltd., 1999.

Bébéar, Claude, and Philippe Manière. *Ils Vont Tuer le Capitalisme* (They Are Going to Kill Capitalism). Paris: Plon, 2003.

Bebchuk, Lucian, and Jesse Fried. *Pay Without Performance: The Unfulfilled Promise of Executive Compensation.* Cambridge: Harvard University Press, 2004.

Becker, Charles M., Trevor Bell, Haider Ali Khan, and Patricia S. Pollard. *The Impact of Sanctions on South Africa: The Economy.* Washington, DC: Investor Responsibility Research Center, 1990.

Benston, George, Michael Bromwich, Robert Litan, and Alfred Wagenhofer. *Following the Money: The Enron Failure and the State of Corporate Disclosure.* Washington, DC: AEI-Brookings Joint Center for Regulatory Studies, 2003.

Berle, Adolf A., and Gardiner C. Means. *The Modern Corporation and Private Property.* Somerset, NJ: Transaction Publishers, 2004.

Birchall, Johnston. *Co-op: The People's Business.* Manchester, England: Manchester University Press, 1994.

Black, Bernard S., Hasung Jang, and Woochan Kim. "Does Corporate Governance Predict Firms' Market Values? Evidence from Korea." *Journal of Law, Economics, and Organization* 22, no. 2 (Fall 2006). http://ssrn.com/abstract=311275

Blair, Margaret M., ed. *The Deal Decade: What Takeovers and Leveraged Buyouts Mean for Corporate Governance.* Washington, DC: The Brookings Institution 1993.

———. *Ownership and Control: Rethinking Corporate Governance for the Twenty-First Century.* Washington, DC: The Brookings Institution, 1995.

Blair, Margaret, and Steven M. H. Wallman. *Unseen Wealth: Report of the Brookings Task Force on Intangibles.* Washington, DC: Brookings Institution Press, 2001.

Bogle, John C. *The Battle for the Soul of Capitalism.* New Haven: Yale University Press, 2005.

Bollier, David. *Citizen Action and Other Big Ideas: A History of Ralph Nader and the Modern Consumer Movement.* Washington, DC: Center for the Study of Responsive Law, 1991. www.nader.org/history/.

Bompoint, Patrick, and Bernard Marois. *Le Pouvoir Actionnarial: Relations Sociétés-Investisseurs Face à la Mondialisation des Marchés* (Shareholder Power: Company-Investor Relations in the Context of Globalization of Markets). Paris: Editions JVDS, 1998.

Brancato, Carolyn Kay. *Institutional Investors and Corporate Governance: Best Practices for Increasing Corporate Value.* Chicago: Irwin Professional Publishing, 1997.

Brown, Gordon, and Tony Wright, eds. *Values, Visions and Voices: An Anthology of Socialism.* Edinburgh: Mainstream Publishing. 1995.

Bughin, Jacques, and Thomas E. Copeland. "The Virtuous Cycle of Shareholder Value Creation." *The McKinsey Quarterly,* no. 2 (1997).

Burrough, Bryan, and John Helyar. *Barbarians at the Gate.* New York: Arrow Books, 1990.

Bush, Tim. *Divided by Common Language: Where Economics Meets the Law: US versus Non-US Reporting Systems.* London: Institute of Chartered Secretaries and Administrators, 2005.

Cabot, Louis, "From the Boardroom." *Harvard Business Review,* Autumn 1976.

Cadbury, Sir Adrian. *Corporate Governance and Chairmanship.* Oxford: Oxford University Press, 2002.

Campbell, Andrew, and Robert Park. *The Growth Gamble: When Leaders Should Bet Big on New Businesses and How They Can Avoid Expensive Failures.* London: Nicholas Brealey International, 2005.

Carlsson, Rolf. *Ownership and Value Creation: Strategic Corporate Governance in the New Economy.* Chichester, England: John Wiley & Sons, 2001.

Carter, Colin B, and J. W. Lorsch. *Back to the Drawing Board: Designing Corporate Boards for a Complex World.* Boston: Harvard Business School Press, 2003.

Center for Working Capital. *The Challenge and Promise of Cross-Border Capital Stewardship.* Washington, DC: Center for Working Capital, 2002.

Chancellor, Edward. *Devil Take the Hindmost: A History of Financial Speculation.* London: McMillan, 1999.

Chandler, William B., III, and Leo E. Strine Jr. "The New Federalism of the American Corporate Governance System." NYU Center for Law and Business Research Paper No. 03-01; University of Pennsylvania Institute for Law & Economic Research Paper 03-03, March 13 2003, available at SSRN: http://papers.ssrn.com/sol3/papers.cfm?abstract_id=367720 or DOI:10.2139/ssrn.367720.

Charkham, Jonathan. *Keeping Better Company: Corporate Governance Ten Years On.* Oxford: Oxford University Press, 2005.

———. *Keeping Good Company: A Study of Corporate Governance in Five Countries.* Oxford: Clarendon Press, 1994.

Charkham, Jonathan, and Ann Simpson. *Fair Shares: The Future of Shareholder Power and Responsibility.* New York: Oxford University Press, 1999.

Clearfield, Andrew. "'With Friends Like These, Who Needs Enemies?' The Structure of the Investment Industry and Its Reluctance to Exercise Governance Oversight." *Corporate Governance* 13, no. 2 (March 2005), 114.

———. "Young Financial Analysts' Views on Environmental, Social and Corporate Governance Issues," UNEP Finance Initiative and World Business Council for Sustainable Development (2005). http://www.unepfi.org/fileadmin/documents/ymt_summary_2005.pdf.

CLSA. *Saints & Sinners: Corporate Governance in Emerging Markets.* Hong Kong: CLSA, 2001.

Cogan, Douglas G. *Corporate Governance and Climate Change: Making the Connection.* Boston: Ceres, 2003.

Collins, Jim. *Good to Great: Why Some Companies Make the Grade and Others Don't.* New York: Random House, 2001.

The Conference Board. *The 2005 Institutional Investment Report: US and International Trends.* New York: The Conference Board, 2005.

Cornelius, Peter K., and Bruce Kogut, eds. *Corporate Governance and Capital Flows in a Global Economy.* Oxford: Oxford University Press, 2003.

Crawford, Leslie. "Spain Sets First with 'Lover's Guide' to Boardrooms." *Financial Times,* May 10, 2005, 10.

Crystal, Graef S. *In Search of Excess: The Overcompensation of American Executives.* New York: W.W. Norton and Company, Inc., 1991.

Damsma, Marvin L., Jon Lukomnik, Maarten L. Nederloff, and Thomas K. Philips. *Alpha: The Positive Side of Risk: Daring to Be Different.* New York: Investors Press, 1996.

Davies, Adrian. *A Strategic Approach to Corporate Governance.* Aldershot, England: Gower Publishing, 1999.

Davis, Stephen. "Corporate Downsizing: Let Shareholders Vote." *Pensions & Investments,* April 29, 1996, 14.

———. *Shareholder Rights Abroad.* Washington, DC: Investor Responsibility Research Center, 1989.

Davis, Stephen, Corinna Arnold, and Rachel Ongé Lerman. *Global Voting.* Washington, DC: Investor Responsibility Research Center, 1993.

Davis, Stephen, and Karel Lannoo. "Shareholder Voting in Europe." *Center for European Policy Studies* 3 (Summer 1997): 22.

Davis, Stephen, and Jon Lukomnik. "Who Are These Guys? Welcome to the Hedge Fund Era." *Compliance Week,* April 5, 2005.

Deloitte Touche Tohmatsu. *In the Dark: What Boards and Executives Don't Know About the Health of their Businesses.* New York: Deloitte Touche Tohmatsu, 2004.

Demb, Ada, and F.Friedrich Neubauer. *The Corporate Board: Confronting the Paradoxes.* New York: Oxford University Press, Inc., 1992.

De Soto, Hernando. *Why Capitalism Triumphs in the West and Fails Everywhere Else.* New York: Basic Books, 2000.

Drucker, Peter F. *The Unseen Revolution: How Pension Fund Socialism Came to America.* New York: Harper & Row, 1976.

———. *Management: Tasks, Responsibilities, Practices.* New York: Harper Business, 1993.

Eccles, Robert G., Robert H. Herz, E. Mary Keegan, and David M. H. Phillips. *The Value Reporting Revolution: Moving Beyond the Earnings Game.* New York: John Wiley & Sons, 2001.

Eichenwald, Kurt. *Conspiracy of Fools*. New York: Broadway Books, 2005.

Elkington, John. *Cannibals with Forks: The Triple Bottom Line of 21st Century Business*. Oxford: Capstone Publishing, 1997.

Feldman, Amy, and Joan Caplin. "Is Jack Grubman the Worst Analyst Ever?" CNN-Money.com, April 25, 2002. http://money.cnn.com/2002/04/25/pf/investing/grubman/

Fels, Allan. *The Australian Financial Review*. October 2003. http://www.anzsog.edu.au/news/article2_oct2003.htm

Francis, Ivor. *Future Direction: The Power of the Competitive Board*. Melbourne: FT Pitman Publishing, 1997.

Franks, Julian, Colin Mayer, and Luis Correia da Silva. *Asset Management and Investor Protection: An International Analysis*. New York: Oxford University Press, 2003.

Frentrop, Paul. *A History of Corporate Governance 1602–2002*. Brussels: Deminor, 2003.

Freshfields Bruckhaus Deringer. *The Legal Limits on the Integration of Environmental Social and Governance Issues into Institutional Investment*. New York: United National Environment Programme, 2005.

Gandossy, Robert, and Jeffrey Sonnenfeld, eds. *Leadership and Governance from the Inside Out*. New Jersey: John Wiley & Son, Inc., 2004.

Garratt, Bob. *Thin on Top: Why Corporate Governance Matters and How to Measure and Improve Board Performance*. London: Nicholas Brealey Publishing, 2003.

Gaved, Matthew. *Institutional Investors and Corporate Governance*. London: Foundation for Business Responsibilities, 1998.

Giddens, Anthony. *The Third Way: The Renewal of Social Democracy*. Cambridge: Polity Press, 1998.

Glasius, Marlies, Mary Kaldor, and Helmut Anheier, eds. *Global Civil Society 2005/6*. London: Sage Publications, 2005.

Gompers, Paul A., Joy L. Ishii, and Andrew Metrick "Corporate Governance and Equity Prices." *Quarterly Journal of Economics* 118, no. 1 (February 2003): 107–155.

Goodman, Susannah Blake, Jonas Kron, and Tim Little. *The Environmental Fiduciary: The Case for Incorporating Environmental Factors into Investment Management Policies*, Oakland, CA: Rose Foundation for Communities & the Environment, 2002.

Gourevitch, Peter A., and James Shinn. *Political Power & Corporate Control: The New Global Politics of Corporate Governance*. Princeton: Princeton University Press, 2005.

Gourevitch, Peter A., and James Shinn, eds. *How Shareholder Reforms Can Pay Foreign Policy Dividends*. New York: Council on Foreign Relations, Inc., 2002.

Government Accountability Office. *Pension Plans: Additional Transparency and Other Actions Needed in Connection with Proxy Voting*. Washington, DC: US Government Accountability Office, 2004.

Graham, Carol, Robert Litan, and Sandip Sukhtankar. "The Bigger They Are, the Harder They Fall: An Estimate of the Costs of the Crisis in Corporate Governance." Policy Brief 102. Washington, DC: The Brookings Institution, August 30, 2002.

Grant, Gavin. *Beyond the Numbers: Corporate Governance in Europe*. London: Deutsche Bank, 2005.

Greider, William. *One World, Ready or Not: The Manic Logic of Global Capitalism*. New York: Simon and Schuster, 1997.

———. *The Soul of Capitalism: Opening Paths to a Moral Economy*. New York: Simon and Schuster, 2003.

Gugler, Klaus. *Corporate Governance and Economic Performance*. Oxford: Oxford University Press, 2001.

Hallqvist, Bengt. *Private Institute for Corporate Governance: The Brazilian Experience.* Pompéia, Brazil: Bless Gráfica e Editora, 2002.

Hammer, Michael, and James Champy. *Reengineering the Corporation: A Manifesto for Business Revolution.* New York: HarperBusiness, 1993.

Harrington, John C. *The Challenge to Power: Money, Investing, and Democracy.* White River Junction, Vermont: Chelsea Green Publishing Company, 2005.

Harrison, J. F. C. *Common People: A History from the Norman Conquest to the Present.* New York: Flamingo, 1984.

Hawley, James P., and Andrew T. Williams. *The Rise of Fiduciary Capitalism: How Institutional Investors Can Make Corporate America More Democratic.* Philadelphia: University of Pennsylvania Press, 2000.

Healy, Joseph. "Corporate Governance and Shareholder Value." ANZ Investment Bank study. Auckland, March 24, 2000.

———. *Corporate Governance and Wealth Creation in New Zealand.* Palmerston North, New Zealand: Dunmore Press, 2003.

———, "The Shareholder Value Performance of Corporate New Zealand." ANZ Investment Bank study. Auckland, February 24, 2000.

Hofmeyr, Jan, Stephen Davis, and Merle Lipton. *The Impact of Sanctions on South Africa: Whites' Political Attitudes.* Washington, DC: Investor Responsibility Research Center, 1990.

Hopt, K. J., H. Kanda, M. J. Roe, E. Wymeersch, and S. Prigge, eds. *Comparative Corporate Governance: The State of the Art and Emerging Research.* Oxford: Clarendon Press, 1998.

Huffington, Arianna. *Pigs at the Trough: How Corporate Greed and Political Corruption Are Undermining America.* New York: Crown Publishers, 2003.

Hummels, G. J. A., and David Wood. *Knowing the Price, but Also the Value.* Boston: Nyenrode Business Universiteit and Boston College, 2005.

Hutton, Will. *The Stakeholding Society: Writings on Politics and Economics.* Cambridge: Polity Press, 1999.

———. *The State We're In.* London: Jonathan Cape, 1995.

———. *The World We're In.* London: Abacus, 2003.

Innovest Strategic Value Advisors. *Value at Risk: Climate Change and the Future of Governance.* Boston: Ceres, 2002.

Institute of Directors. *King Report on Corporate Governance for South Africa—2002.* Johannesburg: Institute of Directors, 2002.

Institutional Shareholders' Committee. *The Responsibilities of Institutional Shareholders in the UK.* London: Institutional Shareholders' Committee, 2003.

International Finance Corporation. *Towards Sustainable and Responsible Investment in Emerging Markets.* Washington, DC: International Finance Corp., 2003.

Isaksson, Mats, and Rolf Skog, eds. *The Future of Corporate Governance.* Stockholm: The Corporate Governance Forum, 2004.

Jacobs, Michael T. *Short-Term America: The Causes and Cures of Our Business Myopia.* Boston: Harvard Business School Press, 1991.

Jenson, Michael, Eric G. Wruck, and Kevin Murphy. *Remuneration: Where We've Been, How We Got Here, What Are the Problems and How to Fix Them.* Finance Working Paper 44. Brussels: European Corporate Governance Institute, July 12, 2004.

Johnson, Gerry, and Kevan Scholes. *Exploring Corporate Strategy: Texts and Cases,* 3rd ed. Upper Saddle River, New Jersey: Prentice Hall, 1993.

Johnson, H. Thomas. *Relevance Regained: From Top-Down Control to Bottom-Up Empowerment*. New York: Free Press, 1992.

Johnson, H. Thomas, and Robert S. Kaplan. *Relevance Lost: The Rise and Fall of Management Accounting*. Boston: Harvard Business School Press, 1987.

Kay, John. *The Truth about Markets. Their Genius, Their Limits, Their Follies*. London: Allen Lane, 2003.

Kedia, Simi, and Thomas Philippon. *The Economics of Fraudulent Accounting*. Washington, DC: National Bureau of Economic Research, 2005.

Kennedy, Allan A. *The End of Shareholder Value: Corporations at the Crossroads*. Cambridge: Perseus Publishing, 2000.

Keong, Low Chee, ed. *Corporate Governance: An Asia-Pacific Critique*. Hong Kong: Sweet & Maxwell Asia, 2002.

Lan, Luh Luh, and Loizos Heracleous. "Shareholder Votes for Sale." *Harvard Business Review*, June 2005, 20–24.

Landes, David. *The Wealth and Poverty of Nations: Why Some Are So Rich and Some So Poor*. London: Abacus, 1998.

Learmount, Simon. *Corporate Governance: What Can Be Learned from Japan?* Oxford: Oxford University Press, 2002.

Ledgerwood, Grant, ed. *Greening the Boardroom: Corporate Governance and Business Sustainability*. Sheffield, England: Greenleaf Publishing, 1997.

Lev, Baruch. *Intangibles: Management, Measurement, and Reporting*. Washington, DC: Brookings Institution Press, 2001.

"Measuring the Value of Intellectual Capital," *Ivey Business Journal*, March/April 2001, 16.

Levitt, Arthur, and Paula Dwyer. *Take on the Street: What Wall Street and Corporate America Don't Want You to Know—What You Can Do to Fight Back*. New York: Pantheon Books, 2002.

Lewin, C. G. *Pensions and Insurance Before 1800: A Social History*. East Lothian, Scotland: Tuckwell Press Ltd., 2003.

L'Hélias, Sophie. *Le Retour de l'Actionnaire: Pratques du Corporate Governance en France, aux États-Unis et en Grande-Bretagne* (The Return of the Shareholder: Corporate Governance Practices in France, the United States and Britain). Paris: Gualino Éditeur, 1997.

Liddle, Roger, and Maria João Rodrigues, eds. *Economic Reform in Europe: Priorities for the Next Five Years*. London: Policy Network, 2004.

Low, Chee Keong, ed. *Corporate Governance: An Asia-Pacific Critique*. Hong Kong: Sweet & Maxwell Asia, 2002.

Lucier, Chuck, Rob Schuyt, and Edward Tse. "CEO Succession 2004: The World's Most Prominent Temp Workers." *Strategy + Business Special Report*, Summer 2004.

Lydenberg, Steven. *Corporations and The Public Interest: Guiding the Invisible Hand*. San Francisco: Berrett-Koehler Publishers, 2005.

Maatman, René. *Dutch Pension Funds: Fiduciary Duties and Investing*. Deventer, The Netherlands: Kluwer Legal Publishers, 2004.

MacAvoy, Paul W., and Ira M. Millstein. *The Recurrent Crisis in Corporate Governance*. New York: Palgrave Macmillan, 2003.

Mace, Myles L. *Directors: Myth and Reality*. Boston: Harvard Business School Press, 1986.

Mackenzie, Craig. *The Shareholder Action Handbook: Using Shares to Make Companies More Accountable*. Newcastle upon Tyne, England: New Consumer Ltd., 1993.

MacKerron, Conrad. *Unlocking the Power of the Proxy: How Active Foundation Proxy Voting Can Protect Endowments and Boost Philanthropic Missions.* New York: Rockefeller Philanthropy Advisors, 2004.

Mallin, Christine A. *Voting: The Role of Institutional Investors in Corporate Governance.* London: Institute of Chartered Accountants in England and Wales, 1995.

———. *Corporate Governance.* New York: Oxford University Press, Inc., 2004.

Manheim, Jarol B. *Biz-War and the Out-of-Power Elite: The Progressive-Left Attack on the Corporation.* Mahwah, NJ: Lawrence Erlbaum Associates, 2004.

Manière, Philippe. *Marx à la Corbeille: Quand les Actionnaires Font la Révolution.* (Marx in the Bin [*or* On the Stock Exchange Floor]: When Shareholders Start a Revolution). Paris: Stock, 1999.

Marshall, Alfred. *Principles of Economics,* 8th ed. London: McMillan, 1946.

Marx, Karl, and Friedrich Engels (trans Moore 1888). *The Communist Manifesto.* London: Penguin, 1967.

Mathiasen, Carolyn. *The SEC and Social Policy Shareholder Resolutions in the 1990s.* Washington, DC: IRRC, November 1994.

McAlister, Debbie Thorne, O. C. Ferrell, and Linda Ferrell. *Business and Society: A Strategic Approach to Corporate Citizenship.* Boston: Houghton Mifflin, 2003.

McCahery, Joseph A., Piet Moerland, Thei Raaijmakers, and Luc Renneboog, eds. *Corporate Governance Regimes: Convergence and Diversity.* Oxford: Oxford University Press, 2002.

McKinsey & Company. *Global Investor Opinion Survey on Corporate Governance.* New York: McKinsey & Co., 2002.

"Measuring the Value of Intellectual Capital," *Ivey Business Journal,* March/April 2001, 16.

Melvin, Colin, and Hans Hirt. *Corporate Governance and Performance: A Brief Review and Assessment of the Evidence for a Link Between Corporate Governance and Performance.* London: Hermes Pensions Management Ltd, 2004.

Metzger, Barry, ed. *Global Corporate Governance Guide 2004: Best Practice in the Boardroom.* London: Globe White Page, 2004.

Micklethwait, John, and Adrian Wooldridge. *The Company: A Short History of a Revolutionary Idea.* New York: Modern Library, 2003.

Monks, Robert A. G. *The Emperor's Nightingale: Restoring the Integrity of the Corporation.* Oxford: Capstone Publishing Limited, 1998.

Monks, Robert A. G., and Nell Minow. *Corporate Governance.* 3rd ed. Malden, MA: Blackwell Publishing Ltd., 2004.

———. *Watching the Watchers: Corporate Governance for the 21st Century.* Cambridge, MA: Blackwell Publishers, 1996.

Morison, Samuel Eliot, and Henry Steele Commager. *The Growth of the American Republic,* New York City: Oxford University Press, 1962.

Oakley, C. A. *The Second City.* Glasgow: Blackie & Co., 1947.

O'Brien, Justin. *Wall Street on Trial.* Chichester, England: John Wiley & Sons, Ltd., 2003.

One World Trust. *Power Without Accountability?* London: One World Trust, 2003.

Opler, Tim C., and Jonathan Sokobin. "Does Coordinated Institutional Activism Work? An Analysis of the Activities of the Council of Institutional Investors." Working papers Series 95-5. Columbus, OH: Dice Center for Research in Financial Economics, October 1995.

Organisation for Economic Co-operation and Development. *OECD Principles of Corporate Governance 2004.* Paris: Organisation for Economic Co-operation and Development, 2004.

Peters, Thomas J., and Robert H. Waterman. *In Search of Excellence: Lessons from America's Best-Run Companies.* New York: Harper and Row, 1982.

Petschow, Ulrich, James Rosenau, and Ernst Ulrich von Weizsäcker, eds. *Governance and Sustainability: New Challenges for States, Companies and Civil Society.* Sheffield, England: Greenleaf Publishing, 2005.

Pitt-Watson, David, and Watson, Tony. *The Hermes Principles: What Shareholders Expect of Public Companies—and What Companies Should Expect of Their Investors.* London: Hermes Pensions Management Ltd., 2004.

Plender, John. *A Stake in the Future: The Stakeholding Solution.* London: Nicholas Brealey Publishing, 1997.

Raaijmakers, G. T. M. J. *European Regulation of Company and Securities Law.* Nijmegen, The Netherlands: Ars Aequi Libri, 2005.

Rajan, Raghuram, and Luigi Zingales. *Saving Capitalism from the Capitalists: Unleashing the Power of Financial Markets to Create Wealth and Spread Opportunity.* New York: Crown Business, 2003.

Richard, Bertrand, and Dominique Miellet. *La Dynamique du Gouvernement d'Entreprise* (Dynamics of Corporate Governance). Paris: Éditions d'Organisation, 2003.

Roberts, John. *The Modern Firm: Organizational Design for Performance and Growth.* Oxford: Oxford University Press, 2004.

Roe, Mark J. *Political Determinants of Corporate Governance: Political Context, Corporate Impact.* New York: Oxford University Press Inc., 2003.

Rosenberg, Hilary. *A Traitor to His Class: Robert A. G. Monks and the Battle to Change Corporate America.* New York: John Wiley & Sons, 1999.

Schwartz, Jeff. *The Purpose of Profit.* London: Tomorrow's Company, 2005.

Sidebotham, Roy. *Introduction to the Theory and Context of Accounting,* 2nd ed. Oxford: Pergamon Press, 1970.

Silver, Don. *Cookin' the Book$: Say Pasta la Vista to Corporate Accounting Tricks and Fraud.* Los Angeles: Adams-Hall Publishing, 2003.

Singer, Peter. *How Are We to Live? Ethics in an Age of Self-interest.* Oxford: Oxford University Press, 1997.

Smith, Adam. *An Inquiry into the Nature and Causes of the Wealth of Nations.* Edinburgh: Nelson & Sons, 1827.

———. *The Wealth of Nations.* New York: Alfred A. Knopf, Inc., 1991.

Sonnenfeld, Jeffrey. *The Hero's Farewell: What Happens When CEO's Retire.* New York: Oxford University Press, Inc., 1988.

Stapledon, G. P. *Institutional Shareholders and Corporate Governance.* Oxford: Clarendon Press, 1996.

Stewart, James B. *Disney War.* New York: Simon and Schuster, 2005.

Strenger, Christian. *Corporate Governance Kapitalmarkt.* (A compilation of speeches and articles.) Frankfurt: Christian Strenger, 2004.

Sustainability. *The 21st Century NGO.* London: Sustainability, 2003.

Sustainability, International Finance Corp. and Ethos Institute. *Developing Value: The Business Case for Sustainability in Emerging Markets.* London: Sustainability, 2002.

Swensen, David F. *Unconventional Success: A Fundamental Approach to Personal Investment.* New York: Free Press, 2005.

Sykes, Allen. *Capitalism for Tomorrow: Reuniting Ownership and Control.* Oxford: Capstone Publishing Ltd., 2000.

Talner, Lauren. *The Origins of Shareholder Activism.* Washington, DC: Investor Responsibility Research Center, 1983.

Thomas, Alison. "A Tale of Two Reports." *European Business Forum* 16 (Winter 2003/2004). www.ebr360.org/downloads/ebf_issue16.pdf.

Tong, Lu, ed. *Corporate Governance Reform: International Experience and China's Practice.* Beijing: Institute of World Economic and Politics, 2004.

United Nations Global Compact. *Who Cares Wins.* New York: United Nations, 2004.

Useem, Michael. *Investor Capitalism: How Money Managers Are Changing the Face of Corporate America.* New York: Basic Books, 1996.

Voorhes, Meg, Carolyn Mathieson, and Jennifer Sesta. *Investor Responsibility in the Global Era.* Washington, DC: Investor Responsibility Research Center 1998.

Walmsley, Keith, ed. *Corporate Governance Handbook.* London: LexisNexis Butterworths, 2005.

Ward, Ralph D. *21st Century Corporate Board.* New York: John Wiley & Sons, Inc., 1997.

Waring, Kerrie, and Chris Pierce, eds. *The Handbook of International Corporate Governance.* London: Institute of Directors and Kogan Page, 2005.

Whitley, Richard, and Peer Hull Kristensen. *Governance at Work: The Social Regulation of Economic Relations.* Oxford: Oxford University Press, 1997.

Williams, Anthony. *Who Will Guard the Guardians? Corporate Governance in the Millennium.* Chalford, England: Management Books 2000, 1999.

Williamson, Oliver. *Markets and Hierarchies: Analysis and Antitrust Implications: A Study in the Economics of Internal Organization.* New York: Free Press, 1975.

World Bank. *World Development Indicators 2005.* Washington, DC: World Bank, 2005.

World Bank. *Reports on Standards and Compliance.* Washington, DC: World Bank Group.

World Economic Forum. *Mainstreaming Responsible Investment.* Geneva: World Economic Forum, 2005.

Young, Patrick. *The New Capital Market Revolution.* New York: Texere, 2003.

Zadek, Simon. *The Civil Corporation: The New Economy of Corporate Citizenship.* London: Earthscan Publications, 2001.

Index

About the Authors

Stephen Davis, PhD, is President of Davis Global Advisors, a consultancy specializing in international corporate governance, and publisher of the weekly *Global Proxy Watch* newsletter. Davis cofounded the International Corporate Governance Network and is a member of the UNEP steering group on responsible investment; the International Advisory Board of Euronext; and Policy Network's working group on economic reform. He is also a founding partner in GovernanceMetrics International, g³ [global governance group], and Beacon Global Advisors. Dr. Davis earned his doctorate at the Fletcher School of Law and Diplomacy, Tufts University. An earlier book, *Apartheid's Rebels*, was nominated for a Pulitzer Prize.

Jon Lukomnik is Managing Partner of Sinclair Capital, a strategic consultancy focused on the investment management industry. He previously served as Deputy Comptroller for the City of New York, where he was investment adviser for defined benefit plans totaling US$80 billion in assets, as well as the City's own treasury. He has served on the official creditors committee for the WorldCom bankruptcy, as Chair of the Executive Committee of the Council of Institutional Investors, on the World Bank/International Finance Corporation's Investor Task Force, on the Risk Standards Working Group, and as the only non-lawyer on the Bar Association of the City of New York's Committee on Corporate Law. He cofounded the International Corporate Governance Network and Governance-Metrics International, serves on the International Advisory Board of Euronext, and is a partner in g³ (global governance group).

David Pitt-Watson is Chair of Hermes Equity Ownership Service (HEOS) and formerly Chief Executive of Hermes Focus Asset Management (HFAM), Europe's leading shareholder activist fund and the only one in the world to be owned and sponsored by a major investment institution. Backed by some of the largest of the world's pension funds, HFAM and HEOS have been instrumental in the turnaround of more than thirty major British and continental European companies. Pitt-Watson is author of "The Hermes Principles," the first attempt by any major investment institution to define its expectations of the companies in which it invests.